Performance Contracting: Expanding Horizons

Shirley J. Hansen, Ph.D.
Jeannie C. Weisman

PerformanceContracting: Expanding Horizons

Shirley J. Hansen, Ph.D.
Jeannie C. Weisman

Published by
THE FAIRMONT PRESS, INC.
700 Indian Trail
Lilburn, GA 30047

Library of Congress Cataloging-in-Publication Data

Hansen, Shirley J., 1928
    Performance contracting : expanding horizons / Shirley J. Hansen,
    Jeannie C. Weisman.
    p. cm.
    Includes index.
    ISBN 0-88173-276-1
    1. Energy industries. 2. Conrracting out. I. Weisman, Jeannie C.,
    1950-. II. Title.
    HD9502.U52H365   1998   658.2--dc21   97-35101
                                                                            CIP

Published by The Fairmont Press, Inc.
700 Indian Trail
Lilburn, GA 30247

Printed in the United States of America

10 9 8 7 6 5 4 3 2 1

ISBN 0-88173-276-1 FP

ISBN 0-13-095819-0 PH

Distributed by Prentice Hall PTR
Prentice-Hall, Inc.
A Simon & Schuster Company
Upper Saddle River, NJ 07458

Prentice-Hall International (UK) Limited, London
Prentice-Hall of Australia Pty. Limited, Sydney
Prentice-Hall Canada Inc., Toronto
Prentice-Hall Hispanoamericana, S.A., Mexico
Prentice-Hall of India Private Limited, New Delhi
Prentice-Hall of Japan, Inc., Tokyo
Simon & Schuster Asia Pte. Ltd., Singapore
Editora Prentice-Hall do Brasil, Ltda., Rio de Janeiro

Contents

Foreword

The publication of this book marks the end of one era and heralds the start of another. The energy services industry has grown from niche participation in the energy field to be an important provider of a broad range of service to end users. While ESCOs still provide performance based energy efficiency and water conservation services, increasingly they provide a much broader menu of services. At their core, ESCOs are problem solvers which customize solutions to almost all energy challenges that a facility owner might face, including energy supply, fuel switching, demand profile control, and the development of power plants, cogeneration, and district cooling and heating systems. ESCOs also offer energy management services, predictive and preventive maintenance services, end-use metering and energy tracking, environmental services, security and fire prevention services, and a host of other value-added problem solving services.

ESCOs possess competitive advantages which will serve them well in a changing marketplace. These include market agility and decisiveness, speed of project implementation, and the ability to integrate project design elements, assess and ameliorate risk, and provide the technical and management capabilities critical to successful project development .

As Executive Director of the National Association of Energy Service Companies (NAESCO), I am proud to say it is a trade association which has worked hard to expand market opportunities domestically and internationally, and to promote the impressive accomplishments of the industry while at the same time working to assure the reliability, competency, and high quality of industry participants. NAESCO is especially pleased with its accreditation program, under which, as of this printing, 15 ESCOs and one lighting service company have already been accredited.

The industry is thriving and is poised on the cusp of another period of change and market expansion. To paraphrase an old proverb, ESCOs are living in interesting times, and happily for the industry, in profitable times as well!

Terry E. Singer
Executive Director
NAESCO

Acknowledgements

In the years since the first book on performance contracting was written, the world of energy performance contracting has expanded and merged into the global economy. To embrace these dramatic changes, the writing of this book has been a challenge. The authors are truly grateful for the support and participation we have received from so many involved in the field. This book, and the work it represents, would not have been possible without the devoted help of our many colleagues.

Our sincere thanks, therefore, go to the contributing authors, (introduced in the lead for each section), who took great time from their own demanding schedules to provide us with their valuable insights. They have given the book a much broader perspective than the authors alone could have offered. Our sincere appreciation also goes to those from the municipal, state and federal governments, energy service companies, and the international community who provided us with case studies which so enriched our text.

To the enterprising ESCOs, such as Energy Masters and EPS, the World Bank and U.S. Agency for International Development with whom we have worked internationally, and others who are venturing overseas to seek international challenges, thank you for expanding the scope of all our visions.

To our clients from whom we learn daily—from ESCOs to end users and all points in between—our deep appreciation. Our experiences working with you in the US and in 20 other countries around the world have provided the resources for us to gain greater knowledge about our industry and continue our own growth.

To Ms. Terry Singer, Executive Director of the National Association of Energy Service Companies, our thanks for her leadership to the industry and for her encouragement and support of this effort so kindly offered in the introduction.

Finally, to Ms. Hope Worley, without whose patience and skill this book would never have been possible.

To all of you, who continue to make our own horizons expand, we thank you.

Shirley J. Hansen
Jeannie C. Weisman

Performance Contracting Today

> Since the 1970s, the way we have been meeting our energy efficiency needs has been in a state of evolution... Sharing the excitement of a growing performance contracting industry has been rewarding. Today, performance contracting is poised on the threshold of even greater opportunities to work with government, utilities, institutions and commercial establishments. In the words of Cervantes, echoed by many vaudeville fanciers of *Don Quixote* through the years, "Thou hast seen nothing yet."

So closed the book, *Performance Contracting for Energy and Environmental Systems*. Every word is just as true today. Perhaps even more emphatic, as the words today represent greater changes and greater opportunities. If the past is indeed prologue, "Thou [still] hast seen nothing yet."

The challenge is to summarize the performance contracting state of the art and lay the ground for changes not yet fully envisioned. Section I offers a digest of those parts of the earlier book on performance contracting, which readers have indicated have been particularly valuable, as well as an update of what is relevant in today's market place.

A few brief segments are almost verbatim as they appeared in the previous book, such as portions of "The Money Side of Energy." After all, the numbers and their importance have not changed all that much. Another section on "Communicating Energy Needs" has received such an enthusiastic response from people, who found they needed a few tips on communicating energy needs and performance contracting opportunities, that we subscribed to the old adage, "If it ain't broke, don't fix it."

Much is completely new, such as the internationally accepted measurement and verification protocol. We have added a Planning Agreement, which has become a commonly accepted part of the solicitation and selection process today. The final chapter of the first section reveals a painful truth, which the survivors know full well, performance contracting projects must be managed; not just administered.

Other areas of performance contracting have changed dramatically in the six years since the first book was written. Some of those changes appear in updates of Section I while others are reflected throughout the book.

Chapter 1

The Energy Opportunity

We are moving toward a new millennium. And whether you believe that new millennium begins on January 1, 2000, or believe, as some purists do, that it begins January 1, 2001, it will be here. That is a fact. That is the future.

But, what are the facts about the need for energy efficiency in the future? Is that need as certain as the coming of the millennium? While energy costs in your neighborhood may be low, or stable, the International Energy Outlook, in 1995, predicted that world energy consumption will shoot up 44% by the year 2010. The impact will be global, major, and long term. As a result we will see energy efficiency positioned as a competitive resource, with more focus on non-price issues. Energy efficiency will mean providing at least the same, and hopefully better, energy services using less of our energy resources.

With the restructuring of the utility industry in the United States and much of the rest of the world, energy uncertainty is already upon us. Price volatility, retail access, predictions of dropping energy prices, and loss of rebates are all issues facing both the demand and supply side of energy.

In the face of domestic turmoil, overseas markets and opportunities will become more attractive. The move toward Central and Eastern Europe (CEE), which previously had centrally planned economies, is already here. And the opportunities in Asia and Latin America dwarf those in the CEE.

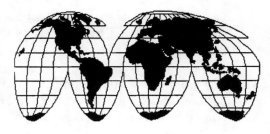

There are many opportunities on the horizon, if you are willing to think globally (in a broader sense and internationally), as well as personally, that point to energy efficiency as a sound practice and a good economic opportunity for the future.

Consider:

- In March of 1997, John Stapleton, Director of the Kentucky Division of Energy, stated that his state could save as much as 25% of the $52 million that Kentucky spends annually on energy for state facilities, including the University of Kentucky. That's as much as $13 million annually that could be used for services to citizens and students.

- At a World Bank meeting in April of 1997, an official of Thailand's Demand-Side Management Office said his country has one of the fastest growing industrial economies in the world. Energy demand is expected to double within the next ten years. The additional investment needed to meet this future demand is projected to reach $18 billion. Thailand expects to offset the billions in capital investment required to meet the demand through a wide variety of energy efficiency efforts.

- At a public hearing on deregulation of the utility industry in Atlanta, Georgia, the Vice President of the Municipal Electric Authority of Georgia expressed concern about the potential for power shortage, once the industry is fully deregulated. He stated that the "obligation to serve" now expected of utilities likely would not survive.

- With the deregulation of the utility industry facing the United States, utilities have become acutely aware that the term "rate payer" must now be replaced with "customer." In the last five years we have seen more than 65 Energy Service Companies (ESCOs) developed by utilities, as they seek new ways to serve their customers.

- The US General Accounting Office has estimated that more than 30% of schools need at least $1 million each to return to a good overall condition, and at least 25% of the schools in 48 states require HVAC upgrades.

- The Association of Physical Plant Administrators (APPA), an organization of higher-education facilities officers, reports that the
  physical components of U.S. institutions of higher education represent an investment exceeding $500 billion. Recent research by
  APPA indicates that U.S. colleges and universities are threatened
  by a backlog of deferred maintenance equating to nearly $70 billion
  requirement for capital investment.[1]

- In a presentation to the World Bank, Richard Sedano, Commissioner of the Vermont Department of Public Service spoke on the
  uncertainty of energy costs, "We know that energy prices in Vermont are low. But that's now. And we know that can change. And
  we know that the buildings we're improving will long outlast the
  current energy situation. It's a long term strategy for our investments." No matter what the cost of energy, efficiency is an investment in the future.

Energy efficiency reduces operating costs and frees up funds for
capital improvements. It purchases text books, buys new medical equipment, hires a new teacher. It lowers costs for consumers, enables enhanced industrial competition, and has the potential of significantly reducing energy-related pollution. Energy efficiency can very likely save
more money more quickly than any other measure to reduce pollution.

Even if you do not have money to invest, now more than ever, the
opportunity to have a more efficient operation is great. An entire industry designed to find the "$120,000 hidden in your boiler," to reduce the
25% of your utility cost that goes to lighting, and find the resources
willing to invest in those improvements, is here to serve your needs.

The concept is simple. It is called performance contracting, a contract with payments based on performance. Historically, it has been
based on guaranteed future energy savings. Performance contracting allows the customer; e.g., industry, state agency, hospital, school or a commercial business, to use future energy savings to upgrade facilities and
cut operating costs now.

An Energy Service Company (ESCO) will inspect a building or industrial facility for energy saving opportunities, recommend energy efficiency measures, and implement those measures acceptable to the owner
at no up front cost *to* the owner. The ESCO then guarantees that the
value of the energy savings will cover the cost of the capital modifica-

tions provided the price of energy does not go below a specified floor price.

PERFORMANCE CONTRACTING—
HOW FAR WE'VE COME!

Like any developing industry, the business of performance contracting suffered through growing pains in the 70's and 80's.

Initially, most projects were based upon each party sharing a percentage of the cost savings generated by retrofits. During the life of the contract, the ESCO expected its percentage of the cost savings to cover all the costs it had incurred, plus a profit. This concept worked quite well as long as the energy prices stayed the same or escalated.

But in the mid 80's prices dropped and it took longer than expected for the ESCO to recover its costs. Some firms could not meet their payments to suppliers or financial backers. Some ESCOs closed their doors; and in the process, defaulted on their commitments to their shared savings partners. "Shared Savings" was in trouble—and the process became tainted by lawsuits and suppliers' efforts to recoup some of their expenses, while facilities managers tried to explain losses previously guaranteed.

To make matters worse, it was discovered that one of the pioneers in the field had been entering into shared savings with an eye toward benefiting primarily from federal investment tax credits and energy tax credits. The building owner did not necessarily receive any energy cost savings.

Stories traveled and soon the trust vital to accepting a new concept, was badly shaken.

Fortunately, many persisted in their efforts to make the new concept work. Some agreements continued to show savings benefits to both parties. Of even greater importance, some companies had guaranteed the savings and made good on those guarantees.

In spite of this tenuous start, the "shared savings" industry survived, but its character changed dramatically. Those supplying the financial backing and/or equipment recognized the risk of basing contracts on energy price; interest rates went up. The use of true shared savings agreements shrank to approximately 5 percent of the market.

In its place, new names, new terms, new types of agreements, and different financing mechanisms emerged. Perhaps to respond to the negativity that had been generated around "shared savings," the industry focus turned to guaranteed performance. And performance contracting emerged as the favored name.

From its shaky beginnings to its near death when oil prices plunged in 1986, a strong performance contracting industry has emerged. But performance contracting will continue to change and evolve.

We expect to see ESCOs and/or utilities providing the following retail energy services:

* energy performance contracts
* energy management systems
* load management
* power marketing
* facilities management and outsourcing
* risk management

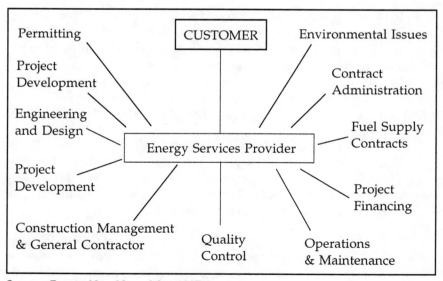

Source: *Energy User News*, May 1997

Figure 1. Potential Services from an Energy Service Provider

Much as we have witnessed in the telecommunications industry, we will begin to see ESCOs and utilities "bundling" their services...offering several or all of the above to their customers. And ultimately, utilities and/or ESCOs are apt to be selling conditioned floor space, as ESCOs and end users look for more efficient means of guaranteeing the return on an investment. Which will bring us full circle back to the first performance contract in the U.S. imported from Europe: chauffage.

We are entering a new era where we will have a blending of energy supply and its efficient use delivered by one entity. Utilities and ESCOs will be drawn together, rather than forced apart, by demand side management in its fullest sense, Performance Contracting.

We can expect to see the concept of energy performance contracting extended to other areas, such as resource management. For example, several ESCOs now offer water management on a performance contracting basis. Just as performance contracting has already been extended to encompass operational savings (begun in the UK), performance contracting will work in any setting where one can define the parameters, establish a baseline and deliver the service cost-effectively for less than the baseline.

In the meantime, those now considering performance contracting—as a consumer, an ESCO, a financier, or a utility—have a history rich in experience. We now have the ability to look at projects which have put the theory of performance contracting into practice.

REAL-LIFE PROJECTS—REAL LIFE OPPORTUNITIES

- The Chet Holifield Federal Building in Laguna Niguel, California, has reduced its energy usage by 30 percent, saving taxpayers more than $600,000 in annual gas and electricity costs. The project was a joint venture of EDISON ENVEST, as a division of Southern California Edison, and the federal government.[2]

- In 1991, a county in Florida faced losing $600,000 of a $900,000 federal grant for energy efficiency in schools and hospitals, because of budget cuts. A creative state energy official, Michael Ashworth, knew there was a way to prevent that loss. Despite the struggles of working in a young and somewhat immature industry, he persevered. This contract, now in its fifth year, is Florida's oldest performance contract in a public school district. Monroe County was able to keep its federal grant and the project has successfully met or exceeded the guaranteed savings every year.[3]

• The first performance based energy savings project in Russia has been successfully negotiated and financed by Energy Performance Services, Inc. The project site is a mining operation with an annual ore extraction of 24 million tons, near the town of Karelsky Okatysh. Project implementation began in April, 1997. The project is expected to be completed in 15 months at a cost of US $11.5 million. Energy Performance Services estimates annual savings of $3.5 million.[4]

• A comprehensive energy analysis of Western State College of Colorado revealed that the college will save nearly $485,000 annually by upgrading the campus' heating and lighting systems. The savings, guaranteed by Viron Energy Services as part of a performance contract, will pay for the on-going $3.3 million renovation project in 10 years.[5]

• In the Czech Republic, Bulovka Hospital in Prague is a large teaching hospital with 1,640 beds, 19 buildings and annual utility costs of approximately $3 million. In a joint venture, EPS, Inc. of the US and Landis & Staefa, Switzerland, developed a $2.6 million energy performance contract, with an estimated annual savings of $680,000 beginning in December, 1995. To date, annual savings have been $696,000. The project will continue through 2003.[6]

• In 1986, the Charleston Area Medical Center in West Virginia implemented its first performance contract for various lighting retrofits. Since then, working with HEC under a 10-year agreement, the hospital has completed more than 80 projects worth over $3.1 million, with energy savings totaling approximately $800,000.[7]

• Good news travels—As a result of their success, an official of the hospital actively involved with local schools, took the concept of performance contracting to Kanawha County Schools. In July of 1987, HEC and Kanawha County Schools began joint development of an energy efficiency program that has lead to projects in 89 schools. This $4 million project has to date resulted in over $1 million in savings.[8]

...and the list goes on. Real life projects with real time savings for those who no longer wish to continue to waste energy and waste resources. And the opportunities are boundless.

PUSHING THE ENVELOPE

Clearly, the "bottom-line" encourages the **commercial world** to pursue energy efficiency, whether the business is a manufacturer, industrial complex, commercial offices, or residential properties. In his book *Lean and Clean Management*, Joseph J. Romm states: "Energy savings are bottom-line savings: Depending on profit margins, that $5000 [...in energy savings] could be better than a $100,000 increase in monthly sales, which entails increased costs for materials, labor, production, and overhead."

At the **local government level**, there are already more than 4,000 performance contracts in place to assist public schools in controlling energy costs and reducing energy consumption.

At the **state government level**, states continue to enact new, and improve current, legislation that encourages savings in public facilities and identifies performance contracting as an acceptable method of financing the projects.

On the **federal government level**, the National Energy Conservation Policy Act, as amended by the Energy Policy Act of 1992, requires government agencies to reduce the consumption of energy by 20% by the year 2000. Presidential Order 12902 also sets targets for federal agencies. Both documents encourage the use of performance contracting. The Federal Energy Management Program of the U.S. Department of Energy has actively helped agencies use performance contracting to help meet the goals of these policies.

Internationally, the U.S. Agency for International Development has been particularly active and effective in making transitional economies aware of the advantages an energy service company (ESCO) industry can bring to the transition to a market economy.

The multilateral development banks, such as the European Bank for Reconstruction and Development, the World Bank, the Inter-American

Development Bank and the Asian Development Bank, have all taken steps to foster and encourage the use of ESCOs in developing countries.

Canada has established an Insured Energy Savings Program (IESP) which reaches beyond the creditworthiness of the owner without placing the full credit risk burden on the ESCO. The IESP provides performance insurance, which creates an "ESCO neutral" financing package by providing 100 percent of the turnkey costs through a non-recourse structure for both the ESCO and the owner. In the IESP scenario, the owner has three options if the retrofit underperforms:[9]

- continue to make payments in anticipation of surplus savings at a later date;

- request the ESCO to make-up the shortfall;

- the Shortfall and Mitigation Fund could be advanced. This would be repaid by stretching the savings period by 10%. This would represent the absolute "worst case" for the owner but nevertheless provides a date-certain termination of the program. It does not create a "pay whatever savings are available situation."

The expanding horizons of performance contracting are not limited to energy. **Water resource management** has found a home in the performance contracting arena. Water savings can be the basis of a performance contract, or in the case of Boston University, it can offer paybacks that make the needed energy work economically viable. Work at the university progressed on a building by building basis, but when they got to Mugar Memorial Library the mechanical work, calculated at 7.62 year payback, would not meet the basic financing criteria of an aggregate payback of six years or less. H_2O Matrix[10] joined the ESCO team and identified water retrofits; i.e., low-flow toilet and urinal flush valves, replacement of all faucet aerators with low-flow models, and the repair of domestic water leaks. The addition of these water conservation measures with a combined 2.82 year payback resulted in a cumulative project payback of 5.6 years, taking the economics below the base criteria.

The opportunities also exist for creative performance contracting that result in business solutions in **wastewater systems**. A manufacturing facility in the Northeast needed improvements to their water and wastewater system, along with significant improvements to their production facilities to increase capacity and lower production costs. By outsourcing their water and wastewater systems, the manufacturer was able to obtain capital, reduce capital requirements, reduce operational costs, and reduce management time on the water and wastewater systems.

The outsourcing partner purchased the existing wastewater treatment facility, installed a water reuse system, and provided facility capital improvements. The manufacturer was guaranteed a reduction of $100,000 annually in operations and maintenance. The outsource partner was able to pay for the system, make improvements and lower the cost of O&M through the energy-efficiency measures.[11]

Performance contracting guarantees savings, and produces results. It is both a simple concept and a complex process. If both parties take the time to understand the options and procedures, negotiate a fair contract, and exercise the necessary commitment, it **WILL** work. There will be satisfaction.

And that's guaranteed!

References
1 *Energy User News*, Volume 22, No. 5.
2 *Energy Efficient Journal*, Volume 4, Number 4.
3 Michael Ashworth, Administrator of State Energy Efficiency Programs, State of Florida.
4 *Energy Efficiency Journal*, Volume 5, Numbers 1 and 2.
5 Viron Energy Services.
6 EPS, Inc.
7 HEC, Inc.
8 HEC, Inc.
9 Richard A. McKenzie, Director, Industrial, Commercial and Institutional Programs Division, Natural Resources, Canada
10 H2O Matrix, Two Oliver Street, Boston Massachusetts 02109, offers water conservation performance contracts.
11 Lombardo Associates/ERI Services, Newton, Massachusetts

Chapter 2

The Money Side
Of Energy

In performance contracting, what a proposed modification will cost and save is the bottom line. Return on investment is usually the motivating force for the end-user, the energy service company (ESCO), and the financing source.

Conversely, the dollars that will be lost if management doesn't act should be a major factor in setting financial priorities. A key consideration is how much the organization will spend if it doesn't reduce energy consumption. This analysis should precede decisions related to energy efficiency and is integral to managing a performance contract effectively once it is in place.

More than one manager has been furious at an ESCO because the organization wasn't achieving predicted "savings," when, in fact, energy savings had been eaten up by increases in the rate schedule. The "front office" may not understand how changing rate schedules can destroy predicted savings. The concept of cost avoidance is essential to weighing and communicating performance contracting benefits.

The guidelines for weighing cost-effectiveness, calculating cost of delay and computing/graphing cost avoidance offered in this chapter are important to the end-user as well as the ESCOs.

Cost-effectiveness

Because every business, every organization, uses a significant amount of costly energy, a wide array of energy conservation opportunities are available to them. However, these opportunities must be weighed to determine which measures offer the greatest financial benefit. This requires not only an evaluation of the cost-effectiveness of the measures, individually and in combination, but a broader financial analysis as well.

Ideally, major modifications will be reviewed by a committee constituted by management so implications for particular programs or impact on the work environment are part of the decision making process. Indoor air quality and other environmental concerns should be considered. At the very least, a cost/benefit analysis requires the sharing of information and techniques between the organization's business officer and the facility manager. If the organization has an energy manager, he/she should definitely be involved. The group should collectively weigh all the energy conservation measures in the light of the financial benefits to the energy program and to the total operation.

Other operation and facility considerations also need to be considered. A new roof is not apt to be the most cost-effective measure. However, if the old roof is leaking, a new roof with increased insulation may be the most critical need. Or, replacing an old boiler that is not only inefficient, but is unpredictable and demands a lot of maintenance, may take precedence over a more attractive controls option.

Sources of funding and reimbursement implications must also be considered. Some utilities may still have rebate programs, for example, to encourage the use of more efficient technologies.

Cost-effectiveness is one measure of economic feasibility. It is an essential ingredient in performance contracting. It answers the question: "How soon can we get our money back from this investment?" There are various ways to calculate the time necessary to recoup the cost of the original investment. These range from simple payback and adjusted payback to the more complicated life-cycle costing (LCC).

SIMPLE PAYBACK

Quick, simple and universally understood, simple payback calculations generally provide sufficient data for low to modest investments. It can also provide a good "first cut" on larger investments. Its purpose is to determine when the funds invested in a particular project will be recovered. The simple payback period (SPP) is found by dividing the value of the initial investment by the projected annual energy savings. SPP is usually given in years and/or tenths of a year.

Simple Payback Formula

$$SPP \text{ (years)} = \frac{I}{ES/year}$$

where,

SPP   = Simple payback period
I   = Initial investment
ES/year   = Projected annual energy savings at current prices

if,

I   = $ 2,000
ES/year   = $ 450

then,

$$SPP = \frac{I}{ES/year} = \frac{\$2000}{\$450} = 4.4 \text{ years}$$

NOTE: In this example and the examples that follow, no attempt has been made to reflect the impact of depreciation, taxes or discount rates.

ADJUSTED PAYBACKS

The simple payback calculations may be modified by any factor management finds critical. The more common adjustments to be factored in are; (1) changes in operations and maintenance (O&M) costs, or (2) projected changes in energy costs.

1.   Changes in O&M costs. The new equipment might require more, or less, O&M work. To the extent the O&M work can be quantified, the Adjusted Payback Period (APP) formula would then read as follows:

Adjusted Payback Formula, O&M

$$APP_{O\&M} = \frac{I}{ES_n + M_n}$$

where,

$$APP_{O\&M} = \text{Payback period adjusted for O\&M}$$

$$
\begin{aligned}
I &= \text{Initial investment for period of analysis} \\
ES_n &= \text{Energy savings for analysis period} \\
M_n &= \text{Differential operations and maintenance} \\
&\quad \text{costs for analysis period} \\
n &= \text{Period of analysis}
\end{aligned}
$$

2.   Changes in energy costs. Since the payback period is a function of energy costs, this approach can more accurately reflect the impact of unstable energy prices. The difficulty comes in predicting future energy costs. Therefore, it is recommended that projections on energy prices be limited to three years and used only for internal discussion, unless the organization has a longer term contract.

Adjusted Payback Formula, Energy Cost

$$APP_e = \frac{I}{X(E_{n1} + E_{n2} + E_{n3})}$$

where,

$$
\begin{aligned}
APP_e &= \text{Payback period adjusted for projected energy costs} \\
I &= \text{Initial investment} \\
E_{n1} &= \text{Projected 1st year energy costs} \\
E_{n2} &= \text{Projected 2nd year energy costs} \\
E_{n3} &= \text{Projected 3rd year energy costs}
\end{aligned}
$$

In the era of utility restructuring it is worth restating the inherent dangers in publicly justifying certain energy efficiency measures predicated on energy price increases (unless you are quoting data supplied by the utility or from a signed contract). If prices don't increase as predicted; or, worse yet, fall, you end up looking pretty bad. Even worse, the justification may become the story. The headline resulting from a university's board of trustees meeting may state, "20% Energy Price Increase Next Year: University Says." And the planned energy efficiency work becomes lost in the hullabaloo.

SIMPLIFIED CASH FLOW

Cost effectiveness is sometimes calculated in terms of Simplified Cash Flow (SCF). In this case, the computation is usually calculated within the parameters of a given fiscal year. SCF weighs the difference in the cost of the fuel consumed plus the difference in O&M costs against the investment for a given time period.

$$SCF = (E_n + O\&M_n) - (I_n)$$

where,

$$
\begin{aligned}
SCF &= \text{Simplified cash flow} \\
E_n &= \text{Energy cost savings for the time period} \\
O\&M_n &= \text{Operations and maintenance savings for the period} \\
I_n &= \text{Initial investment prorated} \\
n &= \text{Period of analysis}
\end{aligned}
$$

if,

$$
\begin{aligned}
I &= \$2,000, \text{ spread over 4 years} \\
E_n &= \$450 \text{ per year} \\
O\&M_n &= \$150 \text{ per year}
\end{aligned}
$$

then,

$$
\begin{aligned}
SCF &= (\$450 + \$150) - (\$2000/4) \\
&= \$600 - \$500 = \$100/\text{year}
\end{aligned}
$$

LIFE-CYCLE COSTING

Incorporating all costs and savings associated with a purchase for the life of the equipment is increasingly being used as a means of judging cost-effectiveness. This approach, Life-Cycle Costing (LCC), may appear to administrators in government to be the antithesis of the required low bid/first cost procurement procedures. If specifications call for LCC as a means of determining cost-effectiveness, then LCC can be compatible with low bid procedures.

LCC's rather rigorous approach can be quite time consuming; however, you will find the effort is usually justified for larger purchases and/

or for relatively limited capital. Life cycle costing addresses many factors which an adjusted payback analysis may miss—salvage value, equipment life, lost opportunity costs for alternate use of the money, taxes, interest, and other factors.

The simplest mode of analysis for LCC is:

Life-Cycle Cost Formula

$$LCC = I - S + M + R + E$$

where,

LCC = Life-Cycle Cost
I = Investment costs
S = Salvage value
M = Maintenance costs
R = Replacement costs
E = Energy costs

LCC is the net benefit of all major costs and savings for the life of the equipment discounted to present value. A building design or system that lowers the LCC without loss in performance can generally be held to be more cost-effective. Other considerations, such as the calculation of present worth, discounting factors and rates, and LCC in new design, need detailed analysis and are more fully discussed in Life-Cycle Cost Manual for the Federal Energy Management Program, prepared by the National Institute of Standards and Technology, United States Department of Commerce.

In considering cost-effectiveness, especially where guarantees are involved, the reader is referred to the discussion on investment grade audits in Chapter 9. Cost-effectiveness cannot be assigned to measures without consideration of the conditions within which it must operate, including the capabilities of the operations and maintenance staff and the condition of existing energy-related equipment.

COST OF DELAY

Some things can be put off without a loss of revenue. Energy efficiency work cannot. Every tick of the clock, every day that passes, represents dollars an organization may have wasted by consuming needless

energy. Every hour of delay forces you to give money to the utility that, through energy management, could have been used to educate students, train sales reps, offer patients additional services, launch a media campaign, meet constituent needs, make a bigger profit, etc. Many administrators tend to treat the utility bill as an inevitable cost. Others find that organizational pressures, which require immediate attention, push energy concerns aside.

But, every day you don't act is a day of wasted energy and, what is more important, a day of wasted money. For example, in Florida, a large state agency with more than fifty sites prepared to enter into a performance contract with the support of the State Energy Office. Despite previous performance contracts for State agencies, a well-meaning attorney took issue with the concept that a state agency would be committing itself to payments to a financial institution, regardless of the status of the ESCO or the performance of the equipment. This one issue delayed the signing of a financial agreement for over eighteen months, at a cost of delay of $106,800 per month in lost energy savings! A loss of at least $1.9m to the agencies—and to Florida tax payers.

Those working in energy management have become accustomed to weighing options by calculating cost-effectiveness as discussed above. The rapidity with which energy savings recover initial investments should be a major factor in weighing energy retrofit *vis á vis* other investments. It is not unusual to find a school district, for example, with a reserve fund earning 7.1 percent interest while energy investments with an ROI of 25 percent or more go begging. Every decision maker in an organization needs to understand fully the "earning potential" in energy efficiency and the lost revenue inherent in delay.

The cost of delay is almost the mirror image of the simplified cash flow formula. The same factors that contribute to energy cost/benefit analysis affect cost of delay calculations, but in a negative sense.

To repeat, the SCF formula is:

$$\text{SCF} = (E_n + O\text{+}M_n) - (I_n)$$

where,

$\quad$ SCF $\quad$ = Simplified cash flow
$\quad\quad E_n \quad$ = Energy cost savings for the period
$\quad$ O&M$_n$ $\quad$ = Operations and maintenance savings for time period
$\quad\quad I_n \quad$ = Initial investment prorated
$\quad\quad n \quad$ = Period of analysis

By totaling the differential costs (the anticipated savings) and sub-tracting the prorated investment, the positive cash flow for a specific cost-effective energy efficiency measure is determined.

The same formula can be used for Cost of Delay (CoD) where the lost savings potential becomes the differential. The lost savings differen-tial is then reduced by the outlay that would have been needed in a given year to achieve those savings, the prorated investment. This nega-tive cash flow figure represents the cost of postponing energy work.

$$\text{CoD} = -(E_n + O\text{+}M_n) + (I_n)$$

where,

$\quad$ CoD $\quad$ = Cost of Delay
$\quad\quad E_n \quad$ = Energy cost savings for period
$\quad$ O&M$_n$ $\quad$ = Operations and maintenance savings for period
$\quad\quad I_n \quad$ = Initial investment prorated
$\quad\quad n \quad$ = A specified period of time

For example, suppose the city government is just starting an energy program and has been advised it can reduce consumption by 25 percent through energy efficient O&M procedures, low-cost retrofits, and the installation of an automated energy management control system. With an annual utility bill of $1.6 million, the avoided costs could be $400,000 per year, less the cost of work. If a $1,400,000 installation prorated over five years (at $280,000 per year) could save $400,000 per year in energy and operations and maintenance costs, the SCF would be $120,000 per year. On the other hand, no action represents a CoD of *minus* $120,000 per year.

Using an annual SCF formula without any adjustment for inflation and with the purchase/installation costs prorated over five years, the calculations would be:

$$\begin{aligned}
\text{SCF} \quad &= (\text{E} + \text{O\&M savings for year}) - (\text{I [prorated]}) \\
&= (\$400,000) - (\$1,400,000/5) \\
&= \$400,000 - \$280,000 \\
&= + \$120,000
\end{aligned}$$

The $400,000 savings would reduce the existing $1.6 M to $1.2 M. In this case, the potentially lower budget is used as a reference point.

$$\begin{aligned}
\text{CoD} \quad &= \text{minus (E + O\&M for the year)} + (\text{I prorated}) \\
\text{CoD} \quad &= \text{The new lower budget minus the existing budget} \\
&\quad (\$1.2 - \$1.6 = -\$400,000) \\
&\quad \text{Plus the prorated investment} \\
&\quad (\$1,400,000/5 = \$280,000) \\
&= -\$400,000 + \$280,000 \\
&= -\$120,000
\end{aligned}$$

In essence, this rather awkward formula looks at what could have been saved less the cost of the work required to achieve those savings over a specified period. To put it more simply, potential savings equal your losses if you do nothing.

The formula does not look beyond the years of prorated investment. In the above example, the CoD becomes $400,000 (exclusive of any O&M costs, depreciation or net present value) in the sixth year and every year thereafter, for the life of the improvement.

Even when using internal resources, you should calculate the Cost of Delay related to various financing options. Using limited resources for other organizational needs may, in the long run, prove to be more costly. If those needs are paramount and the budget is tight, then getting the work done through performance contracting becomes an even more viable option. Figure 2-1 compares the cost of delay a school district might incur by doing nothing to the financial benefits of using traditional bonding or performance contracting. The figure uses simple payback and constant dollars.

An organization is frequently reluctant to use performance contracting because it prefers to do the work itself and "save the service costs." Reality seldom meets expectations. Frequently, the losses due to delays exceed the benefits of internal funding. When an organization is considering the use of in-house labor and funds to save money, it should

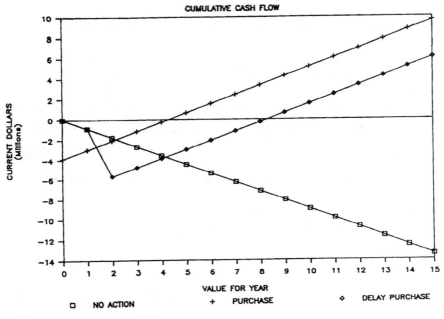

Figure 2-1. Cost of Delay

carefully weigh the Cost of Delay first. And the delayed period should be based on how long it took to get similar work in place in the past—from conception to acceptance of the installation—and not what someone hopes might be the case this time.

In addition to the cash flow impact depicted in Figure 2-1, you need to also recognize the benefit in improving your organization's capital stock, which ultimately enhances its fiscal condition and usually reduces operations and maintenance costs.

To check your understanding of the calculations needed to determine the annualized Cost of Delay you may wish to work through the problem in Figure 2-2.

Using data supplied through energy audits, you can use the same Cost of Delay calculation procedures to determine what you may actually be losing every day, month, or year that your organization fails to act.

After the commitment to secure private sector financing has been made, delays are often incurred because outside support, particularly attorneys, are not familiar with the performance contracting process. These delays can be reduced if your attorney and engineer are involved early in the process.

COST OF DELAY: SAMPLE PROBLEM

Data:

Annual utility bill	=	$1,500,000
O&M on existing equipment	=	600
Projected savings	=	30% energy
		30% O&M
Retrofit investment	=	$1,750,000
Prorated period	=	5 years

Problem:

If the project is put off for one year, what is the Cost of Delay?

First, calculate the projected savings

$1,500,000 × 30% + $600 × 30%

Then, determine what it would cost each year to achieve those savings
$1,750,000 ÷ 5 years

(The net LOSS should be - $100,180/yr)

Now, calculate CoD for 6 years (without considering depreciation, time value of money, or adjustments in O&M.)

Answer Below:[1]

Figure 2-2. Cost of Delay Analysis

COST AVOIDANCE

Rising prices can wipe out all the dollar gains you have made by reducing energy consumption. But think what your organization would have been paying if it hadn't cut back! In order to communicate energy management benefits to others as costs rise, its important to be able to talk about what would have been—the costs avoided.

---

[1]$950,900 ($100,180 × 5 + $450,000 in 6th year, after investment is paid off.)

The joy of counting the dollars that would have gone to the utility makes cost avoidance very real and very gratifying. In order to calculate cost avoidance, a base year must be established. The base year consumption multiplied by the current price per unit will reveal "what it would have cost."

Cost avoidance is what it would have cost minus current costs. Most top management or board members seldom have the time or inclination to wade through a pile of numbers; so it will pay to graph the data when cost avoidance for more than one year is involved.

As an illustration, Figure 2-3 depicts a cost avoidance analysis for Tender Care Hospital. The hospital had cut electrical consumption by 1,002,660 kWh since 1994, but experienced a rate increase of $0.042/kWh over the 1994 to 1998 time period. Even though consumption dropped 25 percent during this time period, costs still rose about $73,000. Without energy efficiency measures, that cost would have increased to $167,000. The top line in Figure 2-3 depicts what it would have cost if consumption had remained at the 1994 level, the middle line indicates actual costs. The shaded area between the top and middle line shows the avoided costs. The bottom line shows the decline in consumption.

The same type of graph as shown on the following page could be used for all the fuels used in a building if total Btu is placed on the vertical axis.

Cost-effectiveness, Cost of Delay and Cost Avoidance are critical components of energy decision-making whether you plan to do your own retrofit work, or ask a performance contractor to provide the service.

ESCOs need to employ these concepts as part of their marketing technique. Cost of Delay is particularly effective.

Cost avoidance numbers, preferably graphs, should be a regular feature in the monthly billing process. Without it, customers quickly forget what the utility bill used to be and why they are paying the ESCO. This becomes particularly critical when there has been a change in administration or top management.

PLOTTING COST AVOIDANCE

Great Eagle Complex   Data: 1998   3,980,760 kWh   Fuel Source: Electricity
                               2002   3,390,200 kWh
                               2006   2,978,100 kWh

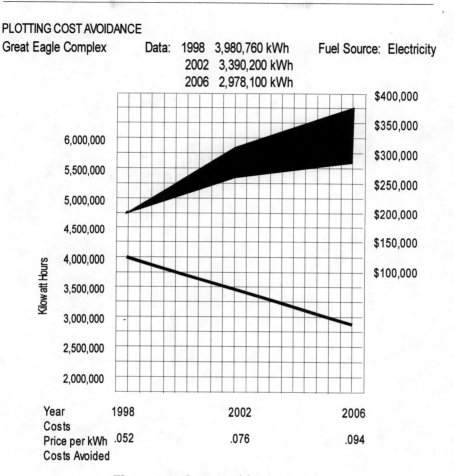

Figure 2-3. Cost Avoidance Graph

Chapter 3

The Fine Art of Solicitation And Selection

A common lament from energy service companies (ESCOs), and those of us who help customers secure ESCO services is, "Please figure out what you want to do first *before* the request for proposal (RFP)[1] is issued." Second-guessing and changing intent in mid-stream create headaches for all. The costs to ESCOs, the frustrating time delays, the owner's cost of delay, the procedural (and legal) problems are legion.

PREPARATION

A few "Homework Rules" will help avoid costly delays and disasters.

Rule #1 for any customer seeking ESCO services is to: *determine the results you want first.* Gather a good cross-section of the organization together to decide what you want out of a performance contract. Since performance contracting rests on techni-

---

[1]We have bowed to the inevitable in this discussion and refer to all requests for ESCO services as RFPs, which is common in the market place. As noted later in this chapter, there is rarely a need for a full blown RFP and a request for qualifications (RFQ) will usually serve.

cal, legal and financial procedures, the team should include facility, legal and financial people.

Many of the problems of securing ESCO services are rooted in the idea that performance contracting is a technical solution; so someone in management thinks the RFP process should be handled by the facility people. Of course, they must be involved. Sound technical services is a key component. But performance contracting is basically a financial transaction and even the very best facility people should not be asked to go it alone.

The customer should, at the outset, recognize who in his or her shop makes the decisions and who influences decisions. Energy managers and facility managers are very influential and can easily kill a deal, but they seldom sign a performance contract. Those who will ultimately okay a contract (lawyer) and sign a contract (CEO &/or CFO) should be involved from the beginning. If they are not represented in the process from the beginning, chances increase dramatically that major procedural changes will occur mid-process.

Results is the by-word for Rule #1. Yes, the customer may need a new boiler or an up-date in the controls system, but the goal is a more efficient, less costly operation that yields a more productive work environment. The organization is buying the ESCO's expertise in reducing operating costs and the associated services to make it happen. Equipment is merely the vehicle used to deliver the savings and services.

Nor should the RFP procedures team lose sight of the need for a productive work environment. The goal is not to cut energy consumption *per se* but to use the energy that must be used as efficiently as possible. Safeguards in operating parameters are essential components of the contract, and need to be reflected in the RFP. Setting acceptable heating and cooling temperature ranges, lighting levels, humidity range and air changes per hour offer occupants the assurances they want and give an ESCO the information it needs to decide whether it should even consider the job.

Sometimes safeguards are situation specific. A very successful ESCO, whose track record in heavy industry is outstanding, may be a disaster in a hospital. For a hospital, a major concern is infection control and *nosocomial* is a dreadful thought. An ESCO, which does not understand the use of positive and negative pressure or isorooms and has not had successful experience in a hospital, should NEVER be selected to do hospital work.

The RFP, therefore, should state the general and more specific criteria an ESCO must meet to be selected.

Rule #2, then, for any customer is to *decide the criteria* the organization will use to determine the ESCO that can best deliver the results it wants. Setting those criteria and how they will be used in the evaluation process is discussed later in the chapter.

For Rule #3, we get really dogmatic. The *evaluation procedures*, which incorporate those criteria, *should be well thought out <u>before</u> the customer issues an RFP*. Each time we have done so, we say we will never again go into a selection process when the RFP has already been issued. A recent experience will explain why.

Recently, an RFP titled, "Request for Proposal for Performance Contracting for Energy Conservation Services" was issued. The first criteria for selection stated in the RFP read, "Preference shall be given to respondents who demonstrate strong capabilities in

terms of experience and reputation in performance contracting,..." But when it came to evaluation time, the owner decided that the proposers didn't need performance contracting experience! The owner still had not made the basic decision as to whether or not the organization wanted a performance contract and an ESCO who had the experience to deliver one. For this and other reasons, we recommended the owner close the solicitation and start over. To do anything else was a gold plated invitation for litigation.

Now that the preliminary homework has been completed, it's time to consider writing the RFP. Even though Oliver Wendell Holmes is said to have observed, "No generalization is worth a damn, including this one," we will generalize that RFPs are inevitably longer than they need to be and ask for far more information than most owners know what to do with. And so we come to Rule #4.

Compliance with Rule #4 would cause a collective sigh in the ESCO industry and create a major drop in consumption of Excedrine for headache 1001.

Rule #4 for soliciting proposals is pretty simple:

- *Keep it short!*
- *Keep it open!*
- *Keep it simple!* and
- *Get only the information you truly need to make an evaluation!*

Proposals that cover all facets of energy financing and services are cumbersome to evaluate and expensive for an ESCO to prepare. The time and cost of preparing a major proposal is apt to discourage some ESCOs from submitting one. This is especially true if the savings opportunities are limited, or the administration or delivery of services relatively burdensome. A cumbersome solicitation process, therefore, definitely limits the options available to smaller organizations—and does not do any favors for larger organizations.

Developing an RFQ/RFP

Prior to structuring the evaluation process, the committee should meet and agree on definitions, scoring and procedures. Preferably, the criteria, weighting, etc. will be set by the committee before the solicitation is issued. The solicitation, such as a Request for Qualifications (RFQ) or RFP, will inform potential proposers of the services required and the criteria that will be used to judge their qualifications. (Assessing the organization's needs and setting criteria are discussed in Chapter 8.)

The following thoughts for RFP writers will make life simpler for everyone involved.

Keep it short! It takes time for your people to prepare big requests for proposals (RFPs). And you don't do yourself any favors by doing so. The only excuse for extensive RFPs is in the case of federal and some state government efforts where acquisition regulations compound the problem. Most RFPs (outside of government) should not exceed 30 pages, plus any appendices.

Keep it open! Detailed specifications are a throw back to "bid/ spec." Performance contracting solicitations should be based on eliciting information as to the ESCO's qualifications—not price. (There are some "price" exceptions, e.g., the federal government insists on some bid prices and the Canadians use an "open book" approach.) Describe what results you want; not how to do it. If you know exactly how to do it, you probably don't need an ESCO. Detailed specifications eliminate options ESCOs can offer. Your organization may lose out on all the rich experiences ESCOs can make available to you. It's their business to identify all cost-effective energy conserving opportunities; not yours.

Precise specifications not only put a box around the ESCO's opportunity to help; it may spell out a project in such a way that the ESCO cannot guarantee the savings.

Keep it simple! Some RFPs raise the question, "Who are you trying to impress?" Or, "You want what!?!" Your organization is more apt to get clean, direct proposals if you issue clean, forthright RFPs.

The obligations imposed on responding ESCOs should be kept within the realm of reason. In the early 1990s an organization with 100+ buildings issued a *preliminary* request for qualifications that required the responding ESCOs to audit facilities and to guarantee a level of savings for all its buildings. At this preliminary stage, the idea was absurd and served no purpose! Since the majority of the buildings were schools, which are seldom all that unique, the request bordered on the ridiculous. Since it was a large organization, some ESCOs did offer qualified responses in the hope that the organization would get more realistic as the process progressed.

GETTING THE BEST

The more you ask for, the more tedious and costly the evaluation process. Most "kitchen sink" RFPs are a testimonial to organizations which have not truly thought through their needs and/or the performance contracting process. Or, managers who must satisfy so many internal masters that the primary purpose of the document is all but forgotten. In "many masters" situations, the use of oral interviews for the pre-qualified few should be considered.

The "get what you need" admonition cuts both ways. ESCOs should be constrained by format and length. Unless it's one of those government things, one must worry about an ESCO that can't tell you who they are, what they can do, and how they package their program in 30 pages or less—excluding appendices and sample audits.

TO TEST OR NOT TO TEST

In the 1970s when this whole process was foreign, test audits were *de rigueur*. The best way to judge the technical capability and approach of an energy service company was to have the owner's engineer review an audit report of the organization's test site. Use of test audits was more important when the industry was young and the abilities of individual firms were untested.

Fortunately, the desire, and certainly the need, for a test audit has faded with time. Unique organizations with unusual operations or peculiar problems may warrant a test audit. Others should resist this cumbersome embellishment if they possibly can.

Owners should keep in mind that ESCOs, who repeatedly succumb to test audit conditions, have to recover their costs somewhere. The test audit costs run up the overhead. Ultimately, those costs must be borne by the customers—particularly those organizations that asked for test audits.

The major difference between a full blown RFP and what has become known as a request for qualifications (RFQ) is generally the technical requirements; and more specifically a test audit.

Today, established ESCOs have proven track records and an increasing number of organizations are accepting sample audits of similar facilities, or well documented references/case studies in lieu of on-site test audits. A test audit is just one more obstacle that may prevent a well-qualified ESCO, who could meet an organization's needs, from even proposing. Audits are costly and ESCOs are increasingly reluctant to audit on speculation.

At the very least, audits should only be requested from a short list of pre-qualified ESCOs. This saves the ESCOs time, improves their odds and reduces the burden on your organization that would result from the evaluation of a large number of test audits.

The most attractive alternative is to ask proposers to submit an audit for a similar facility, which is representative of the work they propose to perform. This sample audit can still be evaluated by an engineer representing the owner's interests and can also be used as a basis for a representative presentation of an ESCO's financial approach. The customer should reserve the right to attach the sample audit by reference to the contract, representative of the ESCO's standard of practice. This reduces the chances of getting a "solid gold Cadillac" as a sample and a Chevy as the delivered product.

PRE-PROPOSAL CONFERENCE

The RFQ/RFP process frequently also involves a conference for prospective proposers, particularly for larger or complex projects. Much like a bidders' conference, the pre-proposal meeting is designed to clarify and expand upon the organization's needs. If it has not been made part of the issued RFQ, you should be prepared to describe the facility(ies) operation (hours, occupancy, processes, square footage, etc.) and offer utility records for at least two years, preferably three, on all candidate buildings. As part of the conference, proposers should be given an opportunity to walk through a representative building while staff respond to questions. Even though the more exacting technical considerations may have been deferred, prospective proposers should have some opportunity to judge the organization's savings potential and whether the job potential meets their criteria.

Unless the project is very large, attendance requirements at the pre-proposal conference should be kept to a minimum, for this is just one more requirement that could discourage ESCO participation.

Required attendance at pre-proposal conferences puts a burden on the industry and reduces the options for the end-user; so required conferences should be well structured and substantive. If the project is awarded to an ESCO that did not attend a pre-proposal conference, then a real question as to the value of the pre-proposal conference must be raised. A required pre-proposal conference, therefore, limits owner's options downstream and should be called only if there are some unique concerns or procedures that may substantially affect the proposals.

Unless the pre-proposal conference is a required part of the selection procedure, a firm's attendance should not, technically, be a factor in making the selection. The conference does provide a subtle opportunity, however, to size up the proposers, and for ESCOs to make a favorable impression. It is also an opportunity for an ESCO to size up a candidate for its services! Since performance contracting has been compared to a marriage, the pre-proposal conference might be viewed as a the first date in a "courting ritual."

INTERVIEWS

After the preliminary selection of qualified firms, an organization can elect to hold oral interviews. If oral interviews are held, the letter of invitation should outline the nature of the presentation expected and any other requirements to be placed on the proposer. It is also helpful if the ESCO is provided information as to who will be representing the organization at the meeting. ESCOs will often ask who the other finalists are and in what order they will be interviewed. Whether this information is supplied is, of course, totally at the discretion of the customer. A good gauge is for the customer to consider what *it* will gain by providing an ESCO such information.

After the interview, many potential customers have found it useful to request a summary statement confirming or clarifying certain points raised during the meeting. This is particularly pertinent if new conditions or offerings have been presented in the interview process.

A TWO-STEP SOLICITATION

There are three disadvantages to relying on a RFQ/RFP two-phase effort: (1) the qualifications proposal usually does not describe the ESCO's full technical approach to the project, or the financial benefits to the organization; so the evaluators will not know for sure whether they have selected the most favorable candidate (the most attractive opportunity, therefore, may be lost); (2) ESCOs may view the two-phase submission as too burdensome, particularly from a smaller organization, and may be discouraged from proposing; and (3) when used with a technical second phase, it protracts the selection process, thus lengthening the time the organization must pay for wasted energy. A two-step selection process also lengthens the sales cycle, which ultimately adds to product/ service costs. A two-step process is only warranted in very large and/or complex facilities; or, in pre-qualification procedures used in federal government solicitations.

REQUESTS FOR QUALIFICATIONS FORMAT

Since the firm's qualifications to deliver the results are the most important single criterion, the accepted practice in many instances is a brief request for qualifications (RFQ) procedure as a stand alone effort, or prior to any in-depth consideration of technical competence. If your organization is inclined to use this approach, exercise care that this pre-liminary screening does not yield qualified firms that look good on paper, but in practice offer inexperienced teams to do the work. Ask for, and expect, a listing of who will be assigned to your job, their assigned responsibilities and their qualifications to fulfill those responsibilities. An estimate of the amount of time they will actually spend on the job is also key. Otherwise, you are apt to have a high powered engineer breeze through leaving Engineers in Training (EITs) in his wake to do the work.

The RFQ procedure can identify the selected ESCO; or, at the least, narrows the focus to a select group of candidates. A second stage, request for technical proposals, oral interviews, and/or sample audits may then follow.

It pays to remember the first law of RFQ writing: the more you ask for the less you get. Defining the results rather than the means will reduce the burden of RFQ preparation and encourage more innovative responses.

In Figure 3-1, the basic elements of an RFQ are presented. A sample RFQ is presented in Appendix A. In using the language in the sample RFQ, you need to remember it only offers a starting point for developing an RFQ that meets your organization's particular needs. You are encouraged to modify it by expanding or deleting certain sections to reflect your precise needs.

REQUEST FOR QUALIFICATIONS

1. Purpose and scope—As briefly as possible, offer the over-all purpose of the project, the range of services you are looking for, and any limitations of importance to an ESCO.

2. Proposal procedures—submission information and expectations regarding the RFQ or later submission requirements; e.g., whether an audit will be expected from the pre-qualified firms.

3. Pre-proposal—(bidders) conference information.

4. Selection criteria and any weighting.

5. Brief case study references which include:
    a)   demographics;
    b)   projected and actual costs;
    c)   measures implemented;
    d)   predicted and actual savings; and
    e)   contact information.

6. Contract requirements pertinent to costs to be incurred by contractor.

7. Proposal format and content
    a)   Contractor background and qualifications.
    b)   Trade references.
    c)   Personnel designated to participate in the project, responsibilities, qualifications, experience in similar facilities and percentage of time each person will devote to the project.
    d)   Sub-trades performed and reliance on joint venture or subcontractors; qualification information on joint venture and/or major subcontractors.
    e)   Prior relevant experience and references.
    f)   Annual report or audited financial statements for the ESCO's most recent fiscal year.
    g)   Demonstrated capability to finance the project.
    h)   Demonstrated level of performance bonding; professional liability insurance.

8. Assurances, qualifications, limitations.

9. Proposal format instructions.

Figure 3-1. RFQ Contents

REQUEST FOR PROPOSALS FORMAT

Should an organization wish to use a broader request for proposal (RFP), the RFQ presented in Appendix A can be converted to an RFP by adding components that solicit information on the technical approach and associated financial calculations. Language eliciting technical competence should set the auditing and financial parameters. Should your organization decide a test audit must be done on a given facility(ies), language similar to that placed at the end of Appendix A should be incorporated in the solicitation document.

Other Modifications

In converting the RFQ to an RFP, the document should be carefully reviewed for any cosmetic changes needed to make the solicitation consistent throughout. Other procedural changes, such as the time specified in the deadlines, should consider the longer time period required for ESCO to conduct a test audit.

Whatever process is used, the key to effective solicitation procedures is to ask for the information that will enable the customer to judge the proposers' qualifications and competence to meet the organization's particular needs as established in the criteria.

ESTABLISHING CRITERIA

In actual practice, the process of evaluating proposals will follow the solicitation procedures discussed earlier in this chapter. The intended evaluation procedure, however, precedes a discussion of solicitations because evaluation criteria and process concerns should influence the way the request for qualifications and consequent responses are developed. As Abraham Lincoln once observed, "If we could first know where we are and whither we are tending, we could better judge what to do and how to do it."

Evaluating the qualifications of an energy service company usually requires a multiple disciplinary approach, including technical and financial expertise. The evaluation process, therefore, typically involves a committee. Unless the organization soliciting an ESCO's services has in-house performance contracting experience, it pays to support the committee's deliberations with a consultant.

Before putting pen to paper, an honest appraisal of in-house performance contracting capabilities is warranted. Customers often seek performance contracts because they do not have the funds to do the needed work on their own. This frugal posture may cause resistance to hiring a consultant. Unless someone in the organization is thoroughly familiar with performance contracting, this is an exceedingly expensive way to "save money." The costs of a performance contract consultant, and/or an engineer as a technical consultant, can be assigned to the project, and the costs covered by future savings.

To establish consistency among evaluators, scoring procedures need to be determined at the outset.

Proposals are generally scored on a 0 to 10 scale for each criteria and are entered on an evaluation form, usually a worksheet for each of the major criteria. Those scores are then transferred to a summary sheet. At this point, the total score for each major criterion is multiplied by the agreed upon weighting to reflect the relative importance of the criterion. The sum of the weighted scores for each criterion provides the total score.

The scores are usually based on a frame of reference as follows:

0) Criterion was not addressed in the proposal or the material presented was totally without merit.
1) Bare minimum.
2) Criterion was addressed minimally, but indicated little capability or awareness of the area.
3) Intermediate Score between 2 and 4.
4) Criterion was addressed minimally, but indicated some capability.
5) Intermediate Score between 4 and 6.
6) Criterion was addressed adequately. Overall, a basic capability.
7) Intermediate Score between 6 and 8.
8) Criterion was addressed well. The response indicates some superior features.
9) Intermediate Score between 8 and 10.
10) Criterion was addressed in superior fashion, indicating excellent, or outstanding, capabilities.

Worksheets for each criterion can be broken out into factors to be considered. A detailed listing of these factors makes sure the evaluator considers each aspect—and that the proposer has not omitted, whether purposefully or inadvertently, any important information. Examples of the above criteria applied to team qualifications are shown below.

EXAMPLES

Criterion: Qualifications of the Proposing Team

Factors To Be Considered:

a) Experience of the prime contractor with previous projects of similar size and type.

b) Experience of the joint venture partner (or suggested subcontractors in the team) with previous projects of similar size and type relative to their stated special expertise.

c) Experience of the proposed project manager as it relates to this project, as well as the qualifications of the assistant project manager; site manager; financial specialist; engineers for design; etc. Percentage of time suggested personnel will devote to the proposed project.

d) Resources (other than financial) available to the team for computer-aided design, equipment fabrication, test/checkout, on-site assembly/erection, commissioning training, etc.

Score:

10 = Fully-qualified and experienced personnel; comprehensive facilities experience, particularly qualified to perform designated duties, sufficient time allotted, excellent resources.

8 = Generally experienced personnel; allotted time adequate, some unique facilities, adequate resources.

6 = A majority of the personnel proposed are experienced in the general fields required; adequate resources; allotted time barely adequate.

4 =   Personnel proposed appear competent in their fields; some re-
      sources are available; allotted time marginal.

2 =   Some personnel proposed appear marginally capable; resources
      appear limited; allotted time questionable.

0 =   Personnel appear inexperienced; resources appear insufficient for
      the job; allotted time inadequate.

Criterion: **Adequacy of Financial Arrangement and the Net Present
Value of Cost Savings to the District**

Factors To Be Considered:

a)   Soundness of the estimate of the cost of services and equipment for
      the work proposed.

b)   The degree to which the cost savings are guaranteed and the form
      of the guarantee.

c)   Degree to which cost savings are based on measurable quantities,
      projections of baseline values or estimated quantities.

d)   Use of energy price escalation; discount rates.

e)   Terms of the sample contract provide optimum benefit to the orga-
      nization (length, return on investment, payment schedule, share of
      savings, etc.)

f)   Ability to finance project.

Score:

10 = Firm (or investor partner, joint venture partner, or subcontractor)
      has indicated that extensive capital and cash flow resources are
      available; terms of the sample contract are extremely favorable; the
      firm proposes the highest net present value of cost savings substan-
      tiated by documented case studies of similar results; the savings are

fully guaranteed; and the organization risks no financial exposure.

8 = Financial resources are more than adequate; terms of the sample contract are favorable; the firm proposes a reasonable net present value of cost savings and they are based on quantitative measurements, reasonably solid estimates, or projections of baseline values and a history of delivering such value to its customer; the savings are mostly guaranteed and organizational risks are minimal.

6 = Financial resources appear adequate: terms of the sample agreement are adequate; the proposal offers strong cost savings with good references; the savings are mostly guaranteed or are reasonably sure of being achieved; and the organizational risks are limited.

4 = Financial arrangement and resources appear marginal; net present value of cost savings is low; and the organizational risks are of some concern.

2 = Financial arrangement and resources appear inadequate.

0 = There appear to be no financial resources for the firm; no cost savings are given in the proposal; or they are not likely to be achieved.

The following criteria are offered without scoring, with the suggestion that the evaluation committee develop its own scoring to affirm that the process is well understood by all committee members.

Criterion: Technical Performance Estimate
Factors To Be Considered:
a) Comprehensiveness of approach.
b) Adequacy of the equipment to provide the services proposed and its integration into existing system.
c) Adequacy of the proposed operation and maintenance concept, including training of facility personnel.
d) Degree to which the proposed system meets all work environment requirements.

Criterion: Management, Schedule and Quality Assurance
Factors To Be Considered:
a) ESCO has been established as an entity long enough to be sure it can deliver promised services and back them up. (Experience of

individuals in a new ESCO are not sufficient and further assurances must be obtained.);

b)   The organizational structure is clear and well-defined; the lines of communication are direct; and the management appears to be well informed and responsive.

c)   The proposed schedule appears to be reasonable without being either too tight or dilatory, and allows for reasonable meshing of parallel and sequential activities.

d)   The proposed management structure and quality assurance program can identify problems promptly, and take effective remedial action.

e)   The proposal clearly defines the organization's supplied resources; the proposed resources are reasonable for the project.

THE EVALUATION PROCESS

Prior to structuring the evaluation process, the committee should meet and agree on definitions, scoring and procedures. Preferably, the criteria, weighting, etc. will be set by the committee before the solicitation is issued. The solicitation, such as a Request for Qualifications, will inform potential proposers of the services required and the criteria that will be used to judge their qualifications.

The criteria should grow out of the identified needs by a cross-section of the organization—based on a fundamental and objective assessment of in-house capabilities.

Since the details in a proposal seldom fit preconceived molds, the decision-matrices used in the suggested evaluation format provides flexibility. The approach shown in Figures 3-2, and 3-3, offer the flexibility to highlight particularly attractive features or some strongly held reservations. This decision-matrix summary sheet and the supporting worksheets allows the evaluator to view and compare at a glance, the ways each firm treated certain criteria. For more complex projects, the decision-matrix approach is preferred.

Criteria/Firm			Decision-Matrix—Summary Sheet
Proposal Presentation	___ × 5 = ___	___ × 5 = ___	___ × 5 = ___
Firm's Qualifications	___ × 30 = ___	___ × 30 = ___	___ × 30 = ___
Technical/Service	___ × 20 = ___	___ × 20 = ___	___ × 20 = ___
Management	___ × 15 = ___	___ × 15 = ___	___ × 15 = ___
Financial Benefit	___ × 30 = ___	___ × 30 = ___	___ × 30 = ___
Comments:			
Evaluator	Total	Total	Total

Figure 3-2. Proposal Evaluation Decision Matrix Summary Sheet

Financial Benefit Worksheet

CRITERIA/FIRM				
PROJECTED LEVEL OF TOTAL ENERGY SAVINGS AND CAPITAL INVESTMENT				
ORGANIZATION'S SHARE (% OF SAVINGS)				
INNOVATIVE ENERGY FINANCING —Payment Schedules —Interim Construction —Financing				
CONTRACT YEARS & RELATION TO —Savings —Services				

Financial Benefit Worksheet (page 2)

FORMULA
Establishing Baseyear
Billing Calculations
Demand charges
Floor price

BASELINE ADJUSTMENT
—Occupancy
—Weather
—Energy prices
—Operating hours

**(%) LEVEL OF
INVESTMENT IN
CAPITAL EQUIPMENT &
MODIFICATIONS**

**EXPLICITNESS AND
FAIRNESS OF
METHODOLOGIES**

ESCO FEE
—in guarantee pkg.
—partly in excess savings
—all in excess savings

Financial Benefit Worksheet (page 3)

CRITERIA/FIRM				
RISK EXPOSURE				
OWNER REQUIREMENTS				
—Insurance				
—Operational control				
—Guarantees				
—Payments for maintenance				
	TOTAL	TOTAL	TOTAL	TOTAL
PROJECT TERMINATION				
—Buyout provisions				
—Return to original status				
OPERATIONAL SAVINGS				
CALCULATIONS				
—clearly documented				
—real budget savings				
—requires owner to reduce manpower to achieve savings				
	TOTAL		TOTAL	TOTAL
COMMENTS				
EVALUATOR _____				

Figure 3-3. Proposal Evaluation Financial Benefit Worksheet

The criterion and weightings suggested in these figures are just that—suggestions. They tend to reflect actual practice, but every organization needs to decide the relative importance of certain criterion. For example, the weight of "5" for the proposal presentation is established to encourage proposers to follow the format prescribed in the RFP to facilitate evaluation. The object of the effort, however, is to select a firm, not a proposal. If too much weight is placed on the proposal presentation, the process could defeat the purpose.

CHECKING REFERENCES

As part of the evaluation process the customer should always ask for, and check, a potential ESCO's references regarding work they have done in similar facilities. The references cited by an ESCO, of course, are usually the best they have to offer. Therefore, it pays to dig deeper on the finalists.

Several sources are available to the enterprising procurement office. Colleagues are always good sources. The state energy office in the ESCO's home state may be a viable source. The state personnel cannot endorse a private firm and are not apt to rule out any firm; however, listening to what they "don't say" can help. If they suggest you contact people who have used the proposer's services, do it. Indirectly, you'll find out in a hurry whether the energy office is high on a certain firm. Or otherwise.

If you still remain uncertain as to the potential performance of a proposer, members of the committee can resort to the ultimate check-up: ask the competition in the area to identify any project where other proposing firms did not perform as promised.

CONTRACTOR SELECTION

While not essential, it is usually valuable to have the committee meet again after independent judgments have been made and submitted. This removes the possibility that committee members misunderstood the instructions, allowed biases to intrude, or overlooked a key area that might be brought out by another committee member during the discussion.

After the contractor has been selected by the committee, it is generally necessary to have top management or a board ratify this action.

This ratification is generally followed by a letter of intent to the selected firm. This letter notifies the contractor of his/her firm's selection and stipulates the time frame and conditions for contract negotiations.

Typically, a Planning Agreement for the investment grade audit and/or a master contract is then established. In the typical Energy Service Agreement, specific recommendations, associated maintenance costs, etc. for specific buildings or complexes are treated in addenda or schedules. These procedures are more fully discussed in the chapter on contracts.

The evaluation and selection process for securing the services of a performance contractor is unique. Potential customers are sometimes reluctant to enter this process without outside support. Ironically, customers often seek performance contracting because they do not have the funds to do the needed work on their own. As noted earlier, the costs of a performance contract consultant, and/or an engineer as a technical consultant, can be assigned to the project, and the costs covered by future savings.

The most costly evaluation, selection process is an attempt to proceed with in-house staff that do not understand the needed procedures and safeguards. It is reminiscent of the old oil filter commercial, "You can pay me now; or you can pay me later." In, performance contracting, "later" is a lot more expensive.

Chapter 4

Measurement
And Verification

The history of savings verification has blotted the industry's copy book. In retrospect, it's amazing how long ESCOs were able to tell customers, "This is what you saved; now pay me." It was all made possible by the reality of the day: owners got needed equipment without any up-front capital and even some positive cash flow out of avoided utility costs. If, however, all of us in the industry were put to the test behind closed doors, we would have to admit that the verification was often based on shaky data and conflict of interest did rear its ugly head.

Once the utility industry discovered that performance contracting could effectively meet their demand-side management (DSM) needs, the world started to change. Utilities wanted to compare costs of delivered ESCO savings to those savings claimed by utilities for the rebates they had provided customers. Since the utilities blithely handed out lamps, or rebates for them, without any assurance the light bulb ever saw the socket in their respective service territories, the utility savings claims were open to question. About this time, the term "vaporwatts" was coined, which summed up the problem very well.[1]

Concerns regarding vaporwatts caused regulators to want the utility "savings" verified for reimbursement. Ultimately, questions regarding the savings claims of ESCOs became open to question. The industry, however, had no uniform protocol for measuring and verifying savings.

A History of Uncertainty

For many years, we have struggled in the quagmire of *NOBLE PURPOSE*. It seems we have "always known" it was a good thing to use

51

energy more efficiently. The economic and environmental value of energy efficiency remains undisputed. But too often we simply did not know (and sometimes do not know today):

(a)   if energy was really saved;

(b)   who should receive the credit (and payment) for any savings;

(c)   if the most cost-effective measures were being implemented;

(d)   if the predicted environmental benefits were achieved; or

(e)   if the utility could, or should, receive the rate adjustment, reimbursement, or other claimed benefits.

(f)   if the specific measures the ESCO implemented saved the energy, or if something else was cutting energy consumption in the facility or process;

(g)   if the savings from the ESCO measures were being reduced by energy consuming actions by the owner.

The need to quantify and verify energy savings went well beyond performance contracting. To those who see a business in measurement and verification (M&V), they can also look beyond the ESCO industry. The mention of a few such needs might suggest other opportunities. Consider:

1.   Owners who question the consulting engineer's savings prediction; or who are unsure about savings-based payments to energy service companies;

2.   Engineers, who wish to offer clients third party validation of their predictions and the added value of their services;

3.   Utilities, who need savings verified for reimbursements, or CO_2, NO_x and SO_x credits;.

4.   Business managers and organization administrators, who need to convince their boards or publics of their
    —environmentally responsible actions, or
    —sound business practices;

5.   ESCOs who want equitable resolutions of customer concerns re-
      garding savings so they can achieve the partnership quality so nec-
      essary for effective projects;

6.   Government ministries and agencies, including environmental or-
      ganizations, who wish to document environmental benefits; or

7.   Investors, who want the security of energy cost and consumption
      savings verification.

Today, an M&V protocol has emerged that is gaining wide acceptance. The initial steps were taken in the United States by a cross section
of representatives of the government, utilities, M&V companies, the energy efficiency and performance contracting industries under the U.S.
Department of Energy's sponsorship. With some modification, this protocol can be used in any country. The U.S. DOE protocol is a work in
progress; so regular revisions are expected. A copy of the International
Performance Measurement and Verification (IPMVP) initially referred to
as the North American Energy Measurement and Verification Protocol,
(and briefly as the Building Measurement and Verification Protocol
[BMVP]) can be obtained off of the World Wide Web by accessing the
DOE Measurement and Verification Protocol Homepage http://
www.bmvp.org. Or, you can obtain a printed document by faxing your
name, address and telephone number to the "Efficiency and Renewable
Energy Clearing House" (EREC) at (703) 893-0400, requesting the "International Performance Measurement and Verification Protocol." A guidance document has been developed by the DOE Federal Energy Management Program (FEMP) office to accompany the IPMVP.

M&V Options

Before discussing the four main M&V approaches provided by the
initial U.S. DOE effort, it is important to stress one area that is not adequately treated: *establishing a baseyear* and identifying variables needed
to modify the baseyear into an annual adjusted baseline. Suffice it to say
here, no one can verify savings if they do not have a solid basis for
comparison. The baseyear data should not only give historical consumption data, but it must describe the existing conditions, such as hours of

operation, that caused the consumption. Only when the major facility/ process conditions have been identified and signed off by both parties have we got a defined basis for measuring any losses or gains.

The following is a summary of the four options presented in the 1997 DOE M&V version.

> **Option A**
> **Percentage of construction cost 1-5%**
> **Accuracy ±20%**

OPTION A: MEASURED CAPACITY, STIPULATED CONSUMPTION APPROACH

This option is intended for energy efficiency measures where end use capacity, demand or power level (kW) can be measured using one-time, *in-situ* end use measurements, or accurately assessed from manufacturer's measurements; and energy consumption or hours of operation are known in advance or stipulated and agreed upon by both parties.

Option A usually involves a one-time measurement of instantaneous energy use before (baseline) and after the retrofit. In-situ measurements can also be used, particularly where multiples of identical units are installed.

This option also calls for some performance verification; i.e., the equipment is installed and performing as specified.

Estimates of energy savings using Option A with measured capacity can be adversely affected by:

- variation in operating efficiency;

- operational changes following measurements;

- malfunctions or lamp outages;

- related equipment changes; or

- failure to account for heating /cooling interaction.

```
Option B
Percentage of construction cost 3-10%
Accuracy ±10-20%
```

OPTION B: MEASURED CAPACITY;
MEASURED CONSUMPTION APPROACH

Option B is intended for energy efficiency measures where end use capacity, demand or power level can be established by a measured baseline before the retrofit, and continuous energy consumption of the equipment or sub-system can be measured post-installation for a selected period of time.

The energy consumption under this approach is calculated by developing statistically representative models of the energy end use *capacity*; i.e., kW, and *consumption*; i.e., kWh.

As with Option A, performance verification once the equipment is installed is needed. Periodic inspections may also be warranted.

```
Option C
Percentage of construction cost 1-10%
(a) Accuracy ±5-10% (hourly, daily)
(b) Accuracy ±20% (monthly)
```

OPTION C: WHOLE-FACILITY, OR MAIN
METER MEASUREMENT APPROACH

This approach is most appropriate where whole-facility baseline and post-installation data are available to measure savings. Option C usually relies on *continuous* measurement of whole-facility energy use and electric demand for a specific time before retrofit (baseline), and *continuous* measurement of the whole-facility energy use and demand post-installation.

Energy consumption calculations rely on statistically representative models of whole-facility energy consumption; i.e., kWh, Btu or kv. Typically, utility billing data and methods using hourly whole-facility baseline and post-installation analysis are used. This approach is generally limited to projects where the expected savings will exceed 20 percent, but not sufficiently large to install permanent hourly data loggers.

The baseline development generally requires regression analysis. The approach is sometimes referred to as "a system identification, parameter identification or inverse modeling approach." Certain assumptions are made and important parameters are identified through statistical analysis. The simplest steady-state inverse model can be calculated by statistically regressing monthly consumption data against average billing period temperatures [(a) in shaded box].

The DOE M&V protocol further explains this approach, stating:[a]

Although simple in concept, the most accurate methods use change point statistical procedures that simultaneously solve for several parameters including a weather-independent base-level parameter, one or more weather-dependent parameters, and the change point or points at which the model switches from weather-dependent to non-weather-dependent behavior. (ASHRAE 1997) In its simplest form, the 65°F (18.3°C) degree day model is a change point model that has a fixed change point at 65°F.

Figure 4-1 shows steady-state, single variable inverse models appropriate for commercial facility energy use as follows:

- (a)   One-Parameter Model
- (b)   Two-Parameter Model Shown For Cooling Energy Use
- (c)   Three-Parameter Heating Energy Use Model (Heating)
- (d)   Three Parameter Cooling Energy Use Model (Cooling)
- (e)   Four-Parameter Heating Energy Use Model (Heating)
- (f)   Four-Parameter Cooling Energy Use Model (Cooling)
- (g)   Five-Parameter Heating And Cooling Energy Use Model (With Distinct Heating And Cooling Modes)

This figure depicts several types of steady-state, single variable inverse models. Figure 4-1(a) shows a simple one-parameter, or constant model, and equation (4.3.1) gives the equivalent notation for calculating the constant energy use using this model. Figure 4-1(b) shows a steady-state two-parameter model where B0 is the y-axis intercept and B1 is the slope of the regression line for

---

[a]BMVP, March 1996, pages 43-47.

positive values of x, where x represents the ambient air temperature. Figure 4-1(c) shows a three parameter, change point model. This is typical of natural gas energy use in a single family residence that utilizes gas for space heating and domestic water heating. In equation (4.3..3), which is given for the three-parameter model, B0 represents the baseline energy use, B1 is the slope of the regression line for values of ambient temperature less than the change point B2. In this type of notation, the exponent (+) indicates that only positive values of the parenthetical expression are considered. Figure 1(d) shows a three-parameter model for cooling energy use, and equation (4.3.4) gives the appropriate expression for analyzing cooling energy use with a three-parameter model.

Figures 4-1(e) and 4-1(f) illustrate four parameters for heating and cooling, respectively. Equations (4.3.5) and (4.3.6) indicate the respective expression for calculating heating, Figure 4-1(e) and cooling, Figure 4-1(f), energy use using a four-parameter model. In a four-parameter model, B0 represents the baseline energy exactly at the change point B3. B1 and B2 are the lower and upper region regression slopes for ambient air temperature below and above the change point B3.

There are several advantages to these steady-state linear and change point linear inverse models, including:

- The application can be automated and applied to large numbers of facilities where monthly utility billing data and average daily temperatures are available.

- It has been shown that linear and change point linear models have physical significance to the actual heat loss/gain mechanisms that govern the energy use in most facilities (Fels 1986, Rabl and Riahle 1992, Claridge et al. 1994 and Rable 1988).

Disadvantages of the steady state inverse monthly models include:

- Insensitivity to dynamic effects; e.g., thermal mass.

- Insensitivity to variables other than temperature; e.g., humidity and solar.

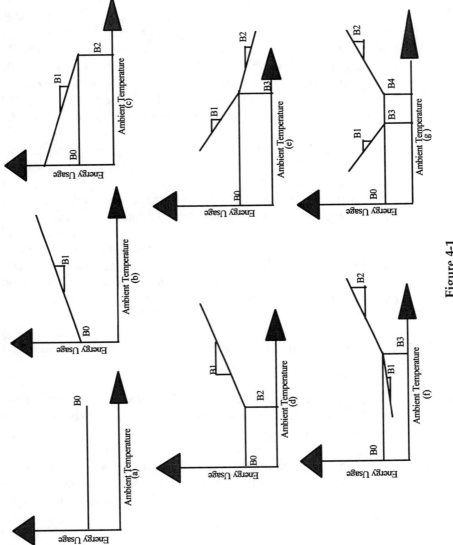

Figure 4-1

• Inappropriateness for certain facility types; e.g., facilities that have strong on/off schedule dependent loads, or facilities that display multiple change points. In such cases, alternative models will need to be developed such as hourly or daily models.

Option C's expected accuracy using: (a) daily and hourly baseline and post-installation models can achieve a ±5-10 percent accuracy; and (b) monthly baseline regression model is ±20 percent for facilities without any major schedule changes. The expected cost is 1-10 percent of construction for each method, varying with utility billing. Installed monitoring equipment ranges from 3-10 percent depending instrumentation and documentation needs.

> **Option D**
> Percentage of construction cost 3-10%
> Accuracy ±10%

OPTION D: CALIBRATED SIMULATION MODEL

Option D was added to the 1997 IPMVP to be used where calibrated simulations of the baseline energy use and/or calibrated simulations of post-installation energy consumption can be used to measure savings. The simulations can be used for whole building or equipment subsystems analysis. This option may be used to confirm equipment, performance, and may include one-time or "snap shot" measurements of performance on an as-needed basis. A range of simulation programs are available; the protocol discusses several.

Periodic inspections of the equipment may also be warranted.

Major input variables that influence simulation results include:

• building plug and lighting loads;
• interior conditions;
• HVAC primary & secondary system characterizations;
• building ventilation and infiltration loads;
• building envelope & thermal mass characterization; and
• building occupant loads.

The protocol warns that there is no conclusive evidence that variables found to be important for one building will necessarily apply to another building.

A WORK IN PROGRESS

The IPMVP is a vital living document with revisions underway and others expected in the future. Three additional areas not covered in the original document—water conservation, new buildings and applications of the protocol to specific projects—are in the 1997 version. The next IPMVP is expected to address the indoor environment.

APPLYING M&V OPTIONS

The selected M&V option will vary depending on a number of factors, including:

a)   the facility (or process) and the consistency of usage (or production) patterns;

b)   the energy efficiency measures installed;

c)   the size of the project;

d)   whether or not payments are related to savings achieved;

e)   the types of savings documentation needed;

f)   instrumentation available and whether permanent installation is warranted; and

g)   the level of accuracy desired weighed against the cost for achieving that accuracy.

Each of these factors have several considerations implicit in the criteria. We can begin to see the range of issues if we examine the measurement implications of a single measure, lighting, under Option A, compared to a chiller project under Option C as described in the original protocol.

Option A: Lamp Replacement

The simplest M&V procedure is probably lamp replacement where we know the change in wattage and can determine the operating hours.

The savings can be stipulated in advance and all that is required is: (1) verification of performance; and (2) verification of the burn hours.

If one thousand 40-Watt fluorescents lamps are replaced with 32-Watt fluorescents, then simple subtraction (40-32=8) multiplied by the number of lamps (8×1000=8000) provides the total Watts saved. Performance verification can be provided by an inspection to ascertain the lamps were installed and operating as specified.

Establishing the hours of operation can be more difficult. If a M&V firm asks both management and O&M personnel, it is apt to get two different answers. Often *very different* answers!! Instrumentation, such as the portable data logger, can quickly decide the hours of operation— baseline and post-retrofit if necessary.

Once the hours are established, the Watts saved are multiplied by the hours to establish saved kWh. The cost savings is determined by multiplying the kWh by the current tariff. [Note: In tariffs with declining block rates, it is the cheapest kWh that is saved; not the average cost per kWh.]

Option C: Chiller Project

Chiller project savings can be analyzed using monthly baseline and post-installation utility billing data provided the savings are greater than the uncertainty of the regression model, and that chiller operating conditions and other building functions have remained essentially the same. Existing baseline conditions should be documented according to established procedures. It is important to note the loading of the chiller, chilled water supply temperatures, condenser return temperatures and flow rates through the chiller. This documentation is important because the efficiency of the chiller, i.e., kW/ton or COP, dependents on the percent load on the chiller, temperature of the chilled water supply, condenser return temperature and flow rates through the chiller.[2]

For those retrofits where such parameters are uncertain or cannot be ascertained, it may be necessary to measure the baseline and post-installation. In-situ chiller efficiency can also be measured. Hourly baseline and post-installation measurements can be used if the loading and temperature have remained relatively constant, and if the chiller output and electricity input are being measured.

For chiller replacement projects that have constant baseline and post-installation loading conditions and operating temperatures, obtaining utility billing data for twelve months prior to the retrofit is recommended. If electricity savings and electric demand are being evaluated, a separate demand analysis needs to be performed that compares the demand for a given month with the demand in the same month of the year prior to the retrofit.

The DOE M&V protocol suggests the following calculation procedures:

Calculating Electricity Savings. Electricity savings from a chiller retrofit that has constant baseline and post-installation loading profiles and operating temperatures can be determined in the following fashion. First, develop a baseline model using the methods previously described. Second, calculate the retrofit electricity savings by comparing the electricity use predicted by the baseline model to measured post-installation data. Savings are determined to be significant if the difference between baseline and post-installation energy use is greater than model error.

Calculating Electric Demand Reductions. Electric demand reductions from a chiller retrofit can be determined in the following fashion. First, develop a baseline demand model using the methods previously described. Second, calculate the post-installation electric demand savings by comparing the monthly demand predicted by the baseline model to measured post-installation demand data. Demand savings are determined to be significant if the difference between baseline and post-installation electric demand is greater than model error.[b]

Limitations Of Calculating Savings From A Chiller Retrofit Using Utility Billing Data. In most cases it may not be possible to accurately assess chiller retrofit savings by comparing monthly utility billing data. This is due to the fact that most chiller retrofits are usually accompanied by changes to the chilled water pumping systems, chilled water setpoints, downsizing of the chillers or staging of the chillers, etc. Therefore, most

---

[b]BMVP, *op. cit.*, pages 54-55. Note: the DOE term "baseline" is the same as base year used elsewhere in this book and also refers to the annual adjusted baseline as defined in the glossary.

chiller retrofits require baseline and post-installation efficiency measurements and load profiles be developed.

Even in such cases where all of these variables have been held constant, savings from a chiller retrofit project can be adversely affected by the following:

- Savings in electricity consumption can be affected when the chiller operates at different baseline and post-installation chilled water setpoint conditions or condenser temperatures, because of additional work which is required to produce colder evaporator temperatures, or shed heat in the condenser at higher temperatures.

- Savings in electricity consumption can be affected if the baseline and post-installation loading on the chiller is substantially different. This is due to the fact that chillers tend to have a non-linear increase in kW/ton ratios as the loading drops below approximately fifty percent (50 percent).

- Savings in electricity consumption can also be affected by flow rates through the evaporator and/or condenser.

All of the above operating conditions should be noted carefully during both the establishment of baseyear and post-retrofit periods.

MEASUREMENT DEVICES

Each of the following measurement devices has benefits and can be applied with success if the purpose and limitations are clearly understood.

PORTABLE DATA LOGGERS (PDL)[3]

The most simple devices are portable data loggers, about the size of a calculator, these battery operated devices most often record hours of operation, although there are a few that record temperature and consumption.

The use of PDLs is normally limited to fixed load, variable hour of operation measures. Occasionally they have been used for more complex applications. Typically these devices are used to record hours of operation of light fixtures. Retrieval of the data is a manual process. As technology improves more complex PDLs are appearing that can record hours of operation according to a utility rate schedule, these data are retrievable via a laptop PC.

Costs associated with an M&V plan using a PDL are dominated by the labor required to place the devices and retrieve the data. These devices can be cost effective for short term measurements to verify quickly estimated hours of operation in a facility.

The biggest drawback to these devices is that they generally do not permit analysis of operation by billing rate period. Energy rates are complex, and it is often necessary to determine when savings occurred in order to accurately assess the value of those savings. The 'snap shots' generated by PDL's will not be sufficient for this purpose.

PERMANENT MICROPROCESSOR BASED
UNIVERSAL DATA RECORDERS (UDR)

These devices are multi-channel microprocessors that accept industry standard signal inputs to measure almost any variable in real time and record values for later retrieval over an auto-dialed telephone link. The great benefit of these devices is that the values are recorded at user definable intervals and permit peak coincidence analysis.

UDRs are the preferred device for most contracts where payment is savings based. They have been shown to provide the best value. UDRs are designed specifically for use in M&V applications and, importantly, have integrated security functions that ensure maintenance of the integrity of original data. An independent auditor can access the data and ensure that the savings reports are accurate.

The universal nature of the signal inputs, combined with the interval recording capability allows UDR devices to meet the needs of all M&V protocols. To date they have been used primarily in lighting applications to verify hours of operation. The reduction in load is fixed for the equipment change from the original lighting source. A photocell is installed in each monitored fixture and connected to the digital input channel of the microprocessor. A digital input records on/off status of the channel. UDRs are particularly appropriate for constant load variable hour, non-weather dependent measures.

More complex applications of UDR devices are becoming more common, they include the variable load, variable hours of operation, weather dependent loads, such as HVAC systems. In these applications many variables will be recorded to be combined in sophisticated algorithms. Extensive database features are a prerequisite for these applications. Some manufacturers offer the database features, others simply offer the data retrieval capabilities. The applications experience of the system supplier becomes critically important when purchasing these systems.

One important feature of a UDR is its ability to measure electrical load. Most of the devices that are commercially available today require a separate kilowatt-hour meter with a pulse output. This tends to add significant cost and reduce accuracy. A few offer the ability to read ac voltage and current signals directly at a frequency high enough to determine load. It is very important to match the measurement frequency to the wave shape of the load. Most energy efficiency improvements tend to distort the sinusoidal nature of the wave. If the wave is not sampled correctly the results could be very inaccurate.

BUILDING AUTOMATION SYSTEMS (BAS)

Another type of measurement device is the BAS. They may be used to log control variables to determine the energy savings that have resulted from the control algorithms. There are several problems with the use of BAS for M&V. The cost per point for a BAS system is often more expensive than that of a UDR. Typically, one has to pay for the development costs of the control functions in addition to the measurement features. Security is often a problem. BAS are designed to record the performance of the control algorithms for tuning purposes and rarely include security features on the data. The logging capabilities of BAS are also very limited. In order to meet the needs of measurement protocols compromises are usually required, often sacrificing calculation of peak coincidence.

CIRCUIT BREAKER SOFTWARE

Software has been recently developed by both of the major international circuit breaker companies, Cutler Hammer and Square D. Cutler Hammer has been particularly attentive to M&V applications. The software is attached to the circuit breaker and reads energy down to machine level. It is usually less costly than submetering and can be used proactively to manage energy as well as passively to document M&V. This software is also valuable in measuring other electrical qualities of interest, such as harmonics.

This software can be used in a proactive fashion to manage energy use (compared to the passive use of the other measurement procedures described above). In some instances, the circuit breakers software can serve as a cost-effective energy efficiency measure.

DATA DRAG

The enthusiasm which surrounds the M&V data gathering could very well create more than one wants to know. Unneeded data are a drag on the monitoring procedures and on the project, and adds unnecessary cost.

All M&V gathered data need to pass an acid test: Exactly what will be done with the information once it is in hand? If a clear need for specific data cannot be established, avoid succumbing to a zealous M&V specialist's enthusiasm.

Weigh carefully the need to have particular information that falls in the "someday if" against the cost and burden of securing it and saving it. If the data can be stored in computer entrails, never to see the light of day unless that dire need emerges, it may be worth it. But if the data have to be waded through in a routing search for needed information, resist. The pertinent data is more apt to be used effectively and on a regular basis if the information is kept short and sweet.

Nothing replaces the key initial step of identifying the specific indicators that can provide the most meaningful data for a particular facility. Planning at the outset saves costs and downstream headaches.

Where do you go to get the needed guidance? Engineering and facility management associations have been working diligently to benchmark key performance indicators... a valuable checklist. Ask people in the organization, who will work with the information, what types of information they need, not just want. Also check with them as to what format they would like to have the data presented. Check with other managers in your industrial area.

Once the bare bones needs have been established, let the M&V specialists do their persuasive best. But pepper the conversation with "Why do I need..." and "How will that help?" If the information can't document operational performance, significant energy savings (or the lack thereof), or help make management decisions, chances are it is not worth the time or the cost.

Not all data are information.

In summary, M&V protocol may seem complex, but it has a logical order. With a little homework, the process can easily be mastered. It is worth the effort for customers and ESCOs alike. The market niche is real and the business opportunity could be exciting for those looking to specialize in this service.

In the final analysis, anything can be measured and any savings can be verified if one spends enough money. There is an inclination to overplay M&V aspects, which in turn places a burden on the project. If M&V becomes too costly, the measure will no longer make economic sense. It is always a question of cost vs. accuracy. The owner and ESCO (and perhaps the financier) should sit down and agree on what constitutes a *reasonable* level of accuracy. The bottom line is: Just how much accuracy can the owner/ESCO/financier afford?

References

1 Lynn Sutcliff, President of Sycom.
2 Gordon and Ng 1994.
3 Adapted from David McGeown's "M&V in Performance Contracting" prepared for seminar manual *Performance Contracting for Energy and Environmental Systems*, Shirley J. Hansen, Ph.D.

Chapter 5

Financing Energy Efficiency

Getting a project financed should be a shared effort between the ESCO and the customer, but the perspectives are different. It is the ESCO's responsibility to put together a bankable project. The ESCO typically arranges the financing. Its reputation and history often add surety, which offers financiers added confidence. The customer usually incurs the debt and needs to know the financing options available. This chapter will first address what constitutes a bankable project from the ESCO perspective. Then, the types of financing available to owners will be explored.

ESCO's, who have been in this business for a few years, remember knocking on the financial doors until their knuckles were bloody. Today, the financiers knock on the ESCO doors ... if, and it's a big **IF**, ESCOs can put together *bankable* projects.

CREATING BANKABLE PROJECTS

What is a "bankable" project? Simply put, it is a clearly documented economically viable project.

Building a bankable project starts with sorting out the pieces that make a project economically viable. The first step is to examine the key components and make sure each aspect is properly assessed and the plan to effectively manage that aspect is clearly presented. Each component carries a risk factor, which is discussed more fully in Section II, and each risk factor carries a price tag. An effective ESCO knows how to assess the components and how to package them into a project that can be financed.

THE CUSTOMER

Pre-qualifying customers is an art. The critical aspects for the ESCO are developing the criteria, asking the right questions and *learning to walk away* when a "lucrative" project doesn't match those criteria.

Ironically, one of the major drivers of performance contracting is the owner's need for financing; so it seems like a dichotomy that a primary pre-qualification for a customer that needs financing is to be creditworthy. But a customer can be cash poor and creditworthy at the same time. In fact, a potential customer who is creditworthy and cash poor is an especially promising candidate for performance contracting. A school district, for example, is typically creditworthy and legally backed by the state, but its revenue stream is often sparse.

Most ESCOs have an understanding with a financial house (or houses) as to what constitutes acceptable credit standing. Some even have prescribed forms for the ESCO's sales people to fill out; so all the pertinent information is acquired and presented in a routine fashion. The credit check at this stage is like most others. Financiers want the information that can reasonably assure them that the loan will be paid back.

The range of information a financial house will need regarding a potential customer will typically include:

- the type of transaction proposed, e.g., equipment title provisions, purchase options, and payment terms;

- the organization's tax status;

- longevity of the customer's organization; ownership;

- its business prospects;

- evidence that the customer can keep the savings, the all important revenue stream from which the payments and the incentive to participate are drawn;

- financial condition with three years of complete and current financial statements i.e., bond rating, 10K, audited financial statement; and

•   preliminary project calculations.

The critical financial information needs to be adequately documented. No matter how charming, persuasive and attractive a potential
customer may be, the financials must be in print—and signed. In their
zeal to make a sale, sales people are sometimes tempted to take the
customer's word for credit standing. But the financier won't. Don't do as
one major ESCO did with a seemingly lucrative opportunity—a 22-story
building in San Francisco with major energy efficiency opportunities. The
ESCO became "savings opportunity blind" and spent a lot of money developing the project based on false financial assurances only to eventually
learn the building was owned by a foreign firm, which just happened to
be going bankrupt.

In addition to the customer's creditworthiness, financiers are more
inclined to loan money when larger ESCOs are involved. Their size and
track record often offer the surety needed to lower interest rates. Smaller
firms, however, need not be discouraged by this apparent market advantage; for the small firm can typically get performance bonds or insurance
to cover the savings guarantees and even with these added costs and
higher interest rates can still compete with the margins charged, for example, by an ESCO affiliated with a controls manufacturer.

The above concerns relate to the financial pre-qualification of the
customer. Once the ESCO is satisfied with the customer's creditworthiness, consideration can be given to other criteria which will be used to
weigh the customer's partnership quality, including the administrative
commitment to the project, the attitudes and abilities of the operations
and maintenance people, etc. These "people factors" and other critical
concerns are generally folded into a scoping audit that assesses project
potential. The scoping audit is little more than a walk-through audit with
a very educated eye. The purpose is to be sure that further pre-qualification and marketing efforts are warranted.

Start-up ESCOs, or "WISHCOs" as they are sometimes called, too
often do not pay sufficient attention to the people factor risks. It is vital
to project success and is touched on below as well as in detail in Chapters 7 and 9.

Once the other pre-qualification criteria has been met and the potential customer has accepted the concept, then a full feasibility study is
needed. Before the ESCO incurs the expense of a premium quality energy analysis, an agreement to cover the costs of the audit if the project

does not go forward is increasingly used to protect the ESCO's investment. The content of this planning agreement is discussed later in the contracts chapter.

ENERGY AUDIT QUALITY

A standard energy audit with its "snap shot" of current conditions is not good enough for performance contracting. These audits typically assume present conditions will prevail for the life of a project. When an ESCO bets money on predicted *future* savings, these assumptions must be tested through a careful risk assessment procedure.

Only an *investment grade audit* that adds specific risk appraisals to the standard name plate/run calculations will meet performance contracting needs. In recent years, energy engineers have learned to look at facility and mechanical conditions and determine the ability of the remaining equipment and energy consuming subsystems to accept the recommended measures. An investment grade audit (IGA) goes beyond these engineering skills and requires the art of assessing people; the level of commitment of the management to the project, the extent to which the occupants are informed and supportive, as well as the O&M staff's abilities, manpower depth and *attitude.*

A key aspect of a quality IGA is a carefully detailed baseyear with the average energy consumed over several years *and the current operating conditions,* which affect that consumption. (See Chapter 9 in the Risk Management section for a full discussion of baseyear issues.)

The ESCO that consistently delivers a quality IGA, which in turn accurately predicts potential savings, builds a track record that financiers find very heart warming. A good IGA is at the heart of a bankable project. When the total project plan is wrapped around a quality IGA and delivered by an ESCO, who can back its predictions with a solid history of successful projects, financiers smile.

EQUIPMENT SELECTION AND INSTALLATION

Predictive consistency comes from knowing what works. And what doesn't! To support a guarantee, ESCOs must have considerable control over the equipment specifications and the selection of the installation subcontractors. Generally, this control manifests itself in order of preference from the ESCO's point of view in (1) working as a general contractor or construction manager, which supplies all the equipment and installation; (2) having primary responsibility for developing the specs in cooperation with the owner and making the final equipment selection; and (3) preparing specs in cooperation with the owner and identifying acceptable bidders for the owner's final selection. For the owner these options offer him or her progressively more control and increasingly transparent costing. The more control an owner exerts, however, the more risk the ESCO assumes, the lower the project economic viability becomes, and the project bankability drops accordingly.

A financier's due diligence carefully assesses the ESCO's ability to make good on its guarantee and to control the variables that threaten the savings and the guarantee. As always, money follows risk. Interest rates are directly related to the project risks as perceived by the financier.

For both parties, the predicted benefits must outweigh the expected risks or the project is not bankable. It follows that the control exercised by the owner directly affects the project benefits—inversely. The owner control level translates directly into ESCO risks, project viability and interest rates. Money that goes to pay interest is not available to buy services and equipment, which produce the savings.

What the industry needs, but presently lacks, is the equivalent of the insurance industry's actuarial tables for the considered measures against specific conditions that significantly impact savings projections. Manufacturer warranties may ameliorate ESCO risks, but the ESCO can't carry performance claims to the bank. The data are building up, but the science has a way to go.

PROJECT MANAGEMENT

One of the great appeals of performance contracting is the extent to which the ESCO's fee, and profit, rides on the project's success. The truly successful ESCOs know the project is only beginning once the construction/installation/commissioning is done. There are three key components to managing a project which are closely related to its success. A good bankable project presentation pays close attention to each one; and so does the knowledgeable financier. They are summarized here in terms of presenting a bankable project, a more complete discussion of project management is presented in Chapter 7.

1. *A planned effective partnership.* This critical aspect is the most obvious and most frequently ignored. It rests on a carefully orchestrated communication strategy where:

    a)   problems are aired, not hidden, and resolved collectively;

    b)   successes and the means of communicating them to the customer's internal and external publics are developed in concert;

    c)   day-to-day incidents are shared and resolved with a sense of camaraderie;

    d)   the ESCO's Project Manager identifies problems and offers business solutions as an adjunct to the customer's operation; and

    e)   the communications strategies are reviewed and enhanced as needed for the life of the project.

2. *Maintenance* (and operations to a lesser extent.) Maintenance and operations must be carefully planned and executed in a routine fashion appropriate to the installed equipment. This maintenance may be performed by the ESCO, its trained representative, or the owner's personnel. A checklist and routine policing are needed in all cases.

    An evaluation of the federal energy grants program for schools and hospitals underscores the critical need for effective operations and maintenance (O&M). A study for the U.S. Department of Energy revealed that in an effective energy management program up to 80 percent of the energy savings are due to energy efficient O&M practices; not the hardware. Without a good O&M program, guarantees are impossible.

    Owners frequently want to keep the maintenance responsibilities for a variety of reasons, including a sense of control, personnel needs, or union issues. If the primary reason is a perceived economic advantage, owners should be aware that ESCOs view reliance on owner maintenance as a significant risk and will financially structure their projects to protect themselves against this risk. In the long run, an owner budgets so much for maintenance, which it could have outsourced for a little more money. In the process, the owner receives a smaller project. The financials for both scenarios should be worked through and compared before owners decide to "save money" by doing their own maintenance. Using computer-based maintenance management may offset the ESCO risk sufficiently to make owner maintenance an economically viable option.

No matter what procedure is used to achieve a quality maintenance program, a solid computer-based maintenance management system (CMMS), can be an extremely valuable tool.

3.   *The Project Manager.* It is impossible to overstate the key role a good Project Manager plays in achieving energy savings and in fostering a strong sense of project partnership. From the start, he or she should help with the risk assessment, help determine customer needs, document needed O&M staff training and personnel augmentation, merge ESCO and owner staff into one team, and become the link between the ESCO and owner management.

SAVINGS VERIFICATION

When money changes hands based on the level of savings achieved, all parties should be comfortable with how the achieved savings are verified and attributed to the work performed by the ESCO. This issue, addressed more fully in Chapters 4, has become the "hot button" in the industry and is in great danger of being over-played. Under the financiers' general guidance, the ESCO and owner should jointly decide on the level of verification and attribution necessary. It is basically a case of cost vs. accuracy, and it is possible to reach the point of diminishing returns rather quickly. With measurement and verification it's easy for the tail to start wagging the dog... with the verification burden becoming so great that a measure is no longer economically viable.

The financier wants some sense that the project benefits are measurable and they are measured through accepted protocols. Too often verification procedures are basically passive, a negative drain on the cash flow, and investors are not interested in funding a gold plated M&V approach that offers little or no return on investment.

In the final analysis, a bankable project is one you, as an individual, would want to invest in if someone else were doing it. An economically viable, bankable project, when all is said and done, is simply one which demonstrates good business sense.

THE OWNER'S PERSPECTIVE

The first step for an owner in achieving the most effective financing is to get an ESCO that can deliver a bankable project. The ESCO's track record and its bank relationships can tell the owner a lot about that.

Roughly 95 percent of the performance contracts in the United States are currently structured for guaranteed savings with the owner typically accepting the debt thorough third party financing (TPF). TPF is especially attractive if the owner qualifies for tax exempt financing. Since the debt will be on the customer's books, owners have some important choices to make regarding that financing.

1. For a *tax-exempt* organization, the project costs can be reduced by thousands of dollars if tax-exempt financing is used. Notice the words used were "tax exempt;" not "if you don't pay sales tax." *Tax-exempt* is clearly defined by the Internal Revenue Code, in 103a, as an organization that can levy taxes, raise a police force and/or condemn property. A school district in Maryland, for example, is not tax-exempt; however, it may be possible for that district to ride on a county's tax exempt status.

2. Leases come predominantly in two forms: operating leases and capital leases.

    If debt ceilings or greater indebtedness is a problem, an operating lease, which is off balance sheet, can be attractive. But the qualifications for an operating lease are pretty narrow; so a certified public accountant needs to be consulted prior to the agreement.

    The majority of energy equipment leases are capital leases. If a lease meets any of the following criteria, it is considered a capital lease:

    •   the lease term meets or exceeds 75 percent of the equipment's economic life;

    •   the purchase option is less than fair market value;

- ownership of the equipment is transferred to the customer (lessee) by the end of the lease term; or
- the present value of the lease payments is equal to 90 percent or more of the fair market value of the equipment.

Conversely, if a leasing arrangement meets any of the above criteria, it cannot be an operating lease.

Leases work very effectively with guaranteed savings programs. Articles in the popular press too often imply that guarantees are available only with shared savings. Not so. Shared savings is only one type of performance contract. Any performance contract can be structured to use lease financing. In a guaranteed savings program the debt service obligation rests with the owner, but it is backed by the ESCO's guarantee that the savings will cover this obligation. The ESCO's surety may reduce interest rates as well.

3.   When the financing is carried by the ESCO, it usually uses a shared savings approach. Shared savings is defined as a performance contract where the percentage split in the energy cost savings is predetermined and the ESCO typically carries equipment ownership until the end of the contract. Shared savings is typically not the best option for the ESCO or the owner. The customer will pay more for the money and less of the investment goes into equipment and services. Since the deal rests on sharing cost savings, it bets on the future price of energy. Risky business, so the money costs more. The ESCO carries both the credit risk and the performance risk; so they get more money to cover those risks.

On the other hand, what happens if the owner, under shared savings, is obligated to pay 80 percent of the savings for five years and energy prices go up, or the savings are greater than expected? This is a major pitfall in shared savings, for the owner is paying far more than expected for the equipment. If shared savings must be used, the owner needs to have the foresight to put a ceiling on the total amount to be paid.

Financial houses may like this financing since the interest for them is higher, but generally it is not in the ESCO's, or the owner's, best interest. ESCOs, who survived the shared savings era of the late 1970s and early 1980s, are quick to point out another major drawback of this approach: the ESCO gets too much money tied up in financing the project. Soon the ESCO becomes too highly leveraged to take on any more debt.

Energy project financiers have stepped in with their capital to free up the ESCOs to do more projects. Using a single purpose entity (SPE) to carry the financing can help. With established M&V protocols, shared savings has become a little more attractive, particularly to owners who need off balance sheet financing.

THE BUY-IN; THE BUY-DOWN

As a final cornerstone to this financing business, owners should not overlook the value of taking an equity position in the project. It is a way to get non-energy related projects incorporated, and/or reduce ESCO and financier risks. A little owner equity can be a powerful leveraging force and make a bigger project possible.

The bottom line for owners seeking to finance energy efficiency is: ask your banker. Find out what the men and women with the money need. Then use their guidance to develop a project. The financier's due diligence, in the end, is the ESCO's and the owner's best guarantee that they have a doable project. In today's U.S. market, if an energy efficiency project can't get financed, the first step is to rethink the project.

A Primer on Financing

There are a number of financing mechanisms available. Some are only available to government agencies. They differ primarily in the purposes for which they can be used, and in the legal steps required to effect them.

Everyone is familiar with conventional loans available from commercial banks. The other major types of financing vehicles are discussed below. Some do not lend themselves as easily to performance contracting and are cited here as a basis of comparison.

FINANCING MECHANISMS

General Obligation Bonds
Definition: *GOs are bonds secured by a pledge of a government agency's full faith, credit and taxing power.*

General obligation bonds are payable from ad valorem property taxes and require voter authorization. State laws stipulate the conditions to be met. For example, they cannot be issued in California without a 2/3 vote of a municipality's constituency. They are considered the most creditworthy by bond investors; and, therefore, are the least expensive form of financing for issuers. General obligation bonds can only be used to finance acquisition and improvement of real property, as prescribed under the respective state law.

Special Assessment And Mello-Roos Bonds:

Definition: *Bonds issued to fund projects conferring a benefit on a defined group of properties. The bonds are payable from assessments imposed upon the properties (in the former case) or from special taxes levied upon the properties (in the latter case) which receive the benefit.*

Special assessment financings are generally used for infrastructure projects; e.g., roads and sewers, while Mello-Roos bonds fund facilities and services, such as libraries and library services. These types of bonds have been, and continue to be, very controversial in the eyes of the general public.

Revenue Bonds:

Definition: *Bonds secured by a specified source of revenue or revenue stream.*

Revenue bonds have numerous uses. Bonds for water, hospitals, airports, etc. are all examples of revenue bonds, where the revenue from a specific source; e.g., airport, water enterprise, hospital is pledged to repay the bonds. Sometimes a third party is established to collect revenues and to administer the promised repayment for a fee.

Lease-Based Financing:

Definition: *Financing in which the fundamental legal structure is a lease. These include Certificates of Participation, Lease Revenue Bonds, and privately placed municipal leases.*

Lease-based financing differs from debt financing primarily from a legal perspective. The obligation to make debt payments is unconditional. Lease payments, on the other hand, are conditional: they need only be made if the lessee has full use and possession of the asset being leased. Restrictions on issuing debt vary by state and may impose significant conditions. These do not apply to leases. All lease-based financings share an underlying structure, described below.

Lease financing is the most common type of local government financing in most states. Generally, the lessee is an owner with a project to fund; e.g., a municipality. From a legal perspective, the lessee undertakes the project; i.e., buys the equipment or makes capital improvements, on behalf of the lessor. The lessor leases the project to the owner, which makes regular lease payments. When the term of the lease is over, the owner purchases the project for a nominal sum, often a token dollar, from the lessor.

Investors fund the lease made by the lessor, in exchange for which they receive the lease payments made by the lessee. This may be done through certificates of participation, lease revenue bonds or the lease document itself. The money investors pay for these instruments goes to a lease administrator (for simple municipal leases) or an underwriter, which deposits it (less the underwriter's fee) with the trustee bank. The lease administrator or underwriter, in turn, makes the funds nominally available to the lessor but, in fact, makes them available to the lessee for its project.

As mentioned above, the lessee is not required to make lease payments until and unless it has full use and possession of the project. When the lessee has completed the project and there is something in place to lease, the owner begins to make scheduled lease payments. The lessee deposits its lease payments with the trustee bank, which makes the required interest and principal payments to the investors.

Special provisions are offered should the leased equipment or building be damaged. Under such conditions, the lessee may stop payments, until the project is repaired or replaced. The legal documents require that the repair be made as quickly as possible, so that investors wait as short a time as possible for repayment to commence. Because of this abatement risk, lease-based financings carry a higher interest rate than other types of financing.

There are a number of lease-based financing vehicles:

Municipal Leases.
This term is often applied to leases even when a municipality is not involved. This may be nomenclature for tax-exempt entity and is frequently used as a legal definition. It is usually a simple lease, which is funded by one investor, typically a bank or credit company. The bank

funds the lease, and the lessee makes the lease payments to the bank or credit company.

Master Leases.

This "umbrella" lease is a variant of the municipal lease with general terms and conditions. As the lessee makes individual purchases or begins individual projects, leases or lease schedules are funded and appended to the master lease agreement. If a performance contract is done in phases; i.e. 10 buildings at a time on a 60-building campus, a master lease may be used to fund each successive phase. The Master Lease also serves well when the timing or amount of funds to be needed are not yet known.

Certificates of Participation (COP).

This mechanism allows investors to purchase certificates, which offers evidence of their participation, and enables them to participate in the stream of lease payments being made by the lessee to the lessor. Certificates of participation have much higher costs of issuance than municipal leases, but carry lower interest rates. They are well suited for larger, longer-term projects. In performance contracting, the COP approach may be used as pool financing, which can fund several projects. For the investors, this approach spreads the risk over several projects; thus, diminishing the risks associated with just one project.

Lease Revenue Bond.

Similar to a Certificate of Participation, except that instead of a corporation serving as lessor, one government agency acts as lessor while the jurisdiction needing funding serves as lessee. In these cases, a lessor government issues the bonds, enters into a lease with the lessee jurisdiction, and the lease revenues are pledged as repayment of the bonds.

LEASE AMOUNT

The lease amount begins with the project cost, but it doesn't end there. In general, the following are added to that cost to arrive at the final lease size:

- *Capitalized interest.* The amount of interest that becomes due during the acquisition or construction period. Sometimes referred to as "interim construction financing" in performance contracting deals. Because the lessee cannot be compelled to make lease payments until it has full use and possession of the project, investors are concerned about being paid during the acquisition or construction period. Investors, therefore, require that the interest amount be "capitalized," or borrowed, through the lease, and set aside to be used to make interest payments during that period. The longer the construction/acquisition period, the more capitalized interest is needed. For example, the interim construction interest on a $4 million performance contract project may be $200,000; so the amount financed to include the capitalized interest would be $4.2 million.

Occacionslly, the lessee uses internal funds during construction to avoid this interest cost.

- *Reserve fund.* An additional amount (usually one year's interest and principal payments) added to the lease amount and deposited with the trustee bank. This fund is used to make interest and principal payments to investors if the lessee is late or fails to make its lease payment. A reserve fund is often required for Certificates of Participation and lease Revenue Bonds, but is not usually necessary with municipal leases.

- *Costs of issuance.* Costs of attorneys, financial advisors, consultants, and incidentals, are usually funded though the lease.

When all is said and done, a $1,500,000 lease may make only $1,280,000 available in project costs with capitalized interest, reserve fund, and costs of issuance all taking their toll.

It should also be noted that at least one ESCO, which brags about not sharing the savings, puts its fee in the project costs similar to a Cost of Issuance. Owners should be aware that this ESCO is getting its fee up front from the financier and reducing its risks while the owner pays the financing for this fee for the life of the project.

The above primer gives a flavor of the options an owner can consider. Unless the owner has personnel on staff comfortable with all aspects of financing, consultation with a CPA or the owner's banker is an excellent precaution. The due diligence of the project financier will benefit an owner, but it will not guarantee that the selected financing scheme is the mechanism that would best serve the owner's needs.

Chapter 6

Contracts
And Negotiations

Owners and managers should never lose sight of the fact that energy service agreements (ESAs) **are negotiable**. Some ESCOs hand out contracts like they are cast in bronze and the word processor is yet to be invented. Any firm that comes in with a "take-it-or-leave-it" contract and *attitude* is not a firm that will work *with* its customer to achieve the best results.

The customer need not, in fact should not, "lose control." Every client can, *and should*, first determine the key elements the organization must have in an energy financing contract and the latitude within which it is willing to negotiate. Negotiating strategies are discussed later in the chapter.

Understandably, an energy service provider and the financier have to have some assurance that they can protect their investments and that the savings can be reasonably guaranteed. Contrary to fears engendered by some, this can be achieved without any negative impact on the internal environment. In fact the contract conditions can, and should, provide an enhanced work environment.

It is strongly recommended that any request for qualifications (RFQs) or proposals (RFPs), ask for a copy of a contract recently executed by the ESCO with a similar organization. The contracts submitted with the proposals should be reviewed to get a sense of what the firm really expects. Contracts from the ESCOs in final consideration should also be reviewed by your organization's legal counsel.

Attorneys, who are not comfortable with the performance contracting concept, can be a major impediment to achieving an agreement. For them, a piece of the puzzle may be missing. If an attorney does not normally provide counsel in contract law, it is prudent to seek additional

or outside counsel. Since this type of contract may be without precedent in the
attorney's experience, it will expedite the
process if he or she is provided references
of attorneys of record on successfully
implemented performance contracts. The
state energy office, the organization's consultant, or the ESCO can usually supply
such information. It will also facilitate the
process if the attorney is brought into the
discussions early in the process.

CONTRACTS: LAYING THE GROUNDWORK

Establishing the criteria, preparing the RFP and evaluating the proposals should lay much of the groundwork for the contract. Neither the
solicitation document nor the proposal should be considered all inclusive
or binding. It may be stated in the solicitation that you reserve the right to
make the proposal part of the contract; however, all organizational conditions upon which the proposal was based should remain consistent or
the ESCO should not be expected to comply with this provision.

Items not in the solicitation or proposal can be placed on the table
for discussion during negotiations. Modifications in what the organization asks for or the firm proposes to do are commonplace. Should the
proposal or parts of it, by reference, become part of the contract, a statement should be included in the contract indicating that, in case of con-
flicting provisions, the contract prevails.

PLANNING AGREEMENT

Brutal experience has taught ESCOs that they cannot afford to give
away their energy audits. At one time, the audits were thought to be an
effective sales tool. They were certainly effective in showing the owner
the existing savings potential, but the ESCO did not necessarily get the
work.

As noted later in Chapter 9, auditors, who can perform the investment grade audits (IGA) needed for performance contracting, are in short supply. ESCOs are in the business of selling projects; not audits. An IGA that does not lead to a project denies the ESCO its auditor's time to perform an IGA that would open up a real project opportunity.

Owners have also been on a learning curve and recognize an IGA is a premium grade audit that lays the foundation for guaranteed results. An owner that can get an IGA for the price of a traditional energy audit is smart to do so. Rather than the usual "snapshot" approach which assumes existing conditions will remain the same, an IGA will give the owner a better understanding of how certain energy efficiency measures will behave over time in his or her facility.

To protect the ESCOs interests and to preserve the auditors time for IGAs that will lead to projects, the Planning Agreement has been introduced into the performance contracting process. The Planning Agreement, also referred to as a project development agreement, is a short contract of three or four pages, which addresses:

a) the objectives which have been agreed to by both parties;

b) the conditions the IGA must satisfy for the owner;

c) a statement that if the objectives and IGA conditions are met and the project is not forthcoming, the owner will pay the ESCO a specified amount for the audit; and

d) a statement that if the IGA does not meet the agreed upon objective and conditions, the owner, of course, pays nothing

e) the amount of the audit will be rolled into project costs if the project moves forward.

The IGA cost in a Planning Agreement carries a premium over the cost of a traditional audit, as high as 50 percent above the typical energy audit cost.

The objectives usually specify the working environment that is necessary and that the recommended measures will not have a deleterious impact on that environment.

The audit conditions generally stipulate the expected range of savings as well as any audit procedures and parameters that are key to the facility manager.

This planning agreement typically does not require the ESCO to engage in the project. Obviously the ESCO has pre-qualified the customer and believes a good opportunity exists or it would not tie up its engineer's time, nor incur the costs. Even with the best pre-quals, however, nasty surprises do emerge.

ENERGY SERVICES AGREEMENT

A properly prepared and executed contract assures that a project moves forward with minimum misunderstanding between the ESCO and the customer. If the language is clear and well understood by both parties and if the terms are fair to both sides, the foundation exists for a cooperative effort that will benefit both the ESCO and the customer. A poor contract invites controversy and bad feelings, often leading to project failure.

The following discussion offers a general overview of what an Energy Services Agreement (ESA) covers. It is followed by a discussion as to how it differs from typical contract language.

Topics generally addressed in energy service agreements are:

*   financial terms and conditions;

*   equipment/building modifications and services;

*   user and ESCO responsibilities; and

*   the construction contract provisions.

These items may all be covered in one comprehensive document; or separate schedules pertaining to work in specific buildings, or clusters of buildings, may be added to the contract as work progresses. Generally, an energy service contract is divided into two parts. In the first part, the Energy Services Agreement (ESA), the two parties agree that the firm will supply services to the customer and, in broad terms, outlines the services. This is the basic contract and is the agreement to agree. Attached to the ESA are "schedules" or attachments which, when agreed to, spell out exactly what is to be done, how savings are calculated and other details. The schedules become a part of the contract. With a large campus or installation, these schedules may be repeated for each phase of the project. For example, 40 buildings may be involved in the total project but the plan is to do it in phases of five buildings each. A set of schedules will then be developed for each set of five buildings. These schedules are signed by both parties for each phase.

A tax-exempt organization may enter directly into a installment/ purchase agreement with the financier so it can use its tax-exempt status to obtain the equipment at a lower interest rate. Or, third party financing is used so the ESCO carries only the performance risk—and not the credit risk. Another project financing model is emerging where the lender and/or ESCO create a Single Purpose Entity (SPE), which carries the credit and to some extent keeps the credit off the ESCO's books. In all such cases, a parallel agreement with the ESCO can then be entered into to audit the facilities, install and maintain the equipment, provide other services and guarantee that savings will cover required payments. This arrangement with a third-party financier is a common approach with private sector customers as well.

The term, performance contracting, rests on the stipulation in most contracts that the energy service company must *perform* to a certain standard (level of savings) as a condition of payment. These performance considerations are integral to the contract components and are implied throughout most contract provisions.

TYPICAL ENERGY SERVICE/FINANCING CONTRACT COMPONENTS

1. Recitals (traditional, but not essential)

2. Equipment considerations
   — ownership
   — useful life
   — installation
   — access
   — service and maintenance
   — standards of service
   — malfunctions and emergencies
   — upgrading or altering equipment
   — actions by end-user
   — damage to or destruction of equipment

3. Other rights related to ownership

4. Commencement date and term renewal provisions

 5. Compensation and billing procedures

 6. Baseyear conditions/calculations, baseline adjustment provisions, and a re-open clause

 7. Measurement and verification procedures

 8. Late payment provisions

 9. Energy usage records and data

10. Purchase options; buyout conditions

11. Insurance

12. Taxes, licensing costs

13. Provisions for early termination
    — by organization
    — by firm
    — events and remedies
    — non-appropriations language (for government entities)

14. Conditions beyond the control of either party (force majeure)

15. Default
    — by organization
    — by ESCO

16. Events and remedies
    — by organization
    — by ESCO

17. Indemnification
    — for both parties

18. Arbitration

19. Representations and warranties

20. Compliance with laws and standards of practice

21. Assignment

22. Additional contract management terms
    — applicable law
    — complete agreement
    — no waiver
    — severability
    — further documents, schedules

23. Schedules (by designated group of buildings, or project phases)
    — description of premises; inventory of equipment
    — energy conservation measures to be performed
    — baseyear conditions and calculations, variables and baseline adjustment provisions
    — savings calculations; formulas
    — measurement and savings verification procedures
    — projected compensations and guarantees
    — comfort standards
    — contractor O&M responsibilities
    — O&M responsibilities of organization
    — termination, default value, buyout option
    — existing service agreements
    — calculation of other savings; e.g., existing service/maintenance contracts
    — contractor training provisions
    — construction schedule
    — approved vendors/equipment

A contract offered by an ESCO is designed to ensure that its interests are protected. As in all contract negotiations, it is up to the customer to make sure its interests are protected as well. Prior to negotiating a contract, both parties need to consider the implications of the various key components and the latitudes within which an item can be negotiated. In other words, decide what is not negotiable, what conditions can serve as "trading stock" and in what priority.

KEY CONTRACT CONSIDERATIONS

Equipment Ownership
The financing scheme used, and the point at which the organization takes ownership, can affect the organization's net financial benefit and may affect depreciation benefits.

The useful life of the proposed equipment is a key factor in post-contract benefits.

ESCOs and/or their financiers usually insist on a first security interest in the installed equipment or collateral of equivalent value.

In the case of buy-out provisions, termination and default values, procedures for establishing capitalized equipment cost may be set forth in the original contract. Terms, such as fair market value, need to be carefully defined. The buy-out provisions will typically be greater than the value of the equipment, as the ESCO's fees for services, risks and potential savings benefits need to factored in.

Malfunction
Provisions for immediate, and back-up, service in the case of malfunctions need to be spelled out. This is especially important if the contractor is not a local firm. Local distributors for the selected equipment frequently serve this function with further back-up provided by the ESCO.

Maximum downtime needs to be considered. The allowable emergency response time will vary with the equipment installed and how essential it is to the operation.

ESCOs need to establish an understanding with the distributor or designated emergency service provider as to the timing and extent to which emergency service will be provided before they are committed in the performance contract.

Firm Actions, Damage
Contracts proffered by ESCOs will discuss actions the customer might take that could have a negative effect on savings. The management needs to determine if these conditions are reasonable and determine to what extent the organization should have the same protections.

Consideration should also be given to the impact the ESCO's redress may have on the organization.

Equipment Selection and Installation

The customer should reserve approval rights on selected equipment provided approval is not "unreasonably" withheld.

ESCOs must retain some rights if they are to guarantee the savings. Under some bid procedures, the energy service company may assume the role of a general contractor: writing specs, monitoring bid procedures, and overseeing installation. Again these may be services a given organization needs, but they also serve to protect the ESCO's position on guarantees. In any case, with guarantees involved, an ESCO must retain sufficient control of the specs as well as equipment and installer selection to assure guarantees will be met.

Contractual conditions used in any construction project; i.e., liability, OSHA compliance, clean up, performance bonds, etc., should apply.

Provisions for Early Termination

From the customer's point of view, contract language regarding termination should include equipment removal provisions, including length of time required and a provision for restoration of the facility.

ESCOs incur major exposure early in the contract, for they incur the major expenses at this time and must depend on eventual savings to cover these costs. Buy-out provisions must provide for ESCO recovery of costs incurred and a proportionate profit. Buy-outs may not be offered as an option until a specified period, as long as two years, has elapsed.

For further protection, ESCOs, or their financiers, frequently specify that a tax-exempt organization using non-appropriation language must agree to not replace the equipment with equivalent equipment within a specified time frame.

Conditions Beyond the Control of the Parties

Usual contract language absolves the ESCO of certain contract responsibilities under force majeure, or acts of God. These conditions should be examined, and the merits of similar provisions for the organization should also be weighed. Increasingly, the language is written to absolve both parties equally.

Default Language

Language frequently limits the conditions of default for the ESCO, but may leave it wide open for the customer. When the financial burden is carried by the ESCO, this is not necessarily inappropriate. Similar language for the organization should be considered, especially if the organization holds the debt service contract on the equipment.

Indemnification

Both the ESCO and the customer should be indemnified. Some ESCOs attempt to secure indemnification from indirect and contingency damages. These are frequently too broad and should be analyzed carefully by the organization's attorney.

Assignment

The customer should insist on prior approval for any assignment, changes of service responsibility, or key personnel. Prior approval of subcontractors may also be desirable.

Applicable Law

The ESCO typically presents a printed contract as the basis for agreement. The ESCO is apt to specify the applicable laws of the state in which it is incorporated. Should court action be necessary, the ESCO has a cost advantage and possibly a legal advantage. This places an additional burden on the customer if located in a different state. Since applicable law provisions may just as easily specify the customer's state, this provision may become "trading stock" in the negotiation process.

Savings Calculations Formulas

The reduction in units of fuel and electricity multiplied by the current cost of energy by unit is the standard procedure for calculating cost of saved energy. Attribution of demand charge savings also needs to be negotiated and included. This procedure is frequently made far more complex than it needs to be. Weather or occupancy changes, added computers, etc., can affect savings; however, extensive contract language trying to anticipate every contingency only benefits the legal profession. The simplest way is to have a broad-based baseline and then agree to reopen, or negotiate, changes of greater than ± "X" percent.

Calculation of Baseyear and Adjusted Baseline

Provisions for calculating a baseyear should be clearly presented. In all cases, existing conditions that have a major effect on consumption should be clearly identified along with major anticipated variables for adjusting the baseline. Baseyear consideration should include; (1) mild or severe weather in recent years, (2) recent changes in the structure, building function, occupancy, etc.; (3) recent O&M work to reduce consumption; and (4) any recent renovation which could affect energy consumption. Reopen language should provide for some adjustment beyond the agreed upon variations; so neither party pays for unexpected contingencies, such as window closures or added computer labs.

The share of the savings will vary with the length of payback, the services delivered, the financing scheme selected, the risks assigned to the ESCO, the length of contract, and the like. The interrelationship of these factors needs to be considered in negotiating the organization's share of the savings.

Measurement and Verification

Procedures for measurement and verification (M&V) will vary with the energy efficiency measures installed, the size of the project and a number of other factors. In the ESA, the contract language typically states that the M&V procedures will be decided jointly following the IGA and according to the International Performance Measurement and Verification Protocol.

Energy Prices

Price volatility currently associated with utility restructuring needs to be given careful thought. How the burden of falling prices or the benefit of rising prices is to be shared should be clearly addressed in the contract. Until the utility restructuring sorts itself out, an ESCO would be foolish not to insist on a floor price. If one party insists on a price floor, however, the other party should enjoy the benefits associated with increased prices.

Comfort Standards

The greatest fear employees associate with energy efficiency, and more particularly performance contracting, is the loss of control of the work environment, particularly comfort factors. The frequently voiced supposition that an energy service company will control the building operation is simply not warranted—unless management abrogates its responsibility and gives the control away.

The owner can, and should, establish contractually acceptable comfort parameters for temperature, lighting levels and air exchange as well as the degree of building level control needed (and override required) to assure a quality environment. The owner's latitude of control can reduce savings. In such instances, the ESCO's risk becomes greater; so the customer's share of the savings will be less.

These comfort and indoor environment standards will become more critical when chauffage[1] becomes more common place.

Projected Compensation and Guarantees

The most attractive part of performance contracting is the idea that there is an entity out there who will make sure the organization has new capital equipment *that works*, and can assure the customer sufficient savings to cover the project's debt service obligations. All this without any initial capital cost to the organization.

The manner in which the energy savings are guaranteed to cover debt service payments is a key component of a contract and deserves careful consideration. Since the quality of maintenance on energy consuming equipment affects savings, most ESCOs require specified maintenance provisions and related maintenance contracts. They may, however, not guarantee that energy savings will cover the required maintenance fee. If an organization regularly contracts for maintenance and the ESCO's fee is not greater than the existing fee, this may not pose a problem.

A contract's major purpose is to identify and assign risks and provide appropriate recompense. The "guarantees" are the bottom line in assuring a contract works in the organization's favor. However, the greater the guarantees, or the risks shed, the lower the savings benefits will be to the customer. As discussed in Section II, *money always follows risk.*

As with any contract, your attorney should review the ESA before signing. Through all the negotiations, frustrations and delays, it's well to remember that a good contract is essential to a successful project.

SECTION-BY-SECTION

Model contracts are frequently requested, but can prove dangerous if not carefully modified to meet the unique conditions of state laws, local ordinances and customer conditions. To help avoid this oversight the following section-by-section analysis is provided with the understanding that local attorneys can then develop a contract that specifically meets an organization's concerns.

---

[1]The combined supply and demand services that offer the customer conditioned space costed per square foot.

INTRODUCTION (RECITALS). The opening section states that both organizations are in business and that they desire to enter into a contract to do certain things to improve the customer's energy efficiency.

SECTION 1. *Energy conservation program.* This section describes in broad terms what will be done on the customer's property and usually lists the schedules that will be attached which detail the actual work, savings formulas and other matters that are measure specific.

SECTION 2. *Customer's energy usage records and data.* This section states that the customer will make available the necessary information about energy use and other data needed to calculate potential savings and measure actual savings.

SECTION 3. *Commencement Date and terms.* The calendar dates when the contract begins and ends are in this section.

SECTION 4. *Payments to ESCO and customer.* Language here provides for the customer to pay for the services that will be spelled out in detail in the attached schedules. The schedules will contain the formulas by which savings are calculated and the way savings may be divided between the ESCO and the customer.

SECTION 5. *Coordination.* This section simply states that the ESCO will not cause unwarranted interference with the business of the customer during the installation of the project and that the customer will cooperate during the installation phase.

SECTION 6. *Ownership.* This establishes the ownership of installed equipment and spells out the ownership rights. It also includes any title provisions should the contract may be terminated.

SECTION 7. *Upgrading, altering, removal or damage* of installed equipment or system is covered in this section. Because the ESCO depends upon the correct operation of the installed equipment to produce savings, this section limits what the customer can do to change or modify that equipment and what happens when the system is damaged. In addition, this section states that the ESCO may upgrade or improve installed systems if savings will be enhanced, with the prior approval of the owner.

SECTIONS 9 & 10. *Material change.* These sections address what happens if the organization makes substantial changes to its facilities (or closes a facility) during the life of the contract which alter the energy situation. A second section generally treats notification procedures in the event of material changes.

SECTION 11. *Insurance.* Requirements for insurance are similar to that required on any construction project.

SECTIONS 12 & 13. *Conditions beyond control of the parties.* These force majeure sections address matters beyond the control of the parties, such as acts of God, which may disrupt the project.

SECTIONS 14 & 15. *Defaults and Remedies.* These sections discuss what happens if either party fails to live up to the terms of the agreement. The first section specifies what constitutes a default by either party. The second section identifies the remedies available.

SECTION 16 *Termination.* This section establishes the means by which the ESCO or the customer may terminate a contract. It also makes reference to the attached schedules, which sets forth the terms under which a customer may "buy out" a contract before the ending date.

SECTIONS 17 & 18. *Indemnification and Arbitration.* The first of these is a standard "hold harmless" clause in which each party will be equally protected. The second section suggests how disputes between the parties should be handled through arbitration.

Several "housekeeping" and contract management sections generally follow assuring that the parties have the authority to sign contracts, that what they have said in the contract is true and that the contract complies with local laws and standard practices.

SCHEDULES. This section, often located just before the signatures, states that the schedules to be attached are a part of the contract. (Generally the schedules detailing the project are prepared, and negotiated, after the general agreement is signed.)

THE SCHEDULES

The schedules to the general ESA serve to make the contract specific to the project. They establish the details of the work to be done and the conditions under which the work will be accomplished. They include the manner in which savings will be calculated, measured and verified, and services that will be provided for specific measures.

The content and number of schedules may vary. Usually the following types of questions must be addressed, each of which may be the subject of negotiation:

A. *Equipment.* What equipment will be installed? What is the projected cost of the equipment? Who will install it? Who will maintain the equipment?

B. *Warranties.* Who will maintain the equipment? How will the maintenance tasks be monitored? Some contracts couple guarantees with warranties.

C. *Savings formula.* What are the assumptions and formulae that are the basis for the energy savings calculations. Allocation of demand charge savings and positive cash flow are treated here. Changes prompted by utility restructuring; i.e., real time pricing, also need to be addressed.

D. *Measurement and Verification.* Are the savings to be stipulated or measured? How will the savings measurements be done and verified? Actual procedures, equipment and assigned responsibilities are set forth varying with the measures installed.

E. *Guarantees.* What are the guaranteed savings by year? What are the payments to the ESCO from the savings by year? What are the guarantees by the ESCO to the customer? What are the guarantees, if any, by the customer to the ESCO? What are the procedures to adjust the baseline for reconciliation?

F. *Baseyear.* What were the consumption and operating conditions of the customer's facilities, process and equipment prior to project retrofits? What operating conditions and/or assumptions are used in the calculations? How will the baseyear be adjusted to accommodate predetermined variables:

G. *Price variation.* When costs vary due to inflation or other factors, especially energy prices, what happens? Is there a floor price? How are price increases shared?

H. *Performance standards.* What customer operating performance standards must be met by the improvements installed by the ESCO; e.g., lighting conditions, acceptable temperature ranges, steam flow, etc.? What are the equipment installation schedules? To what standard of service?

I. *Ownership.* Who will own the equipment during the life of the project? If the customer wants to purchase the equipment during the project earlier than planned, what are the terms and conditions of the purchase?

NEGOTIATIONS

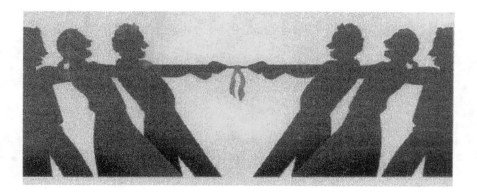

Effective negotiations lead to effective contracts. And more importantly, good projects. Ideally, when the negotiations are over, all parties should walk away from the table feeling they have laid the foundation for a strong partnership of many years.

Before negotiations start, each party should take stock of its own operation and what strengths it brings to the table. Careful consideration should be given to what conditions are negotiable and how much latitude can be allowed on the negotiable items.

It is also important to learn what one can about the other party. Not just what is known that brought you to this point, but what is the other party's negotiating history and behavior at the table. A couple of phone calls in advance can prevent some surprises.

Both parties will profit from a little self-interrogation. What do "they" offer that you must have? What does your organization offer that is particularly attractive to them? What is the best way to position your strengths in the discussion?

Know the process. Ignorance can weigh heavily against you. Negotiations have some uniformity regardless of the topic. Recall previous negotiations, even union negotiations. Consider what your strategies will be, and anticipate what kind of strategies can be expected from the other party.

NEGOTIATING STRATEGIES

Careful thought regarding some very basic negotiating strategies can make you and your organization feel more comfortable, as you head for the table.[1]

1. The customer should carefully review the sample contract submitted with the proposal before the ESCO is initially selected.

2. The customer's attorney should also meet with those negotiating the contract and go over the draft contract submitted by the ESCO. Then, the group can:
   a) set-aside the parts which are acceptable;
   b) note those parts that need slight modifications;
   c) note those parts that might be key to the ESCO, but not necessarily to you;
   d) identify the parts which are unacceptable and what needs to be changed to make it acceptable; and
   e) decide just how much latitude there is on each item and what other parts have some "give" to be sure you get key parts developed to your liking.

---

[1]Some of the following points are derived from Roger Dawson's *Secrets of Power Negotiating,* Published by Career Press, 1995. This book will serve inexperienced negotiators very well.

3. Never accept their first offer. Even "printed" contracts can, and are, revised.

4. Ask for more than you expect to get. The other party assumes you will. Starting where you wish to end up, too often leads to getting less than you wanted.

5. Avoid confrontational negotiation. The other party will be your partner for many years; so start as you mean to go.

6. Display some traits of the reluctant buyer/seller as part of your strategy. Eagerness has its place, but seldom at the negotiating table.

7. Reserve the right to defer to a higher authority; i.e., the boss or the attorney. Generally, attorneys complicate things and too often want to get into legalese. (Remember, attorneys will not be living daily with the project.) Attorneys, however, can be very useful out of the room as the "higher authority."

8. Remove *their* resorting to a higher authority by appealing to their egos or pressing for them to commit to making a recommendation of a certain position to that authority.

9. Be on the look out for their "problem," which you can help solve. Recognize it as a "hot potato" and test its validity.

10. Never, ever offer to split the differences, but you might encourage them to do so.

11. A critical point, which has been noted by Mr. Dawson, is particularly important for performance contracting: perceived values during negotiations go up for materials and down for services. Protracted negotiations can, therefore, diminish the perceived value of services. Considering that performance contracting has a strong service focus, the negotiation process can work for or against a party depending on whether you are buying or selling those services.

12. There are two basic rules on making concessions:
    a) always get something in return; and
    b) start big and taper off.

    If your concessions get bigger, the rewards for the other party continuing negotiations are obvious.

13. If you truly reach an impasse, consider setting it aside to deal with later.

14. Should you reach deadlock on a key issue, consider intervention or mediation.

15. Position a point for easy acceptance by leaving something on the table.

16. Watch out for the "Oh, by the way" when it seems the negotiations are over and everyone is smiling and shaking hands. This last little "nibble" could be bigger than it seems.

17. Never lose sight of the fact that a good contract is one where both parties feel they have a fair and workable contract.

IF I WERE ON "THEIR" SIDE OF THE TABLE

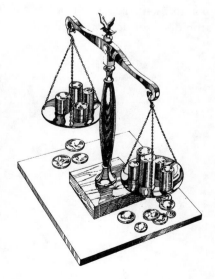

To balance the scales, the customer should picture himself/herself on the ESCO's side of the table. When guarantees are part of the picture and performance is tied to the guarantees, there are some items that are virtually non-negotiable for the ESCO. Recently, a county put out an RFP that glibly stated that the ESCO would carry the financing, make the guarantees and the county would select the equipment. Surprisingly, they got several responses; not so surprisingly most were from very new ESCOs.

In order to make a guarantee on the savings from the project, an ESCO will expect to:

a)   write the specs with owner assistance and participate in the final selection; or

b)   select the equipment with owner final approval; and

c)   select the subcontractors who will install the equipment with owner's tacit approval; and

d)   decree the level of maintenance and tasks to be performed by the owner with some key maintenance provisions reserved to the ESCO.

If the customer feels a strong need to have control of any of these items, they can expect the ESCO to hold back a large financial cushion to cover the risks, which will result in a smaller project and savings. Or, the guarantee provision could be removed from the contract.

If the guarantee that savings will cover the debt service obligation is removed, some performance conditions can still be maintained by developing a shared savings model for the excess savings. In this scenario, there is no assurance that the savings will cover the debt service obligation, but the owner is somewhat assured of the ESCO's continued interest in the project's performance by splitting any savings over and above the debt service payment.

Chapter 7

Managing Performance Contracts

There are several organizational and operational conditions which must be present in order to make the most of the opportunities of performance contracting:

1. Endorsement by management in the form of an organizational statement or policy... commitment;

2. Coordination of project tasks and designated responsibilities through central positions: the owner's Energy Manager and the ESCO's Project Manager;

3. Involvement and support of the occupants, especially the operations and maintenance personnel;

4. Identification of internal and external resources needed to do the job;

5. On-going project assessment;

6. Appropriate attention to detail and schedule to meet project objectives; and

7. A carefully designed communication strategy.

Performance contracting requires effective leadership in each of these areas by both the ESCO *and* the customer. Exercising that leadership in the customer's organization is usually more complex than in the ESCO, primarily because it often involves many people who do not have energy concerns as a major responsibility.

Those energy service companies that have become, or remain, successful on the eve of the 3rd Millenium recognize a strong partnership with the customer as a critical component of any effective savings-based agreement. The level of commitment that is exhibited by management, therefore, becomes a decisive factor in whether or not an ESCO will invest in a certain industrial or commercial facility, university, hospital, or government building.

So, how do you make it work? The critical components are sound management and effective communication.

MANAGEMENT STRATEGIES FOR THE OWNER

A tremendous advantage that accrues to an organization that elects to use performance contracting is the expertise and experience it gains from the ESCO, backed by its guaranteed performance. Unfortunately, this advantage can be so tantalizing that some organizations assume the ESCO can do it all; and, in effect, they abrogate their own responsibilities to manage the process.

The ESCO can bring its expertise to the partnership, but occupant behavior can make all the difference in the level of savings. Uncommitted administrators, uncaring staff and indifferent operations and maintenance personnel can subvert or undermine the best an ESCO has to offer.

ESCOs do not guarantee the maximum savings; that level representing the best that could be achieved under ideal conditions. Understandably, the ESCOs have a vulnerability that causes them to be cautious with their guarantees. Guaranteed savings are apt to be around 80 percent of what an ESCO can reasonably project the savings to be. An organization that does not work hand-in-glove with its ESCO can impede the ESCO from reaching even the 80 percent mark. But with a strong supportive partnership, both parties may enjoy a positive cash flow of up to 100% of the predicted potential; sometimes even more.

Putting the "manage" in energy management requires both administrative commitment and leadership. The real difference between an effective energy program—and one that is not—is the attention paid to the human dimension. It is up to each member of the management team to mobilize this support. Energy leadership qualities draw from the array of management skills already in hand and redefines them within the context of the organization's energy concerns and opportunities.

For most managers, limiting the work day to eight hours sounds like a remote dream. The mere thought of adding to the myriad of administrative responsibilities is enough to make managers shudder. Efficient energy usage, however, is not added to the day. It permeates all activities. Fortunately, once its components have been set in motion, a comprehensive energy management program under ESCO monitoring usually requires only limited attention and reassessment. Visible and continuing attention, however, even if not all consuming, is essential.

Even before management of the project begins, and before the contract is signed, the customer should be aware that an experienced ESCO not only surveys the energy saving potential of a building, but has also assessed the management, administration and staff. The most attractive customers have a written energy policy in place, a designated person responsible for energy efficiency and a demonstrable commitment to both.

SETTING POLICY

Management and administrations can be transitory. Adopting an organizational policy cements energy positions, gives enduring guidance and reassures the ESCO that support is stable. Frequently, the support for performance contracting is made a part of the organization's energy policy, integral to a broad statement of administrative commitment to effective energy management.

Typical policy statements include:

• A statement of the mission of the organization and how energy efficiency relates to that mission; i.e., a commitment to wise use of limited resources, a commitment to implementing all practical ways to increase the bottom line, a commitment to creating a safe and productive environment for employees;

• A statement of concern regarding the broad energy situation and more particularly economic and supply implications for the organization;

• A statement recognizing the advisability and cost-effectiveness of developing energy management procedures;

- •   A statement of commitment to implementation considerations such as;
  - —   authorizing the position of energy manager,
  - —   delegating authority to the energy manager within specified parameters,
  - —   establishing a budget to support the position and process;
  - —   identify funding procedures, and
  - —   requesting that an energy management plan be developed for board and/or administrative approval; the plan to include goals (potential reductions), energy costs (history patterns/ projections), potential savings, suggested procedures, and recommendations; budget, and funding procedures [an investigation and potential implementation of performance contracting may be explicitly mentioned]; and

- •   Reporting requirements to assure the policy is implemented and adhered to, which would incorporate evaluative data and further recommendations.

A policy should be just that, a brief statement of policy. It should not include day-to-day considerations, or the mechanics of implementation. Specific implementation plans, such as temperature settings, belong in an energy management plan.

THE ENERGY MANAGER

If a position has not been designated as the Energy Manager, even for a portion of his or her time, then it is doubtful anyone is managing energy use. For successful performance contract management, one person should be designated as responsible for energy matters and given the time, the authority, and the budget to do the job.

Why does an organization retaining an ESCO need an Energy Manager? The role of the Energy Manager may depend on how comprehensive the contract is and how the Energy Manager's role is defined. But, at the very least, part of someone's efforts need to be devoted to working with the ESCO to make sure the organization and the ESCO are each holding up their end of the partnership.

Specific job descriptions for the Energy Manager position will be

situation specific. But, key
ingredients of an Energy
Manager's job should in-
clude:

- setting up and/or
  implementing an en-
  ergy management
  plan;

- establishing and
  maintaining energy
  records by consump-
  tion and cost;

- identifying assistance available from other sources; e.g., utilities,
  federal/state grants, and exploring ways to leverage such funds or
  assistance;

- assessing future energy needs; overseeing energy audits;

- identifying sources of energy financing and weighing the relative
  financial benefit for various financing options; soliciting performance contracting proposals and evaluating ESCO qualifications;

- making energy recommendations, in conjunction with an energy
  committee, based on such criteria as the prevailing codes, feasibility, cost-effectiveness, financial benefit, health and safety needs,
  and optimizing the work environment;

- implementing approved recommendations: writing specifications,
  overseeing procurement, installation, fine tuning, and operation;

- serving as a liaison to the energy committee and contact point for
  the performance contractor;

- planning and implementing internal and/or external communications strategies, or supplying energy information to those responsible for that function; and

- evaluating the energy program's effectiveness, updating it, and routinely reporting progress to management and/or the board.

An effective Energy Manager needs to have technical expertise and some financial insights as well as communications and leadership skills. Unfortunately, persons with technical expertise do not always have the verbal skills required. The available choices range from a truly fine engineer with limited communications skills to the eloquent leader, who doesn't know a Btu from a cup of coffee.

Given a choice, someone with balance in technical and communications skills is desirable. The ultimate answer obviously varies depending on what is needed, what engineering or communications capabilities are already on staff, and the relative importance attached to hardware vs. user considerations.

The Energy Manager must be in close and constant communication with the people who pay the bills. A brief session involving the financial officer, the energy manager, and the utility representative to assess demand profiles, pricing options, load management issues, etc. and their implications for operation can often reduce energy cost by thousands of dollars. This can, and should be done before a performance contract is entered into, so these easily secured savings do not have to be shared with an ESCO. If it is not already done when the ESCO enters the process, then the ESCO should be asked to facilitate the process and be a party to it. The organization can, and should, keep most of the savings earned through a better understanding of the purchasing process.

With the volatility in the utility industry, this utility consultation practice will need to be done more frequently. A power marketer may be warranted.

To elicit support from the building occupants, the Energy Manager must be able to articulate energy usage and benefits of efficiency in a fashion that strikes a responsive chord in the users. Generally, this means overcoming the frequent perception that "energy conservation" means achieving lower usage by giving up some quality of service or level of comfort.   It can be helpful here to focus on *energy efficiency* as providing the same, or better, energy services and level of comfort while using less energy. Nevertheless, there remain stories such as the Energy Manager who was told by the ESCO that in order to achieve the desired level of efficiency, the building must maintain a temperature of 82 degrees—even during summers of 90-degree heat! Despite his concerns, the

Energy Manager thought he had no choice and ultimately occupants, Energy Manager and the ESCO were miserable. It is important to note here, that the responsibility to implement the strategies that will gain support ultimately rests with the Energy Manager.

Who should an Energy Manager report to? Experience has shown that in order to effect change, an Energy Manager must hold a position of stature within the organization's hierarchy. While situations will vary with personalities and local conditions, it is generally advisable to have the Energy Manager report directly to top management; e.g., the CEO, the hospital administrator, school business official, financial officer, superintendent or president. Some factors to consider in making this decision are:

- Decisions about operations (air exchanges and circulation containment needs, class schedules, athletic events, etc.) frequently necessitate discussions with directors, principals, department heads, deans, medical staff or sales managers, who all have their own worries and goals. Such discussions must be held among individuals with approximately the same organizational stature. It is hard to effect change from a position buried in the facilities or engineering department.

- Implementing an energy program almost always requires changes in past practices and procedures and it is not unusual to find resistance to these changes. If it is the boss' past practices that need changing, making a difference can be exceedingly difficult. If the Energy Manager is to "make a difference" in operations or maintenance, he or she must be on a parallel footing with the director of facilities, chief engineer, etc.—not reporting to him or her.

- The relative position, real or conferred, that the Energy Manager holds in the organization is regarded as an expression of the emphasis management places on the energy program and its commitment to it.

In short, for your organization to have an energy program that makes a difference, the Energy Manager's position must be perceived to be at a level to get the job done.

PROJECT ASSESSMENT

In the early days of performance contracting, the merits of "shared savings" used to be billed as "Their Cash; Your Savings." Like a complimentary dinner guest in a restaurant, the guest doesn't worry about the size of the check. Through the years, however, has come the realization that while you may not pay up front, at some point, you will pay. The funds may be "off balance sheet," money that previously went to the utility, but no matter how one slices it: ULTIMATELY IT COMES OUT OF THE OWNER'S POCKET.

As in all things, the customer should assess what the organization is getting for its money before signing a contract, during the installation phase and throughout the life of the contract. If the organization doesn't have the "how-to-do-it" resources in-house, they are available outside. The owner need not be impeded by the front end cost of such services; for, unless they become too exotic, they can all be assigned to the project. Outside resources may include:

- an engineer with energy efficiency credentials (not an architect unless the training or experience includes mechanics, electricity and energy efficiency);

- a contract attorney with performance contracting experience;

- a financial consultant with an understanding of life cycle costing and energy efficiency;

- an independent assessment group to do periodic checks on the formula, the adjustments to it, and the savings calculations;

- measurement and verification by an impartial third party; and

- a performance contracting consultant, who can look out for the organization's best interests, guide it through the process and put the organization in touch with top notch people who provide the above services.

Effective project management also demands a means of independently assessing the savings achieved over time. A computer-based energy accounting program should be an integral part of your project assessment practices.

CONSTRUCTION MANAGEMENT

Depending on how the contract is structured, either the ESCO or the customer will be in charge of the construction phase. This will demand that the requisite skills reside in whichever organization has this responsibility.

It cannot be stressed too heavily that when an organization decides to engage in performance contracting, it is buying services. The project equipment are merely tools used by the ESCO to achieve the service goals. Remembering this may well require a change in how an organization has traditionally handled the purchasing and installation of equipment.

The construction phase is where projects are most often delayed and customer's routines disrupted. It is essential that the Construction Manager knows how to minimize both of these possibilities. At the beginning of the construction phase, the Construction Manager should have in place a detailed schedule of tasks, and the milestones by which they intend to measure progress. Knowledge of local standards and codes is essential to ensure compliance. Periodic tracking of compliance of quality standards, code compliance, and timeliness of project tasks should be the responsibility of the Construction Manager. Project progress should be tracked by comparing the actual work performed, to both the project budget and the construction schedule.

The Construction Manager must make certain that highly qualified subcontractors are used. This is particularly important if the nature of the project is such that manufacturer of the equipment dispatches a crew to the customer's premises to perform the installation.

Avoid bid/spec. Often, particularly in the public sector, RFPs are issued and low cost bidding for equipment is used. Remember, the ESCO is guaranteeing the energy savings. Low bid means barely acceptable. If the owner requires the ESCO to select equipment based solely on low cost, their risk goes up. That means the customer's savings go down! If the organization's procedures will allow it (or can be changed to allow it), the ESCO should be given authority to manage the construction and purchase the equipment it believes will meet the savings guarantees and perform to the maximum for the customer.

The owner can maintain some control in such a process by participating in specification development and/or approving equipment selections. But the ESCO must play a key role in the development of specifications and in the selection process. This may mean giving up some control for those in the company or organization who have handled equipment and construction purchasing. But in the long term, it might also mean the success of the project!

ESCO MANAGEMENT STRATEGIES

The hit-and-run approach to energy efficiency doesn't work. Performance contracting requires performance over the life of the contract. ESCOs that thought all they had to do, once a sale was complete, was perform a little maintenance and issue a monthly bill are no longer with us. The industry is full of horror stories that can be traced to poor ESCO leadership and poor communications between the customer and the ESCO.

A working partnership will require more than lip service. The effective ESCO looks at the organization's needs and serves them. Service that is directly related to savings should not be farmed out. For example, one ESCO in the 1980s contracted out all of its monitoring, billing and maintenance on existing contracts for a set fee. The ESCO lost contact with its customers. The subcontractor had no incentive to provide the quality of service that meant greater savings. Everybody lost.

Performance contracting should be a way for an organization to address its energy needs, its equipment needs and its energy-related maintenance concerns. The organization, however, should not assign more to, nor expect more of, its ESCO partner than the ESCO has historically offered its previous customers. Grand and glorious promises, which the ESCO does not have the resources to deliver, pave the way for growing disenchantment that can ultimately lead to court.

The best performance contracts today are much more than financing. They offer specialized energy expertise, improved capital equipment, training, monitoring—whatever the customer wants that can be reasonably built into the package. In fact, the effective ESCOs are increasingly laying out a "smorgasbord" of opportunities from which customers can pick and choose services that most precisely meet their needs,

PROGRESS UP THE VALUE CHAIN

↑

Business solutions

Integrated solutions

Chauffage

Supply efficiencies

Comprehensive demand efficiencies

Single measure solutions

and which the ESCO can demonstrate provide added value. ESCOs, which will endure into the next century, must envision progress up the value chain to the point where the ESCO can offer the customer business solutions. Those needs may not include financing. They may, however, include guarantees that enhance the customer's ability to do its own financing.

Most aspects of an effective ESCO's operation are common to any well-run organization; however, energy service companies have a few peculiarities that require special management sensitivities and procedures.

First, ESCOs sell a service, but customers usually think they are buying products. Performance contractors sell cost-effective productive environments; the boilers, chillers and controls that may be installed are merely vehicles to make it happen. The hospital needs a new boiler; from the administration's perspective, getting a more efficient boiler through performance contracting, means the boiler is paid for from future energy savings. This difference in point of view can undermine effective communication between the two organizations and frustrate the sense of partnership.

Second, the ESCO is selling promises; predictions of savings. When those savings are realized everyone is happy. But memories are short. The high utility bills of the past may be forgotten, especially if there has been a change in management, and soon the customer may feel he's paying for "nothing."

One important ingredient ESCOs can, and should, provide their customers is cost avoidance information. A performance contract is designed to save energy; money savings are an important by-product. However, performance contracts sold as "money savers" can become management headaches if the price of fuel goes up. ESCOs, who want to develop and maintain good relationships with their customers, learn how to calculate cost avoidance and to communicate those "savings" graphically with billing procedures, through regular briefings, annual reports, etc. Information on avoided costs are a vital part of a communication's effort. (See Chapter 2 for a description of cost avoidance.)

Third, to the uninitiated, the process may seem to rely on smoke and mirrors. It requires some expertise in both financing and energy technology if the customer is to be comfortable with the performance contracting concept. Bridging the gap from business office to boiler room is not always easy, but can be done if the ESCO and the customer work together effectively.

The performance contracting process also requires an attorney who knows something about contract law, financing, and energy efficient technology. Performance contracting is a relatively new concept and not well understood by all attorneys. Too often, rather than acknowledge their limitations, lawyers drag out the decision-making process or advise against the whole concept. ESCO sales personnel and management must be all things to all people, or draw on independent third party financial, legal and technical contacts to educate their customer's counterparts.

The good ESCO anticipates what the energy manager needs in order to maintain an informed staff and management. Then, the ESCO makes certain that the energy manager has the information when it's needed and in a useful form. Such an effort not only maintains commitment and enhances savings; it paves the way for contract enhancement and renewal.

THE PROJECT MANAGER

Just as it is vital for the customer to have an energy manager, it is equally vital for the ESCO to have a Project Manager. Whether the Project Manager is located on-site or makes regularly scheduled site visits will likely be determined by the scope of the project and other factors of the performance contract. But for the comfort of the customer and the coherency of the project, a single point of contact, a voice for the ESCO with the client, is essential.

Selection of a Project Manager does not mean simply hiring or assigning the best technical person for the job. If this is to be a partnership between the customer and the ESCO, the Project Manager will be key to the partnership. His or her selection should be based on ability, technical management expertise, and communication skills—with some common sense thrown in about how the ESCO relates to the customer. A good Project Manager will walk a fine line between protecting the ESCO's investment and being an advocate for the needs of the client.

The fact is, however, that even if a Project Manager has the best skills, but not the ability to work within a particular environment—from urban to rural, from one part of the country to another—those skills may be useless. A psychological/social fit is also a part of the equation. This becomes particularly important when an ESCO is working nationally or globally. Insensitivity to social and cultural norms can ruin a project and destroy opportunities for future projects.

In this role, the Project Manager will likely be most effective if he or she understands that winning over people within the organization, who might be skeptical of new process, will make everyone's life easier and the project more successful. Informing the operations and maintenance staff about their new roles or new equipment, without achieving their "buy-in" can be deadly. Many a project has been sabotaged because it wasn't considered important to include maintenance staff in project development.

Finally, the Project Manager for the ESCO has to have the authority to adjust the project as unexpected situations arise. Assigning a Project Manager who must always "check back" will diminish his or her relationship with the customer.

An effective Project Manager will:

- be involved as part of the initial IGA risk assessment;

- help determine O&M attitudes as well as training and manpower needs;

- merge the technical people in-house and outside support, into a smooth working team;

- help manage effective energy efficiency communications within the organization;

- serve as a liaison between the customer and the ESCO; representing the concerns of each entity to the other;

- identify and expeditiously resolve any problems in a cooperative and collegial manner; and

- become an adjunct to the effective and efficient operation of the customer's organization—even finding business solutions before the management knows it has a problem (which may not even be related to energy efficiency).

An effective Project Manager often finds upgrade potential or business solution opportunities over the life of the contract that exceed the initial investment.

EFFECTIVE COMMUNICATIONS

The ideas and concepts considered in previous chapters may be quite new to many of the people whose cooperation is essential for energy efficiency and performance contracting success. Members of a management committee, a board of directors, and other managers must understand what the performance contract aims to accomplish, the procedures involved and what the results are apt to be. Many "higher ups" will want to know how this benefits the company or helps the organization achieve its mission. Many, in other departments that will be involved, such as finance, will want to know why they should add on yet another responsibility.

Operations and maintenance staff must understand the "why" as well as the "what" of their role in energy efficiency, or the effort will fail. Care must also be exercised to assure O&M personnel that the new energy effort is not a criticism of their past efforts, and will, in fact, enhance their work.

Building occupants need to know how they fit into the efficiency plan—and how they, in turn, will benefit. Without that understanding and the commitment to help, occupants can defeat the most sophisticated control system or elaborate management plan.

Once management starts the process of seeking an energy service company partner, communication becomes an essential component of the selection process. Once the contract is signed, regular progress meetings and close coordination become essential ingredients of an effective project.

There is nothing magical, nor particularly sophisticated, about the application of communications techniques to the various requirements of an energy efficiency program, or the performance contracting aspect of it. Effective managers know very well how to communicate with their boards, staff, clients, patients, customers or community. The absolute dependence of an energy efficiency program on the human element, however, makes a review of communications fundamentals valuable. An energy efficiency project spends money on hardware, but whether energy and money is actually saved depends on people ... and getting results depends on effective communications with the people involved.

COMMUNICATION STRATEGIES

The two real issues today that bolster the need to do energy efficiency work are MONEY and ENVIRONMENT.

We need to talk MONEY... dollars saved rather than energy conserved. Everyone understands and is interested in money. Few would agree to throwing money out with the garbage; so you just might interest them in what they are burning up. Even though a performance contract is written in terms of energy saved (Btu or kilowatts) talking money gets the message across.

Cultivating and making use of that interest in relation to energy efficiency is the communicator's primary challenge. In fact, if those dollars can be translated into a competitive advantage, enhanced bottom line, computers, band uniforms, etc.—something of great interest to members of the organization—THEN "energy savings" become even more attractive. Look at the people you need to gain support from, consider their individual interests, and move forward to win them over.

A few years ago, Mr. Anil Akuja, former energy program manager for the Los Angeles United School District, described an effective communication's strategy used to gain support for a $15 million energy program. He said the new energy management program appealed to different decision-makers for different reasons:

We sold [the concept of installing an energy management system] to the schools' principals by saying the systems would improve the classroom environment. The board bought it because the systems would have a 3.5-year payback, and the maintenance people bought it because with the alarm functions of the systems, their operations costs are lowered.

Understanding the art of communicating to the needs of specific groups, Akuja concluded that the program received support from all board members because it had saved the district $67 million in avoided energy costs.

As de-regulation looms on the horizon, the cost of energy in the future remains an unknown. Some believe the price will go up, some believe there will be power outages, and some believe customers will be demanding more services for their money. Most agree there is uncertainty. What better reason to save money than the uncertainty of the future!

ENVIRONMENT—there is growing concern about the pollutants emitted by burning fossil fuels. The question of the 1970s was "do we have enough fossil fuels to sustain the economy?" The question for the next millennium is, "Can we afford to burn what we have?" That question is of global concern, particularly as we consider the growing economy of developing countries, such as Thailand, whose energy demand is expected to double in the next ten years.

According to Joseph Romm, in *Lean and Clean Management*, "Efficiency lets a company do very well while doing much good, reducing emissions of nitrogen oxide, sulfur dioxide, and carbon dioxide—gases that cause smog, acid rain, and global warming."

COMMUNICATING ENERGY NEEDS

Effective energy management means that Energy Managers and the Project Manager must understand and fully accept the critical role of communications in all phases of the energy efficiency effort. One attorney involved in a performance contract arbitration commented "nearly all the problems seem to be traceable to in-effective communications." Effective communications is planned and orchestrated; it becomes as much a part of a successful program as does the work accomplished with a wrench or a screwdriver.

The essence of effective communications lies in knowing: (1) the target audience... *Who* do you need to reach? (2) the purpose of the message... *What* action do you want to prompt? (3) *What* (and how much) do they need to know to achieve the results you want; and (4) *What* is the best time, route and format to use to reach your audience. How well these factors are understood and how they relate to each other will determine the degree of success (or failure) of any communications effort.

Target audiences can, and must, be defined. At a minimum, they include top management, staff, building occupants. People in the community are a particularly important group to public institutions. If an organization is to function smoothly and effectively, none of these audiences can be neglected for long.

Bringing the "Board" on Board

No energy efficiency project can be truly effective without solid commitment; therefore, it makes sense to start this discussion of communications strategies with the board, the governing body or top management. Not all organizations have "boards"; however, for simplicity sake, the term board will be used in a generic sense to encompass all governing bodies and the higher echelons throughout this discussion.

The board needs to be informed regarding past energy management successes in similar organizations or companies, and provided with information about the money that can be financed. If any part of that understanding is incomplete, getting backing for any new energy projects can be very difficult.

A few facts can help tell the story. Does the board know what energy costs are for each unit of production? Per pupil? Per square foot? Per bed? Do they have available information about the potential to save? Are utility matters a real part of the budget process, or is it just another line item that can be passed over without discussion because "nothing can be done about it"?

A simple presentation to the board showing the money the organization is losing unnecessarily and the dollars that might be saved through improved energy efficiency is a good starting point. Try out some hypothetical (but reasonable) numbers, say 15 percent or 20 percent savings this year, and then project those savings for 5 or 10 years. Then, ask for support to explore ways to make those savings possible.

Does the board know the environmental damage being caused by the unnecessary burning of fossil fuels? The CO_2, NO_x and SO_2 emissions do not have to be calculated by each fuel exactly—some figures averaged to Btu reduction will get the message across.

A walk-through energy audit of several buildings will provide a good estimate of savings opportunities and suggest the steps needed to get the job done. This should also supply the basis for determining the dollar and environmental costs of doing nothing about the problem. As noted elsewhere in this book, we are not talking about a full scale audit!

"Energy" information needs to be presented to the board in a straight forward manner. Burying board [or bored] members under discussions of Btu or elaborate discussions of variable air volume will only confuse the issue. Also, it's important that the discussion not become a criticism of present or past management of energy resources. A general discussion of what can be done, the dollars that can be saved, and what those dollars could mean to the operation (supported by environmental concerns) should be the basic message.

On almost any board, or in any management group, there will be one or more members who want lots of details about almost everything. In energy, as in other areas, it pays to deliver those details, but only on request. Delivering supplementary materials or having additional discussion outside of board meetings may recruit some solid support, while not turning off those who really don't want to know that much about air intake volume, burner efficiency, or CO_2 emissions.

Every CEO, president, superintendent, financial officer or chief administrator knows how quickly board members learn that anything anyone wants to do costs money. At this stage, it is valuable to introduce the idea that there are a variety of energy financing options available beyond traditional methods—and that several of these options do not require any capital investment, or "new" money. Support to explore those options and develop a plan for their consideration comes next. Keeping up the flow of information and moving ahead steadily, but in rather well defined steps, will enhance the chance of success when it becomes time to "ask for the order."

Performance contracting differs rather widely from traditional financing methods. As every administrator knows, anything out of the ordinary, particularly when it comes to financing, often makes board members uneasy. The ability to explain the options that are available with considerable clarity and confidence takes on added importance. An outside consultant may provide valuable guidance and communications support.

Citing others who have successfully used performance contracting may allay concerns. The fact that both the public and private sectors are using performance contracting with increasing enthusiasm speaks to its effectiveness.

Outside Audiences

Talking to external publics can be very important, especially for public entities. For a public entity, the community is the ultimate boss, paying the taxes, and voting for council members. It pays dividends to let the community know that the administration is doing something about energy costs and the environment. Audits and studies aimed at increased efficiency are news. Training programs to upgrade operations and maintenance skills are news when couched in terms of controlling energy costs and pollution while improving the learning, patient care, or work environment. Stories can be prepared for the local press, or additional opportunities to get the word out can be found.

When the time comes to move forward with a performance contracting project, the information about controlling energy costs and pollution without using local or state tax dollars is good business and good news for local governments, schools, etc. Proceeding in a businesslike manner to do something positive about costs, improving cash flow and freeing up funds for special purposes without adding to the tax burden, is very welcome news indeed.

When a RFQ or RFP is issued, public organizations should let their external audience know about it. It reinforces the fact that something is being done to use resources efficiently. When contracts are signed, publicize the fact that a program is off and running. If it is appropriate, emphasize the portion of the work that will be accomplished by local subcontractors. Work for local companies is always good news in the community. If the project is being financed by an energy service company, it helps to coordinate the development of any news releases with them to assure consistency and accuracy.

Talking to an external public can also be good business for an industrial facility or the operators of commercial buildings. Let people know the organization is a good corporate citizen, saving resources and helping to protect the environment. "Good news" about what you are doing helps with community, and employee, relations.

ESCOs can be very helpful in supplying public information strategies that have worked with similar customers. A performance contractor can become the conduit to networking with other organizations with performance contracts. The beginning of work and the installation of new equipment can provide a "news hook"… an excuse… for communications to all who are interested that things are happening on the energy/dollar front. It provides still another chance to build support for, and an understanding of, the energy efficiency program.

Consider photo opportunities. If the energy savings "bought" new band uniforms, show the students trying them on. If the savings paid for new computers for the college, show them being unloaded. If the savings paid for replanting the atrium at the nursing home, show the planting with residents helping or looking on. If the savings increased the donation your firm can give to the Salvation Army, get a picture of presenting the check—or better yet show the good things that were made possible with the money.

Bring the Staff on Board

Without question, successful communications with staff is vital to the mechanical and financial success of any energy efficiency project. If the staff, at all levels, understands how the energy effort will benefit *them*, they will generally support the program. If not, determined "resisters" can find ways to defeat any plan. It is important to use every opportunity to put across the message that the energy efficiency effort is not just to save energy but to save dollars that could be going for other, much more desirable things.

That is why one portion of an organization's needs assessment should be devoted to developing a "wish list" and calculating ways to show how energy savings can pave the way to getting computer systems, books or new equipment... or cutting product/unit costs. While freed up dollars might not be immediately available to purchase the items on the wish list, seeing the opportunity to do so will make the benefits of the savings more real for many.

Building occupants also need to know that energy efficiency doesn't mean bundling up and freezing during the winter, nor does it mean living with far too much heat in the summer. We are still haunted by the Emergency Temperature Building Restrictions of the late 1970s that were part of the Emergency Energy *Conservation* Act. Since then "conservation" has been equated by many to deprivation. It is good business to use the term energy *efficiency*. After all, it is what we are really about: using the energy that must be used for a safe, comfortable, productive workplace as efficiently as possible. A well engineered and executed energy management program can enhance overall comfort levels. Of course, some buildings will never be totally comfortable no matter what is done to the HVAC system; so it pays to be cautious with any promises in those situations.

And don't forget that the environmental message is just as important to the staff—maybe more so.

The total building population is an "audience" that will experience the results of the program. If heating and cooling systems work better (or worse), what is perceived to be happening will make all the difference in their acceptance of changes that occur. If this audience knows and understands what is going on and feels that the results will benefit each of them respectively, fewer instances will be created where, for example, an instructor, aided by students, destroyed a thermostat with the heel of a shoe. Communications to this vital inside audience can be tailored to fit various segments of building populations, so everyone can be let in on the "secrets" of energy efficiency.

As an important side benefit, it has been demonstrated over and over that effective, internal communications is one of the most effective external communications tools. Nurses talk to patients, staff to friends, students to parents and to other students, plant workers to spouses and the word spreads.

Operations and Maintenance

A critical first step in communication with operations and maintenance (O&M) staff is to affirm the good things they have been doing. They must not view preparations for an energy efficiency program, or a performance contract, as a criticism of their work. Nor should it be viewed as a job threat. Performance contracting can free the staff to do other work that has been put off far too long. (Unless, in fact, the plan is to secure some savings from reducing personnel, which is a decision that should be made totally by the customer.)

O&M personnel should be active participants in the effort from the beginning and should receive a steady flow of information as the project moves forward. Even when the process becomes a matter of RFQs and contract writing, the O&M staff should be kept informed of progress. They have a direct, personal interest, because when the project actually "happens," it will happen to them. Their attitude will have a major impact on results—good or bad.

GETTING THE WORD OUT

Messages need to be kept simple. Most people are not interested in all the details of the project, but they do want to know how it affects them. A few thoughts for guidance include:

- Tell building occupants what it all means in terms of comfort and money saved for other things.

- Tell O&M staff what the changes can mean in improved equipment to work with, perhaps fewer complaints from occupants, better levels of maintenance and control.

- Tell employees about comfort and dollars that can be salvaged from energy bills.

- Tell the board (and the public) that there are ways to increase energy efficiency, gain capital equipment, reduce environmental damage and increase cash flow without the commitment of organizational funds. Those who want all of the details will ask and should be accommodated, but for the most part the real question to be answered is, "What does it mean for me?"

Communications are a key part of energy efficiency planning and should be considered a part of every phase. When the audits are done, publicize the fact, giving credit to those employees who do the work. When consumption drops in particular facilities, recognize the custodians or key maintenance personnel at a board or management meeting.

Projects do not always go smoothly nor precisely follow the plan. Careful attention to communications throughout every phase provides the needed base of credibility if things should go wrong. And if they do, acknowledge problems while they are small and establish the fact that steps are being taken to deal with them. That way, there can be no sudden revelations of CRISIS. The keys to successful passage through the communications mine fields when problems arise are openness, candor, and adherence to the first (and best) rule of press relations: NEVER SPECULATE.

If problems arise, never cut off the flow of information.

GETTING THE JOB DONE

Who should do all of the communications work? And, it is work. If the organization has an information director or public relations person, this effort should be a real part of his or her responsibility; but, it cannot be done alone. There must be a steady flow of information from those directly involved in the project to the person responsible for dissemination. This type of information effort often fails because someone is "too busy" to pass along details of what is happening and/or doesn't realize its communications importance. The information program will be effective only if it is considered as a regular part of the project and planned as carefully as engineering and finance. If communication is handled as an after thought, or "when I get around to it," there is a real risk of project failure.

The day when everything is finally in place and running well is a good time to celebrate. It is time to get the word out yet again. A time to review what has been done and to look ahead to what all the changes can accomplish... a time to "point with pride." It is also an opportunity to salute the staff and recognize those who have helped make it happen. Recognition ceremonies may be appropriate. More than one certificate has found its way to the boiler room wall. Also express appreciation to those who may have been inconvenienced during the project. It's a great time to say thanks.

And when you have results, SHOW THEM. Keep the picture opportunities in mind. If management can demonstrate that the energy efficiency program has saved money for those special items from the "wish list," tell the story. Installing new lab equipment, patient care equipment or new playground equipment in the city park, which were paid for through energy savings, has real visual impact. This is great material for company employee newsletters or magazines.

Communications is the application of common sense to the distribution of information. Successful managers have learned to use the tools and techniques of communications in all sorts of circumstances. An energy efficiency program depends upon the application of the best of those skills if it is to get results. With a performance contract, the partnership is strengthened through planned communication.

Section II

Managing Risks

Risk, perceived or real, is at the heart of performance contracting. It is a key consideration for the potential customer and absolutely critical for the service company (ESCO). The ability to assess realistically and manage those risks is the foundation of an effective project for both the customer and the ESCO.

Section II examines the potential and perceived risks from the customer's viewpoint, presents the essential ESCO risk assessment and management strategies, and concludes with a discussion of the relationship of indoor air quality to energy efficiency.

Prior to exploring the key aspects of risk as they pertain to performance contracting, the nature of risk and how it is managed seems appropriate.

Once a risk is identified, then an assessment is made to weigh the potential risk against expected benefits. Part of the assessment is a careful examination of the variables that can exacerbate or diminish the risk. If this evaluation suggests the benefits outweigh the risk, then some procedure to manage the risk and its contributing variables is engaged.

A range of risk management options exist. In every case, the management of risk involves decisions regarding:

(1) the relative risk/benefit ratio;
(2) whether the risk, or its contributory variables, can be reduced or eliminated;
(3) the level of risk that is acceptable; and
(4) who can best control and bear the risk burden.

The primary internal management strategy to control the risk is through substitution, reduction or avoidance. These options may focus on the risk or the contributory variables. The selected management option(s) will vary with the nature of the risk itself; the relative cost of a specific control; and its impact, if any, on the benefits to be achieved.

A popular strategy to manage risks in energy efficiency matters is assignment. In assigning risks, the decisions rest on:

(a)   who can best accept the risk;
(b)   what, if any, mitigating strategies can be implemented before they are assigned;
(c)   what are the concerns associated with the various in-house strategies available; and
(d)   what are the costs of outsourcing the risk.

Two axioms prevail: (1) risk is typically best assigned to the party that can control it or gain the most from its control; and (2) the benefits from engaging in an activity must outweigh the costs of mitigating/ managing associated risks.

The risk may be assigned in part to a vendor; i.e., equipment warranty. Risks may be assigned to construction firms through performance and payment bonds. Or, risks may be accepted by performance contractors (ESCOs), through performance guarantees for their performance and that of the equipment. Risks may be real or perceived. If a key decisionmaker in an organization perceives a risk as real, then, for all practical purposes, it is real and should be treated as such. In such cases, however, an option may exist to convince the decision-maker that it is a perceived risk and not real. A softer option may be to treat a potential variable of the perceived risk; thus, having "treated" the risk.

Whether risks are real or perceived, they can affect the financing available. Risk factors can constrain the procedural options, limit the availability of financing and determine the cost of money. Risk, and strategies to manage risks, always carry a price for someone. Money follows risk. The insurance model is a prime example; whoever accepts a risk is compensated in some fashion.

At the same time, the due diligence of the financiers in considering the merits of a proposed project in itself offers some safeguards and a second opinion as to the risks that may be incurred. Financiers must perform a due diligence that can offer an owner valuable insights as to the relative merits of certain financing approaches.

Management must also understand that failing to act can carry its own risks—fiscally, professionally and politically. The best course of action is to judge the alternatives prudently and select the course that offers the greatest, or most critical, benefits for an acceptable level of risk.

Chapter 8

Owner Risks and Mitigating Strategies

Owners need to weigh the relative risks associated with each of the performance contracting delivery options within the context of local conditions. The framework presented in this chapter defines the major risks and variables that exacerbate or diminish certain risks. It is designed to help potential performance contracting customers decide whether to bear or transfer certain risks as part of the project delivery strategy. If in-house staff cannot mitigate the particular risks associated with the selected option(s), then an organization may choose to transfer these risks either by selecting a project delivery option that assigns these risks to the service provider or outsourcing directly for services that will mitigate the risks.

Risk factors will vary with local conditions at particular times. Effective assessment and management procedures must reflect local conditions. Once adjusted for the unique local characteristics, the costs associated with accepting or assigning risks can be determined. These "costs" go beyond money and frequently encompass time, manpower, administrative capital, and/or political considerations.

THE RISK ANALYSIS FRAMEWORK

Performance contracting can offer organizations risk shedding opportunities. Evaluating various performance contracting structures requires an understanding of the relative risks each carries. The following framework defines the major risks and variables that exacerbate or diminish certain risks associated with performance contracting. The options examined are vendor financing, shared savings, and guaranteed savings.

The range of out-sourcing opportunities addressed within this framework are those unique to performance contracting. For ease of reference, the following risk management frameworks separate the technical, financial and procedural risks.

The following analysis was first developed at the request of Ms. Christine Vance, Bureau of Energy Conservation, City and County of San Francisco as part of an effective energy efficiency financing decision making model, "Picking Up the Pace," developed under a grant from the Urban Consortium. Information on obtaining the full report is provided in the reference section. Ms. Vance and her associates in the City of San Francisco are to be commended for realizing that potential performance contracting customers, particularly those in the public sector, need a realistic way to identify risks as well as ways to compare and mitigate such risks. The authors gratefully acknowledge the customer perspective provided by Ms. Vance, her colleagues and associates that is incorporated within the following discussion.

PERFORMANCE CONTRACTING OPTIONS

Before the risks related to various performance contracting/financing options are assessed, a quick summary of the energy efficiency financing options available through performance contracting will make the following figures more understandable.

Vendor financing. Typically, the simplest form of performance contracting, vendor financing is generally offered by a manufacturer who wishes to demonstrate confidence in the energy efficiency capabilities of its equipment and offers to take payment of the equipment out of the avoided utility costs. This approach is often referred to as "paid-from-savings." Financing (and equipment selection) is limited to those vendors offering such a service. Bias by the vendor towards his own equipment is a factor.

Shared savings. Prior to project implementation, the owner and energy service company ESCO agree on a percentage split of the energy cost savings. Performance and credit risk are both carried by the ESCO. If there are no cost savings, the ESCO does not get paid. If savings are greater than expected or energy prices go up, the customer can easily pay more than expected for the use of the equipment.

Guaranteed savings. The ESCO guarantees the quantity of energy to be saved and that the dollar value of those energy savings will be sufficient to cover the debt service obligations. The customer incurs a credit risk on the books, but the debt service obligation is guaranteed to be met through the savings unless the price of energy drops below a specified floor price.

TECHNICAL RISKS

The major risks typically associated with energy efficiency work are technical considerations, which run the gamut from equipment selection to technical expertise of in-house staff and outside consultants, energy audit quality, construction/installation matters, maintenance and operations concerns, savings persistence potential, and savings verification. Each of the these risks may vary with the financing mechanism used. These are presented in Table 8-1, with the relative risk associated with the typical energy efficiency financing options, the major contributing variables to the risk, as well as potential mitigating strategies to treat those variables.

Many technical risks can be managed through an analysis of the variables contributing to the level of risk and implementing the appropriate mitigating strategies. All mitigating strategies, however, demand internal resources and/or the expense of outside support. In almost all cases, for example, direct purchase will reveal the highest level of risk to the organization, but requires the lowest total expenditure.

Of the three types of performance contracting presented in Table 8-1; i.e., vendor financing, ESCO shared savings, and ESCO guaranteed savings, the guaranteed financing approach generally offers the greatest level of risk shedding opportunities. Vendor financing is usually equipment specific; seldom offers a comprehensive energy management approach; and is constrained by the vendor's line of equipment, probable equipment bias, and potential "needs" enhancement.

Vendor financing and ESCO shared savings offer off-balance sheet financing, which may make them more attractive when weighing financial risks or in cases where debt ceilings are a factor. Neither approach offers the comprehensive technical support and the risk shedding offered by ESCO guaranteed savings.

Table 8-1. Technical Risk Framework

Technical Risks	Performance Contracting Options			Major Variables	Mitigating Strategies
	Vendor Financing	Shared Savings	Guaranteed Savings		
Equipment performance —longevity —warranty	3	4	1	Quality of specs Selection process Contract conditions	In-house/consultant expertise Legal ability available
Technical expertise	3	1	1	In-house staff experience/training Consultant qualifications	Provide needed experience/training Secure outside consultation Selection process
Audit quality; accuracy	4	3	2	Auditor technical and risk assessment abilities Review capability Vendor bias	Selection process Review a sample audit 3rd party validation Establish procedural criteria & scope of audit

Construction/ installation	1	2	1	Vendor or subcontractor qualifications Contract provisions	Selection process Performance/payment bonds Legal ability Owner construction supervision
Maintenance & operations	3	3	1	Manpower In-house staff qualification Training; experience	Outsourcing Training quality Selection process
Savings persistence	3	3	1	Varies by measure Administrative commitment O&M attitudes, training, experience	Contractual obligations Vendor selection ESCO selection Guarantees offered Deal's financial structure
Savings verification •approach •instruments	5	4	1	Needs vary by measure, guarantee, & needed accuracy	Amount paid for accuracy 3rd party validation

Legend: N/A not applicable; 1 low risk; 2 low-medium; 3 medium; 4 medium-high; 5 high

Since an ESCO carries both the credit and performance risks in shared savings, the cost of money is higher. This in turn drives down the acceptable payback period and frequently removes the big ticket items, such as boilers and insulation, from projects. To gain the benefits of guaranteed savings, particularly technical risk shedding, the owner must accept the credit risk and the associated costs of a more complex and comprehensive approach.

FINANCIAL RISKS

Financial risk factors are paramount in evaluating the best procedures for funding energy efficiency measures. Risks associated with various energy efficiency financing approaches are typically significant factors; including securing the financing, impact on the debt ceiling, the likelihood of achieving the savings, the cost of money (interest rates; use of tax-exempt status, and repayment terms), energy price fluctuations, the extent of the equipment warranties, whether the guarantor will be there to back the guarantee for the life of the project, what hidden costs may exist in package deals, and the higher payment risks specifically related to shared savings.

Table 8-2, presents these risk factors, the typical level of risk associated with the factor by financing option, major variables and usual mitigating strategies. In most cases, the risks for all three performance contract options can be managed through contract provisions. In all cases, the customer's willingness to assume performance risks will typically lower project financing costs.

Before discussing the specific implications of the risk factors revealed in Table 8-2, one other factor needs to be addressed. Since the financing is carried by the ESCO in vendor financing and shared savings, there is a tendency to assume that the owner will not pay any transaction costs or finance charges. All costs incurred by the vendor or the ESCO must be accounted for somewhere. While the financing comes from a larger pool of funds, the transaction costs are apt to be lower; however, the customer still pays for this cost of doing business.

Warranties

Like direct purchase, vendor financing is apt to have the typical manufacturing warranty and nothing else. However, the vendor's interest in getting paid from savings will help assure savings occur—and that

Table 8-2. Financial Risk Framework; Technical Issues

Financial Risk Factors	Performance Contracting Options			Major Variables	Mitigating Strategies
	Vendor Financing	Shared Savings	Guaranteed Savings		
Projected savings not realized	1	1	1	Lack of expertise —specs —selection Vendor claims	Use outside consultant
Warranties —limited; —manufacturer	2	2	1	Contract provisions Equipment selection	Negotiation
—Guarantor "disappears"	N/A	2	3	Contract provisions Assume debt service obligation	Performance bond Organization's financial status
Increased savings or energy prices may make equipment payment too high	2	4	NA	Contract provisions	Be aware Negotiations Set payment ceiling

(Continued)

Table 8-2. *(Concluded)*

Financial Risk Factors	Performance Contracting Options			Major Variables	Mitigating Strategies
	Vendor Financing	Shared Savings	Guaranteed Savings		
Post-contract Savings	2	2	2	Quality of the specs Project scope Equipment useful life	Engineering support Selection process Maintenance quality
Establishing baseyear; baseline adjustments	3	2	2	Availability of historical data Identification of baseyear conditions Clarity of formulas in the contract	Organization's energy management procedures Combined technical & legal expertise
Provisions & cost for M&V	4	4	4	Procedures Accuracy	Instruments & approach used Cost 3rd party validation
Fixed payment	4	5	1	Monthly savings fluctuations	Clear formula Variables established
Cost of delay	1	3	3		

Legend: N/A not applicable; 1 low risk; 2 low-medium; 3 medium; 4 medium-high; 5 high

the equipment will work until the equipment is paid off.

In shared savings and guaranteed savings, the ESCO payment depends on the equipment performing at a certain level for the life of the contract. This assurance is even stronger with guaranteed savings. So in addition to the manufacturer's warranty, which is typically conveyed to the customer under performance contracting, an implied warranty exists.

The ESCO guarantor could disappear, leaving the customer without this additional "warranty" and leave the owner with the debt service obligations. This risk is underscored by the large vendor/ESCOs; e.g., Johnson Controls, Honeywell, Landis & Staefa, Carrier, who point to their size and longevity as a positive factor. These big companies, however, are not without problems. All ESCOs should be investigated as to their organizational and financial stability and when in doubt, a performance bond to back up payments should be required. Keep in mind, however, that the cost of such bonds come out of the project; so a share of the cost is borne by the customer.

Increased Savings Or Energy Price Changes

In a shared savings project, the customer agrees to pay a percentage of the avoided utility costs to the ESCO. In a $1,000,000 deal, this might be 70 percent, or $700,000, which the customer has deemed is a reasonable cost for the equipment and services received. If the avoided utility costs go higher than expected by virtue of greater than expected savings or higher energy prices, the customer may find itself paying 70% of $2,000,000, or $1,400,000. To a lesser extent, this is also possible in vendor financing if the contract stipulates a term rather than just paying off the equipment costs. This concern can conceivably happen to some extent in guaranteed savings if the excess savings is shared with the ESCO. An ESCO's interest in helping the customer secure excess savings generally outweighs this problem. Whether the selected financing is shared or guaranteed savings, this risk can be managed by stipulating the absolute dollar value of the shared or excess savings an ESCO can receive.

Post Contract Savings

The length of time the installed equipment will continue to operate near design and, thus, deliver the desired savings is key when weighing project benefits. This risk can be effectively managed in any financing scheme by stipulating useful equipment life, quality of maintenance and performance criteria in the specifications and/or contract.

Fixed Payment

Not knowing from month to month what the required payment will be can be unsettling and is typically inherent in vendor financing and shared savings options. In fact, these fluctuations in shared savings have frequently created an adversarial relationship between the customer and ESCO to the detriment of the project. The bookkeeping by all parties is a greater burden. Fixed payments are preferable.

Cost of Delay

Small direct purchase items can usually be acquired quickly and the cost of delay risk would, consequently, be very low. Performance contracting generally offers a quicker start-up if the organization's personnel and technical/legal support understand the concept. Increasing complexity typically incurs greater delays.

Intrusion/Interruption

The risks of interrupting operation or intruding on processes and procedures are typically higher in more comprehensive programs; thus, ESCO guaranteed savings carry a higher risk and vendor financing a lower one. Requiring contractors to work outside of regular operating hours is a frequent solution, but the added labor costs are often borne by the project (and shared by owner) and must be weighed against the benefits.

Financing Availability

The creditworthiness of an organization is a factor underlying all financing mechanisms. The repercussions from Orange County, California, are still felt in the market place; so cities and counties, for example, are subjected to greater due diligence and viewed with more caution than previously.

Shared savings options will be affected by the ESCO's creditworthiness and its ability to assume any further debt equity.

Debt Ceiling

If a public sector organization is limited by statute, bond ratings, lack of voter authority or fiscal prudence from assuming more debt, vendor financing and shared savings become attractive options for they are typically off balance sheet. All other financing options will increase debt. If the public sector organization has limited room left to incur debt, the financing options need to be weighed against other needs, which may create demands on the credit available. Similarly, private sector firms must also weigh increased debt, for it can affect the ability to borrow for other purposes.

An organization pays in other ways for the off balance sheet opportunities; vendor financing is usually confined to a specific piece of equipment and does not offer a comprehensive approach. The organization is also limited to the product line available from vendors which offer "paid-from-savings." Relying on vendor recommendations may also allow the "fox to design the hen-house."

The ESCO carries both the credit and performance risks in shared savings; therefore, the ESCO must hold back funds to cover more risks. Financiers remember the number of shared savings projects that went sour in 1986, when energy prices dropped, and view a shared savings approach as a greater risk. In shared savings, the ESCO and financier are, in effect, betting on the future price of energy. With the advent of retail wheeling and the expected price volatility, this risk is greater than ever. The cost of money for shared savings is high and is apt to go higher. As the portion of the investment goes up to obtain money, the dollars available to invest in equipment—and savings—go down.

Cost of Money

Interest rates are always a factor in determining the most attractive financing option. In the United States, tax-exempt financing offers the most attractive interest rates for eligible institutions, but can only be used if a municipality, or other tax-exempt organization, accepts the credit risk. Vendor financing *and* shared savings rely on the manufacturer/ ESCO, which requires commercial interest rates. The amount of interest paid will depend on how the deal is structured. The length of the contract also effects total interest paid as well as the impact of discount rates. The surety offered by large ESCOs can reduce interest rates.

In calculating energy payback periods, or return on investment, the investment is divided by total expected energy savings per year. Seldom, if ever, does the owner consider the reduced dollar value of those energy savings. The dollar value of energy savings can be adjusted to "present value" dollars. "Present value," or "discounted" dollars, are dollar amounts adjusted for the fact that, left invested over time, those dollars would generate income through interest earnings. This is sometimes referred to as the "time value of money." When making this adjustment

Table 8-3. Financial Risk Framework; Money Issues

Financial Risk Factors	Performance Contracting Options			Major Variables	Mitigating Strategies
	Vendor Financing	Shared Savings	Guaranteed Savings		
Financing not available	N/A	4	1	Customer creditworthiness, Performance risk of financing option	Use vendor financing or shared savings, ESCO qualification and surety
Increase debt ceiling	N/A	N/A	5	Statutory ceiling, Voter authority problems	Use vendor or shared savings
Cost of money —interest rates —discount rates	2	4	1	How deal is structured, Length of contract	Contract conditions, Financier opinion, ESCO surety
Tax-exempt not available	4	4	N/A		
Energy prices —fluctuation —negotiate rates; prices may fall lower than floor price	3, N/A	4, 4	2, 4	Contract provisions, Utility restructuring, Contract provisions	Negotiation, Follow state & federal actions, Negotiation
Hidden project costs	3	4	4	Margins, Mark-ups, Profit	Open book pricing, Require transparency, Reserve right to bid equipment

Legend: N/A not applicable; 1 low risk; 2 low-medium; 3 medium; 4 medium-high; 5 high

the dollars are worth progressively less over time. The longer the payback; the greater the discount rate impact. The higher the interest rate; the greater the decline in dollar value. Future interest rates, therefore, become a risk factor that's hard to predict. The best source of assistance is the project financier, whose business relies in part on projecting interest and discount rates as accurately as possible.

The interest and discount rate risks can be limited by shorter contracts. Short contracts predicated on savings, however, force short paybacks. Short payback criteria remove the larger "big ticket" items; e.g., boilers, chillers, window insulation, etc. from consideration. These big ticket items generally have greater savings persistence and, therefore, offer savings and environmental benefits for a longer period of time.

Energy Prices

Predicting the future price of energy is hard, if not impossible. The roller coaster we have been on since 1973 is apt to take some new dips and turns as utility restructuring takes effect. To protect themselves, ESCOs typically guarantee the energy saved will cover the debt service provided energy prices do not go below a certain floor price. This provides a little more risk to the customer, but the obligation to pay the utility falls commensurably; so it is usually a wash.

The greatest risk at present, and probably the hardest of all to manage, in energy efficiency work is predicting how changes in supply costs will weigh against energy efficiency savings. For large organizations a fraction of a cent negotiated on the supply side of the meter can significantly outweigh any proffered efficiency economic gains. It is quite possible that negotiated or bid utility rates may fall lower than a stipulated floor price. This is most apt to happen in large industrial, military bases and big commercial establishments where the owner's power to negotiate with the supplier is greatest.

Hidden Project Costs

When energy efficiency financing moves away from bid/spec, a major fear voiced by owners relates to hidden costs. Thus, the financial structure of a deal must be carefully examined for these costs. On the other hand, it should be remembered that bid/spec is only as good as the quality of the specifications. Further, when "low bid" is required, the bidder is being asked to deliver *minimally acceptable* equipment. Under traditional low bid, post contract savings, which usually accrue totally to the customer, can be very limited. Good business practices suggests the bidder will not invest in equipment, which would normally last longer than a specified and/or contract period, if he can help it.

If management is concerned about hidden costs, it should always back out the numbers in proposed costs and identify the cost of the equipment and the cost of the services received. If in-house expertise is not sufficient, outside consultation is a very good investment, especially on larger projects. If in doubt, a customer can reserve the right to bid the equipment separately after reviewing the ESCO recommendations. An ESCO, however, must approve the specs and participate in final equipment selection if it is to offer a guarantee in such circumstances. A small organization, may not have this luxury if the savings opportunity is marginal. In addition to bid/spec equipment purchase options, there are mechanisms for establishing a framework for comparing prices as well as reference works, such as *Means*[1], which can prove helpful. An organization may also want to consider the open book procedures used in Canada, where prices are listed for categories of service as well as acquisitions.

In the final analysis, the net project financial benefit is a good indicator of the extent to which hidden costs exist or really matter. Too often potential customers get caught up in potential equipment costs and lose sight of the fact that the services and guaranteed savings are the desired result.

PROCEDURAL RISKS

Many of the procedural risks stem from insufficient attention to planning, selection procedures, inadequate equipment and maintenance specifications as well as the lack of project supervision and staff training. Table 8-4 describes these risk factors and assigns the relative level of risk by performance contracting financing option. The major variables contributing to these factors and some mitigating strategies are also identified in the table's two right hand columns.

A review of Table 8-4 reaffirms that careful preparation and planning can effectively mitigate a significant portion of most procedural risks. The variables and mitigating strategies are self-explanatory in the following table with four possible exceptions.

---

[1]Means, R.S., *Means Mechanical Cost Data*. Kingsten, MA.

Project Management

The coordination between an ESCO and the customer is the prime responsibility of the ESCO's Project Manager and the organization's lead person. To make it work, the responsibilities of the Project Manager should be clearly set forth in any ESCO proposal/contract as well as the qualifications by the assigned personnel to meet these responsibilities—in education, training and experience. The percentage of time the Project Manager will devote to the project each year of the project should be clearly stated. Assigning a new Project Manager, should a replacement be necessary, should always carry with it prior customer approval.

Facility Control Problems

Fear of loss of comfort is almost always the greatest concern among board members and occupants. Contract stipulation as to the acceptable range of heating and cooling temperature parameters, relative humidity levels, air changes per hour, lighting parameters, etc., generally satisfy these concerns. The owner should set these parameters; however, the more control of the facility a customer requires, the greater the ESCO risk and, consequently, the greater the ESCO's share of the savings.

Quality Operations and Maintenance Training

The contract should clearly assign which parties are providing certain maintenance tasks and these tasks should be sufficiently detailed to assure the expected quality of maintenance is delivered. Check-off lists or a computer managed maintenance system can go a long way toward mitigating this risk. Training for O&M staff should be offered by ESCOs on installed equipment at a minimum and on related energy consuming equipment wherever feasible. Training should be annual for the life of the contract.

Emergency Response Provisions

The level of risk associated with emergency response will vary considerably based on the measures installed and how critical they are to the operation. The response time on a burned out lamp, for example, is usually not as critical as when a chiller goes down on a hot summer day. The required response time necessitates an assessment of how critical the equipment is and how long the facility can coast. Typically, ESCOs will rely on local distributors as their first line of defense.

Table 8-4. Procedural Risk Framework

Financial Risk Factors	Performance Contracting Options			Major Variables	Mitigating Strategies
	Vendor Financing	Shared Savings	Guaranteed Savings		
Facility selection procedures	3	3	2	Organization leadership	Organization admin. should establish
Poor equipment selection procedures	3	3	2	Planning, Specs —who writes —who approves	Quality in-house or consulting expertise
Audit is not sufficiently comprehensive	N/A	4	2	ESCO selection Auditor selection	Quality in-house or consulting expertise Length of contract
Project management inadequate	N/A	2	2	ESCO selection Project Manager selection	Careful planning & selection

Facility control problems	2	2	2	Contract provisions	Specify acceptable parameters in contract
Quality of maintenance; training	2	2	1	Specification for maintenance Trainer's abilities; cost	ESCO selection Project Manager
Emergency response provision	1	2	2	Contract provisions	Specify acceptable parameter s in contract
Termination conditions & values	3	3	2	Contract provisions	Negotiations Legal abilities
Schedule adherence	1	1	1	Delays	Check past practice of vendor, ESCO penalties, bonuses
Intrusion/ interruption	1	2	3	Variable contract language Size of project	Mitigate through careful attention to operational needs Project Manager

Legend: N/A not applicable; 1 low risk; 2 low-medium; 3 medium; 4 medium-high; 5 high

Keeping Risks in Perspective

Whenever this much attention is paid to potential customer risks there is the inherent problem of enlarging customer perception of the risks to be incurred. And, as a result, it can strike fear in the hearts of the less venturesome. It is appropriate, therefore, to come full circle and once again state that performance contracting is *a risk shedding opportunity*. Less risks should be incurred in performance contracting than in any other energy efficiency financing approach. The biggest risk for a customer, in fact, is selecting the right ESCO.

The Big Risk: Getting the Right ESCO

The risks associated with selecting an ESCO are about the same as in other energy efficiency financing approaches: insufficient attention to planning and selection procedures at the outset. Careful preparation and planning can effectively mitigate many risks. Planning and preparation should include:

(1)   deciding on the desired results and determining the criteria, which will indicate the firm best prepared to deliver those results;

(2)   developing effective selection procedures, including specifications and/or request for proposal language, and evaluation procedures;

(3)   establishing contract language, which reasonably protects the organization, and negotiating reasonable contract terms; and

(4)   realistically examining capabilities of staff and retaining quality outside consultation whenever needed. [Note: In a project of sufficient size and value, these consultation costs can be assigned to the project.]

Concerns related to effective solicitation and selection procedures are more fully developed in Chapter 3, "The Fine Art of Solicitation and Selection."

In the final analysis, risk management answers two questions: What do we get out of it if we proceed? If we go ahead, how can we control any associated problems and costs? When energy efficiency is considered, the answers for an organization may vary; but the principles are the same.

Chapter 9

ESCO Risks and Management Strategies

From the ESCO perspective, performance contracting is risk management. In the final analysis, the ability of the ESCO to identify risks, assess their implications and manage them effectively makes a decisive difference in the level of services and savings an ESCO can offer.

ESCO Risk Vulnerability

The greatest points of risk vulnerability have emerged as the ESCO industry has matured. Today, the experienced ESCOs know more precisely which performance contracting aspects need careful scrutiny and management. Associated horror stories have helped to underscore critical risk aspects. How these aspects manifest themselves, their magnitude

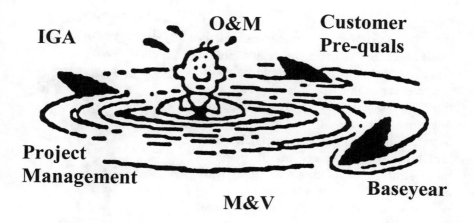

IGA O&M Customer Pre-quals

Project Management M&V Baseyear

and mitigating strategies may vary by market or by country culture, but there is an underlying consistency. The major risk factors that must be managed by an effective ESCO have been established: customer pre-qualifications; project development; energy audit quality; equipment selection and installation procedures; commissioning; operations and maintenance practices and training; measurement and savings verification; and project implementation.

CUSTOMER PRE-QUALIFICATION

For the firm just entering the ESCO business, the most obvious customer qualification seems to be energy savings potential. But that is far too simplistic.

Since performance contracting is primarily a financial transaction, the financial condition of the customer is equally important. The customer must remain in business for the life of the project if the project is to remain an economically viable endeavor. For the ESCO to stay in business, its fees must be paid. To the extent that the customer incurs debt to purchase the equipment, the organization must be in a position to meet the debt service obligations.

Of nearly equal importance is the impact the customer's management and staff can have on the project. As noted in Chapter 7, the "people factor" can make or break a project that otherwise seems very attractive.

Qualification Criteria

To manage the customer risk effectively, each ESCO needs to determine the criteria a customer must meet to be an attractive candidate for performance contracting. The ESCO must also develop the questions, and perhaps a survey form, to ascertain if the criteria are met. The final and most difficult piece of the management strategy is to know when to walk away. It is hard for the sales and marketing people to turn their backs on a potential customer that just oozes energy savings

Just learn to walk away...

potential; but if key criteria are not met, the project won't work.

Pre-qualification criteria can usually be divided into three categories: financial/economic factors, facility/technical factors and people factors. These categories can be further refined into specific criteria as follows:

Financial/economic factors:
- creditworthiness,
- organization's longevity, stability,
- organization's business prospects, and
- supporting documentation.

Specific markets and given customers will prompt additional financial criteria. Many financial houses now have stipulated conditions, even forms, that ESCO sales people need to consider.

Facility/technical factors:
- building age and useful life,
- building function, potential changes,
- occupancy hours, people,
- condition of mechanical equipment,
- existing level of maintenance,
- annual utility bill, and potential project size, and
- energy and cost saving potential.

These criteria will be addressed in depth during the investment grade audit (discussed below) but a preliminary judgment must be made as to whether these criteria are met sufficiently to warrant further project development. The preliminary judgment is usually made with a "walk-through" scoping audit.

People factors
- top management commitment,
- multi-level involvement, team approach,
- evidence that the concept and benefits are understood,
- management has needs, wants, wishes that the project will serve, and
- O&M manpower, abilities, training needs, attitudes are supportive.

Assessing these criteria is very difficult, as ESCO personnel seldom have the needed analysis skills and portions of this assessment are highly subjective. However, ESCOs should do all they can to quantify people factors.

The level of top management's commitment is very important, but an absolutely critical factor is the attitude of the O&M staff. If the director of facilities or maintenance announces that a performance contracting project will not work, the ESCO can be assured it will not work! The person, who has responsibility for the switches and valves, can defeat the best designed project in the world.

Pre-qualification of customers is both a science and an art. The ESCO that does not master this area will spend a lot of time and money chasing empty promises. Time and money that could be spent seeking viable customers. Salespeople also need guidance as to the timing of securing answers to certain criteria as well; so they know when to cut their losses. For example, if the financials are not clear and adequately documented by a specific stage in the sales cycle, internal counsel should be sought before any more sales time is expended.

PROJECT DEVELOPMENT

From the first call through the Project Development phase, the ESCO is investing money in a potential project. The biggest enemy in the ESCO business is time. The more protracted the Customer Qualification and Project Development phases are; the more costly.

The Project Development phases, therefore, should be carefully planned and smoothly executed. Each risk associated with this phase should be acknowledged and addressed. A concern is getting the "buy" decision. At the Pre-qualification phase, the preliminary buy check should determine if further work is warranted.

"BUY" Signals

A crucial early step is to determine who are the decision-makers and the influencers in making a buy decision. Influencers, such as energy managers and directors of maintenance, can often slow down or kill a deal, but they seldom sign the contract. The key considerations at this stage are who are: (1) the decision makers; and (2) can the management make a decision in a reasonably short time. A protracted sales cycle, or a never completed deal, not only slows the day when revenues can flow, but ties up personnel that could be used to make another project happen. Identifying buy/no buy signals is a critical part of a marketing strategy.

By the time the Project Development phase is reached, more ESCO funds have been expended; but no revenue has been realized. Compressing the sales cycle through successful sales strategies is essential.

One ESCO has successfully used a Decision Schedule that lists the tasks leading to a contract, the responsible party for each task and the task completion dates. After the concept sell is accepted, both parties develop and sign the Decision Schedule. Then, should one part lag, a courteous letter saying, "We cannot meet our date for…Task 7… completion because your financial officer still has the material…" generally gets the process moving again.

Deal stoppers during the Project Development phase include:
- Finding the project cannot be financed;
- Recognizing the project cannot be paid for out of the projected savings;
- Determining projected savings cannot be measured effectively; or
- Realizing the savings baseline is too dynamic to be managed.

Anticipating these issues and taking steps to resolve them may avoid such problems. Or, at least avoid the money hemorrhaging on a futile effort. Pre-approved project financing, for example, will make it clear early in the process exactly what the financier expects.

An effective way to move from the Project Development phase to the Investment Grade Audit (IGA) is to prepare a concept report with a benchmark energy analysis and rough numbers as well as the agreed upon project objectives. This document then serves as the basis for a Planning Agreement, which is a preliminary agreement requiring the owner to pay for the IGA if the project does not go forward.

INVESTMENT GRADE AUDITS

ESCOs have learned, often through painful experience, that the traditional energy audit is just not good enough. An audit that incorporates all the name plate data, run times, etc. is only the first step. If an ESCO is going to invest its time and money in developing a project and laying its guarantees on the line, then it must have quality information to justify the investment.

The traditional energy audit has been a "snap shot" approach that typically assumes all current conditions will remain static for the projected payback time of the measures. But buildings are seldom—if ever—static. They are typically dynamic places with changing functions. What's more, they're populated by people who simply will not behave in predictable, consistent ways.

For investors and energy service companies that rely on energy and operational savings to ultimately fund retrofits, the 1970's energy audit has increasingly fallen short of the mark.

We have historically skirted the implications of the human element in energy auditing. "Paybacks" have been assigned to certain measures in multiple applications when we knew full well they would not perform in exactly the same manner under differing conditions. Remember, as stated earlier, that up to 80 percent of the savings in an effective energy management program can be attributed to the energy efficient practices of the O&M personnel. In other words, as little as 20 percent of the savings could be attributed to the actual hardware, but we have continued to make calculations like a piece of hardware was going to always operate in the same fashion under vastly differing conditions.

Frequently, the impact of existing energy related equipment on newly installed equipment has also been neglected. Back when we were all on a steep learning curve, a controls company attempted to duty cycle a 100-year-old boiler in Providence, Rhode Island. With 20/20 hindsight, we now know that was not a good idea.

Over the years, experience has taught those in the performance contracting industry that guarantees require more precise calculations of conditions which surround newly installed energy efficient equipment and the unpredictable element people bring to the equation.

Today, those who wish to predict savings with any degree of confidence must turn to an *investment grade audit* (IGA).

An IGA incorporates the name plate data, run hours, and other information that goes into a traditional audit. Then, a *risk assessment component* is applied which assesses conditions in a specific building, and more importantly, looks at the human aspect. The challenge is to determine how the proposed measures will really behave *over time* given the probable future conditions in a given facility.

The human factor must not only be assessed, but paired with potential energy measures to ascertain the impact occupants, management, maintenance and operational behavior will have on the energy efficiency measures. For example, measures which are practically people impervious, such as insulation, can be looked on more favorably, especially in facilities where the human factor receives a relatively low score. On the other hand, measures such as controls—particularly if overrides are readily accessible—carry a greater risk because of the human factor. All of these factors must be considered while the payback and predicted savings are being forecast.

An IGA is far more demanding, requires greater skills, and necessitates some subjective judgment. The auditor must weigh many key factors, including:

- management leadership and its commitment to energy efficiency
- the resultant occupant behavior based largely on management's visible commitment
- the manpower, skill and training needs of operators and maintenance staff
- the level of equipment sophistication the O&M staff can operate effectively
- the condition of energy-related mechanical equipment
- repairs and replacement budget provisions
- the attitude of O&M personnel towards the energy program.

Once these and other human factors are weighed, an IGA requires that they be converted to risks with price tags. The whole financial structure of an energy project, especially those with savings guarantees, must allow for these risks.

Woven through all the technical/human consideration, is the money component. Life cycle costing, complete with net present value calculations, must be part of an IGA.

General facility upgrades and needed equipment replace-

ment often drive projects. Energy efficiency benefits from these changes are becoming a carefully calculated part of the investment package. The measures must yield the calculated benefits if the package is to be economically viable. Assumptions that things will stay the same just don't cut it anymore.

Engineers who can perform a quality IGA bring in the money. They are in short supply and in increasing demand. The search is always on for auditors, who can perform a quality IGA, thereby reducing the ESCOs' risks. In fact, many ESCOs now charge owners a premium for an investment grade audit if the project does not go forward. This charge is incorporated into a preliminary Planning Agreement as discussed in Chapter 6 "Contracts."

The auditor scarcity is being compounded by growth in the industry. Mark Ginsberg, of the U.S. Department of Energy, has declared performance contracting is the only growth area in the energy efficiency business. The investor owned utilities in the United States alone now boast more than 65 ESCOs. This growth has put added pressure on the limited supply of investment grade auditors.

When all is said and done, a quality energy audit must stand up to the careful scrutiny of bankers and other investors. An IGA is at the heart of a "bankable project." Hence the term, *investment grade audit*. Any thing less no longer adequately serves the owner, the contractor, or the investor.

THE CRITICAL BASEYEAR

Inadequate baseyear documentation can become a bubbling caldron that only gets hotter through the project years. A quality baseyear, as part of the IGA and the contract, deserves special mention, for it is a key part of effective project management and savings verification.

An auditor cannot accurately predict savings without knowing exactly what the existing conditions are. Too often, however, those conditions are not clearly set forth and signed off by the owner. Then, the squabbles start over how long the lights used to be on… and they build from there.

In addition to the energy consumption, all pertinent operating conditions that contributed to that consumption need to be *accurately* noted. Stressing "accurately" seems rather redundant, but we still find auditors who ask management how long the lights are on... and believe what they hear! Or, they ask the custodian and take the response as gospel. Nine times out of ten, the numbers from management and the custodian don't even agree. This is one time when a "little black box" really works. Namely, the portable data logger,[1] if used judiciously prior to the audit calculations, can yield valuable data and avoid later misunderstandings. The same care in documenting other operating conditions is needed.

EQUIPMENT SELECTION AND INSTALLATION

Equipment selection should grow out of the audit recommendations, as it would in any energy efficiency project. The latitude given the ESCO by the owner in this selection process significantly reduces the level of risk the ESCO carries. The greater the customer's say in the matter; the greater the ESCO's risk.

At the very least, the ESCO needs to be fully involved in preparing the equipment specifications. If the owner insists that the equipment be bid to assure competitive prices and/or cost transparency, the ESCO should participate in the final selection process. In this instance, one party may narrow the field of acceptable bidders to two or three; then the other party makes the final selection.

In much the same fashion, the ESCO must have some control over the subcontractors, who will install the equipment, to assure that it is installed correctly and will operate near design.

Risks associated with equipment selection and installation often put the owner and ESCO at odds. The ESCO would prefer to function as

---

[1]See Chapter 4, Measurement and Savings Verification, for more information on portable data loggers.

a general contractor and have full responsibility for all aspects of project implementation. The owner is rightly concerned about the quality of equipment installed on the premise. Frequently, the use of local subcontractors is also important to the owner. In part, because a particular subcontractor is already familiar with the facility and has the owner's confidence. Politically, it is often attractive to use local labor for community relations or to bolster the local economy. Working out an amicable owner/ESCO arrangement at this point can help set the stage for a true partnership—and a successful project.

The construction manager can play a key role in assuring the right equipment arrives at the right time and is installed by those qualified to do so. For the owner and ESCO, a construction manager working closely with the owner's lead person, can effectively hold down risks and costs. An effective construction manager oversees the process, minimizes the delays and the associated costs, and keeps the whole process on schedule. Critical to a retrofit project, the construction manager also keeps intrusion in the organization's procedures to a minimum and keeps existing building and industrial processes in operation as much as possible. A more complete discussion of an effective construction manager is presented in Chapter 7, "Managing Performance Contracts," but is mentioned here to recognize the important risk mitigation role a construction manager can offer.

There is some latitude for the customer and ESCO negotiations regarding equipment and installer selection, but not much. The customer should keep in mind that the more control the organization keeps in this process; the greater the ESCO risks. As we will see later in this chapter, the greater the ESCO risks are; the less the project benefits the customer. In the final analysis, as long as an ESCO guarantee is involved, the owner will pay to some degree for any measure of control the organization chooses to keep.

COMMISSIONING

Difficulties with existing buildings and increasing concerns about indoor air quality have underscored an owner's need for commissioning. Gradually, ESCOs have also recognized that commissioning can help underscore the partnership relationship at the outset, and assure all parties that the design criteria have been met and all installed equipment are operating correctly. Since commissioning is a performance verification procedure, it can also serve as the first key step of the measurement and savings verification process.

The concept of commissioning has been borrowed from the shipping industry. The idea grew from recognition that new boats operate at sea and must operate as designed. Service calls and system downtime are not attractive options when this floating "building" is a long way from port.

While land locked servicing and downtime problems may not be quite so dramatic, occupant health, safety, comfort and productivity has encouraged commissioning as a critical part of owner acceptance of newly installed equipment.

A well designed commissioning process can assure that:

- The new equipment has been tested and its performance verified in the presence of staff and the ESCO's Project Manager; so those responsible for its future operations and savings potential concur on its acceptable performance;

- Calibration procedures, fine tuning, and routine maintenance are performed and clearly understood. Integral to this process is the scheduling of services and the identification of responsible staff and contractors who will perform the necessary procedures;

- The intended benefits and the optimum operating procedures are understood by all involved, including management, O&M staff and occupants. Without this clear understanding, faulty operations may go undetected; or difficulties may be ascribed to the new equipment which are unwarranted;

- All documents; e.g., manuals, cut sheets, building drawings, specifications, etc., should be conveyed to those who will operate and maintain the energy consuming systems; and

- Another cornerstone is laid in the growing sense of partnership between the owner and the ESCO.

For some, commissioning may seem to be inconsistent with "turnkey mentality" in the building industry. It is, however, entirely compatible with a performance contract partnership where maximum comfort and savings are the goal.

The case study by Michael Prittie and Scott Jackson of The Boeing Company, presented in Appendix B, offers some key points on the planning and benefits of commissioning. While this case study is for a new facility, it offers excellent guidance for risk mitigation in performance contracting. The commissioning services were provided by Engineering Economics, Inc. of Solana Beach, California.

Since controls systems are integral to so many performance contracting projects, the second case study offered in Appendix B presents a commissioning procedure on newly installed controls. The case study is written from the owner's perspective, (the University of Washington) by Phoebe Caner, who now works full time for the university as a staff engineer.

These two case studies have been placed in the appendix as they are quite lengthy, but they offer such excellent perspectives on the merits of commissioning as part of a performance contract that we did not want to abbreviate them for inclusion here.

In reviewing these case studies, it also becomes clear that the commissioning process can help lay a strong foundation for the O&M work needed to support the guarantees.

OPERATIONS AND MAINTENANCE PRACTICES

The "up to 80 percent" figure attributable to O&M energy efficiency practices referenced earlier in this chapter is also very scary to ESCOs, who are guaranteeing the energy saving performance of the equipment. It is small wonder that most ESCOs prefer to maintain the equipment themselves; or, designate a contractor, who is also under some performance guarantees, to do it for them.

Setting the O&M tasks and schedule by measure is a key management function whether the ESCO's own personnel perform the work, it is assigned to a contractor, or the customer's staff performs the needed tasks. In every case, some policing of the facility or process is essential to assuring the tasks have been performed on schedule. The risks are greater and the policing more imperative when the O&M functions are further removed from the ESCO.

Some owners think they will save money by having their own personnel perform the O&M tasks. This is questionable and comparative calculations should be made. In such comparisons, consideration must be given to the size of the risk cushion the ESCO must set aside to cover the greater risks associated with O&M work provided by the owner.

While making such calculations, customers should be aware that ESCOs frequently make as much or more from the maintenance contract than they do from the savings and related services. If the maintenance services revenue is denied an ESCO, the project will be less attractive. Some of the lost revenues may be made up in other aspects of the project. Or, owner maintenance may add sufficient risk for the ESCO that the risks exceed the benefits and the project is no longer viable.

Some of the maintenance risks, especially those performed by a subcontractor or by an owner, can be mitigated by using a computer-based maintenance management system (CMMS). These programs are flexible enough to be tailored to the exact measures implemented and have hundreds of tasks detailed for various energy savings measures. It is an automated way to police the quality of the maintenance as well as attribute and document the inadequacies that cause measures to fall short of their promised savings. Both the ESCO and the owner are urged to consider CMMS when a broad range of equipment has been installed and a myriad of tasks are necessary. Software that already contains the broad range of equipment and the associated tasks should be used. If this data-entering task is left to the purchaser, the success rate for CMMS use is a dismal 20 percent.

MEASUREMENT AND VERIFICATION

A well-planned measurement and verification protocol (M&V) can offer strong risk mitigating opportunities. Whenever money changes hands based on savings, some validation of the savings is necessary.

Chapter 4, "Measurement and Savings Verification," describes in detail M&V's current status and recommended protocols. It should, however, be stressed here that inappropriate M&V will actually add to performance contracting risks. When M&V plans are not appropriate to the measure, yield information that is questionable, or are too costly for the value of the data provided, they work against a sound performance contract. And escalate the risks.

Conversely, a good M&V protocol, agreed to in advance by both parties, not only serves as a valuable tool but offers a risk mitigating opportunity.

PROJECT IMPLEMENTATION

All too often, new ESCOs talk about a project being completed once the equipment has been installed and accepted. That's direct purchase/construction project mentality. The successful ESCO and its partner realize the project is *only beginning* when the "stuff is in the ground."

Due to the importance of effective project management through all the years of the contract, Chapter 7, Managing Performance Contracts, has been devoted to this key aspect. The point in bringing it up in this context is to stress the risk implications inherent in this phase of the project.

Technical consideration, such as sound maintenance practices and provisions for upgrades/alterations, seem to be more obvious than the subtle people factors.

Effective project implementation, however, relies on the Project Manager. The principle difference between a partnership with open and effective communications between ESCO and customers, and one headed for the courts, is a quality Project Manager. This is followed closely by the qualities of the customer's Energy Manager—and how well the two project leaders work together.

The ESCO's interest in achieving the full project implementation benefits is largely influenced by where the ESCO's fee is placed in the financial structure. The mechanics of this are discussed later in the chapter. There is a bottom line, however, in the risk area of which potential customers should be fully aware:

The manner in which an ESCO takes its fee out of the project influences its interest in full project implementation and achieving excess savings.

At least one ESCO buries its fee in the guarantee package and claims not to take a share of the savings. This procedure certainly reduces this ESCO's project risks significantly. Such an arrangement, however, offers no incentive to the ESCO to work with its partner beyond achieving the guarantee. As long as the savings don't drop below the guarantee level, that ESCO carries little concern about how the project will perform over time. There is a price, however, as the ESCO incurs a greater risk of customer dissatisfaction.

The owner is better served by an ESCO which takes some or all of its fee out of the excess savings over and above the guarantee.

Overall the ESCO is best served by taking enough of its fee out of the initial financing to cover the costs it has already incurred. In such situations, the ESCO's basic revenue needs are satisfied and the portion of the fee coming from the excess savings offers the ESCO an incentive to assure the excess savings happen.

MANAGING RISKS THROUGH THE FINANCIAL STRUCTURE

Risk management strategies impact the bottom line—for all parties. The way ESCOs use the financial structure to manage risks, described below, substantiates the assertion that performance contracting is a financial transaction.

ESCOs do not guarantee all the savings they expect to achieve in a building and/or industrial process. The level of guarantee is influenced by the perceived risks.

Through the audit process, the ESCO determines what a reasonable level of potential savings will be. Then a percentage of that "reasonable level" is guaranteed as shown in Figure 9-1. The guarantee covers the normal construction costs; e.g., design, acquisition, installation and interest on the money. The risk cushion established by the ESCO (perhaps unknown to the customer) will typically vary the guanantee level from 50 to 80 percent of the expected savings potential. Some ESCOs insist their sales engineers not exceed an 80 percent guanantee mark. A few ESCOs will go above the mark on very secure measures with a highly qualified customer. The difference between the potential guarantee and the actual guarantee is the "risk cushion." The "risk cushion" is the ESCO's protection against the perceived risks. If a project performs as expected, there will be excess savings above the guarantee. This is sometimes referred to as the "positive cash flow."

The level of the guarantee will vary both by the perceived customer-associated risks and by the ESCO's confidence in its own ability to assess the risks and develop effective mitigating strategies. In other

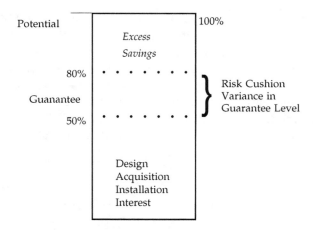

Figure 9-1. Managing Risk Through The Financial Structure

words, as depicted in Figure 9-2, two companies may assess the same facility, calculate the same savings potential, but perceive the risks quite differently. The difference between Company A's and Company B's guarantee level, as shown in Figure 9-2, is their respective risk analysis capabilities.

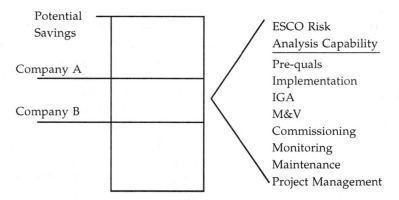

Figure 9-2. Effective Risk Strategies

The IGA risk analysis goal is to have predicted and achieved savings consistently close. Surprisingly, achieved savings should exceed projections by only a slight amount. ESCOs, who consistently show savings far in excess of the guarantee are:

a)   limited in their risk analysis capability;
b)   have basic auditing problems; or
c)   are too cautious.

Some ESCOs have been known to brag about the 40 to 50 percent achieved above their guarantee. This is nothing to brag about. They are hurting themselves and their customers.

An example will demonstrate the losses that come from cautious ESCOs, who are so pleased with their excessive positive cash flows. A customer's energy bill is $10 million per year and Companies A & B both identify energy efficiency measures to reduce the savings by 25 percent, or $2.5 million per year. Company A decides it can place its guarantee level at 75 percent of the expected savings ($2.5 million × 75% = $1.875 million) while Company B puts its guarantee at 60 percent ($2.5 million × 60% = $1.5 million). The level of guarantee per year from the two companies will differ by $.37 million as shown in Figure 9-3. If the payback period is four years, the level of investment in equipment can be $1.5 million greater for Company A... and for the owner. If Company A is right and the mitigating strategies and greater investment in equipment yields $.37 million more per year, the guaranteed savings over 10 years will be greater than Company B's guarantee by $3.7 million. The total guaranteed benefit to the owner would be $5.2 million greater with Company A. Even if both companies, achieve the same potential level of savings the owner will have gained $1.5 million more in capital investments with Company A. And ESCO "A" will have sold and implemented larger project.

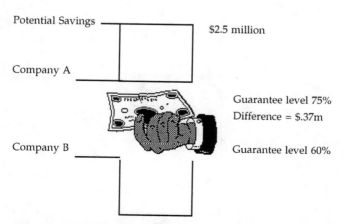

Figure 9-3. Effective Risk Strategies; Implications To Owner

THE ESCO FEE

All ESCOs charge a fee for their services. One ESCO, in a recent article, indicated that the customer should not go with any ESCO that wants a share of the savings. The implication is that this ESCO does not take any money from the savings for its services. Not true. A performance contracting project is funded from the savings. No ESCO to our knowledge is totally altruistic.

If we examine three scenarios, the significance to the owner and the project become very evident. The "altruistic" ESCO #1, as noted above, takes all of its fee out of the guarantee package. ESCO #2 takes some fee from the guarantee package and some from the positive cash flow. ESCO #3 takes its fee entirely from the cash flow. The implications for the ESCO and the owner in these three scenarios are significant.

ESCO #1. The ESCO gets all of its money from the financier up front. The money need not be discounted (See Chapter 5 for impact of discounting). The return on investment is more secure and risks are reduced. As long as the guarantee is met, ESCO #1 has little concern as to how the project performs. Customer dissatisfaction is higher with this approach.

As discussed in the project implementation section, ESCO #1's support to the owner to achieve any savings above the guarantee is less

ESCO #1

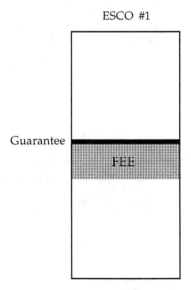

Guarantee

Figure 9-4. ESCO #1 Fee In Guarantee

certain. Since the ESCO fee for all of the years of the contract are buried in the financing, the owner pays interest on the ESCO fees for multiple years. If, for example, the ESCO fee is $100,000 per year on a 10-year contract, the owner is paying interest compounded annually on $1,000,000 that it would otherwise not have to pay.

When the ESCO's sales pitch states the owner gets "all the savings," or "all the excess savings," or "all the positive cash flow," customers should recognize they may get more immediate savings but they are apt to pay for it in interest charges and lost capital investment.

ESCO #2. This ESCO places some of its fee in the guarantee package and gets some of the fee from a certain percentage of the excess savings. For the ESCO, the portion in the guarantee package is a secure return on investment and need not be discounted. The risks are somewhat reduced. The ESCO has some interest in assuring the customer achieves some positive cash flow. Customer satisfaction is apt to be better than with ESCO #1.

For the owner, ESCO #2 is more apt to be an active partner than ESCO #1 for the life of the project. The portion of the ESCO fee in the financed package will be smaller; therefore, interest costs will be lower. The owner will receive most, but not all the excess savings. The savings, however, due to continued ESCO involvement are apt to be greater than

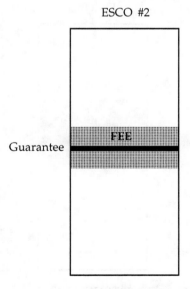

ESCO #2

Guarantee

Figure 9-5. ESCO #2 Fee

with ESCO #1. When an ESCO proposes to take a relatively small portion of the excess savings, the type #2 ESCO is usually involved.

ESCO #3. This ESCO takes all of it fee out of the excess savings. The risks for the ESCO are higher if excess savings are not achieved. The fees are paid out over the life of the contract and need to be discounted. The ESCO is a very active partner for the life of the project.

The owner pays no financing charges or interest on the ESCO fee. The ESCO, however, typically takes 100 percent of the excess savings to a specified dollar amount; so the owner does not have the potential for immediate positive cash flow. The active partnership of the ESCO generally yields greater excess savings.

There is usually greater cost transparency, as a type #3 ESCO clearly spells out exactly how its fee will be paid from the excess savings.

Hybrids of these three scenarios may also be offered. Potential performance contracting customers can rest assured that somewhere in the financial structure is an accommodation for the ESCO fee. Every ESCO gets a fee, even those who characterize themselves as non-profits.

In the final analysis, how risks are assessed and managed financially affect all parties. It is in the interests of the customer, the ESCO, and the financier to work together to develop an effective risk management strategy.

ESCO #3

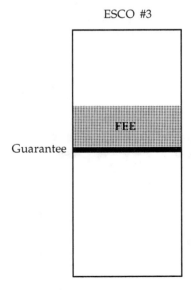

Guarantee

Figure 9-6. ESCO #3 Fee

Chapter 10

Clearing the Air About IAQ and Energy Efficiency

Indoor air quality (IAQ) risks associated with energy efficiency are more perceived than real. Fears that energy efficiency measures may have a negative impact on IAQ affects owners and ESCOs alike. These fears have increased perceived risks, created sales resistance and changed the financial dynamics of a project. It is important to recognize that these fears exist and treat them factually early in the process.

A closer look at where the fears originate and manifest themselves as well as assessment of the real relationship between IAQ and energy efficiency is needed.[1]

A perspective of the owner's dilemma regarding IAQ and energy effi-

Get the facts and fear no more!

ciency can be ascertained by posing the question: Which way does a professional facility manager or real estate manager turn? On one hand, poor indoor air quality can hurt productivity and lose tenants. On the other, there is the constant demand to run facilities as cost-effectively as possible. That means energy efficiency should be a high priority.

IAQ or energy efficiency? The popular press has informed us repeatedly that we can't have both. *They are wrong!*

In nearly every IAQ article the second or third paragraph will mention the energy crisis of the 1970s, the resulting tight buildings and all our IAQ woes. Readers have been left with the impression that, as energy prices soared in the 1970s, those nasty owners and facility managers tightened buildings to save dollars and left the poor occupant sealed in these boxes gagging on stale air filled with pollutants.

ESCOs have found market resistance based on this fallacy and greater risks in making any comfort or health guarantees.

Where did the idea originate that the energy efficient building was at fault? For the answer, let's return to those wonderful days of yesteryear when the ol' leaky, drafty building was supreme. Or, if that's not possible, let's do the next best thing; open the windows and turn up the fans. Somehow the idea that a tight building is not good and uses only recirculated air has permeated the indoor environment thought processes. Ventilation has become THE answer. For the last ten years, the ventilation disciples have almost convinced us that's the way to go. Open the window! Air will just "naturally" get better.

But has it? Will it? The answer, unfortunately, is: **Not necessarily!!**

FINDING ANSWERS

ALL THAT "FRESH" AIR

What if, for example, the air outside is worse? *Natural* air sounds so wholesome. In the good ol' days, we knew without being told that anything "natural" was good for us, including all that natural, fresh air. But what if that fresh air, that *natural* air, is heavily polluted? Try stepping outside of the United terminal at O'Hare International Airport; the air outside is much worse than the air inside. There is no "fresh" air out there. Natural ventilation would be a disaster. Opening the window is really not an option.

Ask hay fever suffers about opening the windows and letting all that wonderful fresh air in. And all the pollen with it.

Or, look at it from another perspective, what happens inside when we open the window? What seemed like a good idea can cause a stack effect. If our room is in a school, we could create negative pressure in the basement. Now if the school has radon problems, that wonderful cross ventilation could cause even more radon to be drawn into the classrooms.

Ventilation is not always the answer.

If we are to clear the air about the relationship between IAQ and energy efficiency, then we need to make that statement even stronger. Ventilation is *seldom* the best answer. Certainly, it is an expensive answer.

Where did we get this idea that ventilation is the great panacea for indoor air quality problems? Why have we been so quick to embrace the idea that ventilation will offer us "acceptable" indoor air quality?

ENTER THE VILLAIN

We have been living with the popular assumption that the energy efficient "tight" buildings just naturally means less ventilation. Ergo, the problem could be rectified by more ventilation.

The ASHRAE 62-1989 standard is titled, "Ventilation for Acceptable Indoor Air Quality." To the uninitiated, that sounds like ventilation will deliver "acceptable" air. It may not. At the very least, the title sounds like the American Society of Heating, Refrigerating and Air-Conditioning Engineers, Inc. has given its blessing to ventilation as **THE** mitigating strategy.

When ASHRAE 62-1989 was formulated, the popular belief was that much of our IAQ problems were created by, and could be cured by, ventilation. Make no mistake, ASHRAE 62-1989 has undoubtedly brought relief to a lot of people, who would have otherwise suffered from "sick building syndrome" … whatever that is. At the time 62-89 was developed, it was very difficult to determine what some of the pollutants were, what their level of concentration was (or should be), and/or what their sources were. Investigation and measurement protocols have come a long way since 1989, even if we are not there yet. Increased ventilation probably gave relief to occupants in an era when we weren't quite sure what else to do.

Ventilation is not the preferred treatment for IAQ problems. It never has been!! EPA has been telling us for years that the best mitigating strategy is control at the source.

In the 1970s and 1980s we reduced outside air, so we wouldn't have to pay the high energy costs of conditioning it and moving it around. With less outside air, we suddenly became more aware of the contaminants that had been there all along. Less outside air meant greater concentrations. Since reduced ventilation was a fairly standard remedy in the 1970s, it is not surprising that the knee-jerk response to the popular dilemma of the 1990s, IAQ, is to increase ventilation.

But blowing more air into the building has not necessarily solved IAQ problems. Sometimes, in fact, it has made things worse.

LOSING GROUND

A couple of cases where more ventilation may create greater IAQ problems can help document the problems this fallacy fosters.

Relative Humidity
Historically, when construction costs have exceeded the budget, the first cut all too often has been removal of the humidifier/dehumidifier equipment from the specs. Today, without those humidifiers or dehumidifiers, it is very hard to correct the negative impact increased ventilation has on relative humidity. To reduce indoor pollutant levels, which may not have been an IAQ problem, increased ventilation invited in all the IAQ problems associated with air that is too dry or too humid. With over 50 years of data on respiratory irritation, even illness, due to dry air, creating drier air is not the answer. With all we now know about microbiological problems and their relationship to humid air, creating more humid air through increased ventilation is not the answer.

The Dilution Delusion
Energy culprit thinking has prompted a heavy reliance on dilution as *the* answer. Maybe we can clear a little of the air if we ask: Is dilution really the answer? Visualize for a moment all those airborne contaminants as a neon orange liquid flowing out of a pipe in an occupied area. Would we be content to dilute it by hosing it down? Just because we can't see our air pollutants, does not mean they are less of a problem. Or that dilution is the solution.

Have we really gotten rid of the problem by reducing the level of concentration? There is still a lot we don't know about chronic low level exposure to some contaminants. There is a very real possibility that we will look back in a couple of decades and see solution by dilution as nothing but delusion. A very serious delusion.

DETERMINING THE VALUE OF
INCREASED OUTSIDE AIR

Using increased outdoor air as a mitigating IAQ strategy also makes several gargantuan assumptions. First, it assumes increased outside air is going to reach the occupants in the building. As recently as the mid-1980s, a study of office ventilation effectiveness found over 50 percent of offices in the United States have ventilation designs that "short circuit" the air flow. Owners and ESCOs should look at the facilities... where is the diffuser... and how does air leave the room. Increasing the outside air may cause a nice breeze across the ceiling, but it may do little for the occupants.

Second, the outdoor air focus has us bringing in air when recirculated cleaned air may be better. Filtration and air cleaning are virtually ignored in 62-89. Bringing in more outside air, which admittedly may be worse than inside air, can cost millions and millions. Should the fresh air fetish totally overrule economics when specified filtration of recirculated air could give us the indoor air quality we need?

When unnecessary fossil fuels are burned to condition all that additional "fresh" air we bring in from the outside, what happens to the quality of the outside air. One study revealed that compliance with ASHRAE 62-1989, increased our nation's public schools energy bill by at least 20 percent. In addition to lost tax payer dollars paying for questionable fresh air, another study revealed that compliance will put approximately 6,303,400 tons of CO_2 in the air—just in the U.S. and just from public schools each year.

This kind of people pollution thinking has its roots back in the Dark Ages when people took a bath once a year whether they needed it or not. People... and that nasty habit native Americans supposedly introduced into our culture ... smoking. Body odor and smoking. If you think that sums up our problems, then you've forgotten a few other ages that have come along since the Dark Ages. Remember the Renaissance? Then, the Industrial Age? How about the Technological Age, Information Age, or whatever it's called, that we are now in?

When we measure our air *per occupant*, we forget about all the pollutants we have managed to make through the years. How many hundreds of new volatile organic compounds (VOCs) do we add to the list each year? As we "progress," people pollutants become less of a

factor, and building materials, furnishings and "new, improved" equipment take on greater importance. Recent European studies have shown that the building pollutant load is much larger than we expected.

Ventilation per occupant just doesn't cut it if pollutant sources other than people dominate an area. Laser printers and copiers, as they operate, give off just as many pollutants whether there are 2 or 20 people in an office. Ventilation *per occupant* simply won't do the job in low occupancy situations.

To "tighten" the noose even further, the National Institute of Occupational Safety and Health (NIOSH) labeled the illness from those energy efficient *tight* buildings, "tight building syndrome." "Sick building syndrome" and "tight building syndrome" became synonymous. Operable windows were remembered wistfully.

Blaming tight buildings gave us charts like the one on the left; so we could compare those minuscule energy savings to the huge personnel losses. "Look," they told us, "at all the increased absenteeism; the lost productivity. What a stupid idea … saving energy … for a few pennies … and losing big dollars. What an expensive idea!"

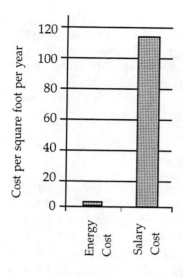

Clearly, the hypothesis is: **lower energy bills make people sick.**

The implication was clear: there is a direct correlation between energy efficiency and indoor air quality problems.

LET'S CLEAR THE AIR! To prove the hypothesis that lower energy bills make people sick, it is necessary to show that all energy efficient buildings have poor air quality and lower productivity.

Or, to state it another way, a tight building is detrimental to people's health. With a little regression analysis, we ought to be able to build a straight line relationship ... the more energy efficient a building becomes, the greater the absenteeism and the lost productivity.

All this talk about tight buildings would lead one to believe there was something really wonderful about those old leaky buildings. Just think ... all those creaky, decrepit old leaky buildings ... weren't they wonderful? Just full of unconditioned, unfiltered, uncontrolled breezes. After all, what was a little draft? You could always move closer to the fireplace, or the pot bellied stove.

Joseph J. Romm's excellent article, "Lean and Clean Management" in the Spring 1995 issue of *Energy and Environment Management* cited a number of instances where energy efficiency had improved productivity, such as West Bend Mutual Insurance's 40 percent reduction in energy consumption *with a 16 percent increase in productivity*.

Casey Stengle told us, "Life ain't what it used to be and probably never was."

The unvarnished truth is "natural" air is not always what it is cracked up to be. Nor is there anything wrong with a tight building; provided that a tight building is well designed and well maintained. Yes, tight buildings more readily reveal professional errors. Yes, tight buildings are less forgiving of poor maintenance. But a well designed, well maintained tight building can provide energy efficiency *AND* quality indoor air.

VIRTUES OF VENTILATION

Ventilation definitely has its place in an indoor air quality program. Ventilation can be a good mitigating strategy when the contaminant or its source can't be determined, as an intermediate step until action can be taken, or when source mitigation strategies are simply too costly. Specific applications of ventilation; e.g., localized source control or sub-slab ventilation to control radon, are valuable control measures.

THAT "52 PERCENT"

Before extolling the virtues of ventilation gives us false comfort, we need to clear the air about the infamous 52 percent. The ventilation advocates were, and are, quick to point out that an early study by the NIOSH stated that 52 percent of the IAQ problems found were due to "inadequate ventilation." Somehow that got translated to inadequate *outside air*. A more careful look at that NIOSH's 52 percent reveals that was a quantum leap. The "inadequate ventilation" problems encountered by NIOSH included:

- ventilation effectiveness (inadequate distribution);
- poor HVAC maintenance;
- temperature and humidity complaints;
- filtration concerns; and
- inappropriate energy conservation measures.

Inadequate outside air was only one of a long list of problems.

NIOSH has pointed out that the 52 percent figure is based on soft data. To the extent, however, that it represents primary problems in the investigated buildings, the NIOSH findings also impart another critical piece of information that is typically overlooked: *48 percent of the problems found by NIOSH will NOT be solved by ventilation*. NIOSH has extensive experience in indoor air problem investigations and a highly regarded protocol. They have determined that nearly half of the problems they have investigated are not related to ventilation. If the NIOSH data and problems identified by other investigation teams are considered collectively, it seems safe to surmise that a great many of our indoor air problems cannot be satisfied solely by increasing outdoor air intake.

Forty-eight percent of the time ventilation did not solve the problem. This fact alone underscores the need for treatment at the source any time it is technically and financially feasible.

THE REAL IAQ/ENERGY EFFICIENCY RELATIONSHIP

A little research does reveal a relationship between IAQ and energy efficiency. First, survey after survey tells us that when the utility bills started climbing in the 1970s, the first place owners, and many facility managers, looked to find money to pay those bills was in the maintenance budget. This was especially true of institutions on rigid budgets, such as schools and hospitals. As the utility bills have gone up through the years, those institutions have progressively cut deeper and deeper into maintenance until our deferred maintenance bills are staggering. Deferred maintenance in just our public schools comes with a very healthy price tag over $100 billion, according to a publication of the Association of School Business Officials.

The second relationship between IAQ and energy efficiency, can also be traced back to energy prices and maintenance. As energy prices climbed, owners bought more sophisticated energy efficient equipment. Unfortunately, O&M training to operate and maintain that equipment did not keep up. Sometimes the training wasn't offered when the equipment was installed. More often, there was a turn over in the O&M personnel and the new staff did not receive the necessary training.

Keeping these relationships in mind, it's really sad to learn that a majority of the IAQ problems found are due to operations and maintenance problems. Table 10-1 offers a review of IAQ problems found by NIOSH, Honeywell and the Healthy Buildings Institute (HBI) at the beginning of the 1990s when ventilation seemed to be the universal panacea. The labels are different; but the commonality of O&M-related problems is very apparent.

THE MUTUAL GOAL OF IAQ AND ENERGY EFFICIENCY

To really clear the air, a careful look at our true goal is needed. Every facility management professional and design professional pro-

Table 10-1. Sources of IAQ Problems

Org.	NIOSH	HONEYWELL	HBI
Bldgs.	529	50	223
Yr.	1987	1989	1989
Inadequate ventilation (52%)[a]	Operations & Maintenance (75%) energy mgmt. - maintenance - changed loads	Poor ventilation - no fresh air (35%) - inadequate fresh air (64%) - distribution (46%)
Inside contamination (17%)		
Outside contamination (11%)	Design - ventilation/ distribution (75%) - filtration (65%) - accessibility/ drainage (60%)	Poor filtration - low filter efficiency (57%) - poor design (44%) - poor installation (13%)
Microbiological contamination (5%)		
Building fabric contamination (3%)	Contaminants (60%) - chemical - thermal - biological	Contaminated systems - excessively dirty duct work (38%) - condensate trays (63%) - humidifiers (16%)

Source: *Managing Indoor Air Quality*, The Fairmont Press.
[a]Percentages exceed 100% due to the multifactorial nature of IAQ problems.

fesses that it is his or her desire to provide owners with a facility that has an attractive, healthy, safe, productive environment as *cost-effectively* as possible. If, indeed, that is the goal, then IAQ and energy efficiency are very compatible. They go hand in hand.

THE 80's GUIDELINES

Assessing the guidelines of the "80s" will help bring these two aspects in line. (And we don't mean 1980s.) First, let's look at what we call the 80-10-10 rule. 80 percent of IAQ problems can usually be spotted with an educated eye and a walk-through of a facility. This walk-through might include some very basic measurements for temperature, humidity, CO_2, etc., but not a sophisticated, in-depth investigation. The other 20 percent of problem facilities require more specialized testing—often a lot of testing. All too often, even with exhaustive, expensive testing, 10 percent of the problems remain unresolved. To summarize, 80 percent of the IAQ problems are detected through a relatively simple walk-through, 10 percent are resolved through pretty sophisticated, expensive testing and nearly 10 percent remain unresolved.

Then we have the energy "80s." Our "up to 80 percent" figure rears its ugly head again. It's worth repeating. "Up to 80 percent of the savings in an effective energy program could be attributed to energy efficient operations and maintenance practices." Not the hardware.

What a bitter pill to swallow. To save money to pay the utility bill, owners cut operations and maintenance. Then, they ended up with maintenance related IAQ problems—and higher energy bills. So the vicious cycle started all over again ... with more cuts in the maintenance budget.

Fortunately, there is a positive side to all this. The same vicious cycle that dug us into this hole can help us climb back out.

IAQ AND ENERGY EFFICIENCY: TEAMING UP

If we can identify nearly 80 percent of our IAQ problems with a walk-through investigation; AND, if we can find up to 80 percent of our energy savings through a walk-through audit that identifies O&M opportunities, can't we put them together and let the energy savings pay for it all?

The answer is a resounding, "Yes!" A non-profit organization, the Indoor Environment Institute (IEI) has established a protocol to perform just such a service, combining energy and indoor environment audits, and is providing the service at cost.[2] Other organizations are now following IEI's lead. The measures, of course, for energy efficiency and IAQ may vary but they can be spotted on the same walk through. An IAQ walk-through investigation is paired with the idea behind performance contracting: let future energy savings pay for the work. It identifies the problems and ways to finance the mitigation. This approach proves once and for all that IAQ and energy efficiency are compatible. When IEI is done, the owners and/or facility managers have the assurance that they are providing a safe, healthy, productive environment as cost-effectively as possible. The combined IAQ/energy efficiency walk through offers tremendous relief from the specter of IAQ lawsuits by assuring owners they have done what the "reasonable man" would do. And in almost every case, it can be done without taking a chunk out of the budget.

LET'S NOT KILL THE MESSENGER

There is one other relationship between IAQ and energy efficiency that deserves careful consideration. When we reduced ventilation and infiltration in the late 70s and early 80s, we did increase the concentration of some contaminants that were already there. Energy efficiency measures, in many instances, were the messengers, but they were not necessarily the cause of the problem. The energy measures only made us aware that we had pollutants in the air that could be injurious to our health. We learned that the sources of those pollutants should be removed or contained whenever possible. Energy efficiency gave us the message. We need not take a page from the King and shoot the messenger.

Consider what will happen as energy prices go up ... and they will ... if for no other reason than we need to start calculating the real cost of energy. Whether our friends in the Middle East run up the price tag, or we start doing a better job of figuring the costs of externalities, we are only kidding ourselves if we think prices will stay low... forever.

When the cost of energy goes up, once again IAQ and energy efficiency are apt to be at logger heads. This does not have to be the case. If IAQ leaders persist in attributing IAQ problems to energy efficient buildings as well as relying on more and more outside air for the answer, we lose. For cost-conscious owners, climbing energy costs will typically outweigh most IAQ concerns. Only regulating expensive, and often unnecessary, outside air requirements can compete against escalating energy prices. And the money could still be wasted.

Environmental concerns, higher energy prices, national security issues and the unnecessary waste of our limited energy resources make increased ventilation, at the very least, a costly answer. Sustainable development means we all put our heads together and work for a quality indoor environment, energy efficiency and a quality outdoor environment.

Our ultimate goal is to produce a comfortable, productive indoor environment as cost-effectively as possible. That puts energy efficiency and indoor air quality on the same side. Good managers and effective ESCOs need to have command of both if they are to do their jobs effectively.

References
1 More information on IAQ can be found in *Managing Indoor Air Quality* by Shirley J. Hansen.
2 Indoor Environment Institute, Mike Crandall, 4302 Floral Avenue, Cincinnati, OH 45212, (513) 531-7110.

Performance Contracting: The Next Generation

Performance Contracting: The Next Generation is about the future. Contrary to those who would like to believe otherwise, the future of the energy industry is unpredictable at best and a picture of chaos at worst. The utility industry is in a state of constant and volatile change as it faces de-regulation, or as we prefer to call it (as you will read in the first chapter of this section), re-regulation. We are indebted to Mr. Richard McMahon and Mr. Steve Rosenstock of Edison Electric Institute, who have contributed so generously to this chapter by giving the utility's perspective on changing energy services.

If there is one certainty about the future, it is that ESCOs will continue to have a role in the industry, albeit a changing one. As we dust off the crystal ball, it seems pretty safe to predict the services offered by energy service companies and utilities will change; customers' options for energy services will broaden; and options for performance contracting will expand.

"Chauffage" will begin to generate more interest. As the major suppliers of energy are no longer limited to utility companies, conditioned space at a guaranteed cost per square foot; or for industry, energy per unit of production, will become more attractive. The concept of paying one company for energy, operation and maintenance and capital improvements will become progressively more enticing to management.

But in the next generation, energy is not likely to be the only area where performance contracts will be viewed as the way to make needed improvements without major capital investments. Bob Payne, Director of Federal Energy Services for Duke Solutions, offers a particularly insightful look into working with industry and developing other opportunities in his chapter "When *"Energy"* Isn't the Answer."

And finally, we certainly cannot address the future without acknowledging the growing presence of the Internet, and the changes we have witnessed in how we communicate and do business. Charlie Douglas, a key player in the areas of operations, industrial relations and human resources in the telecommunications industry for many years, offers a perspective on how we have moved from parchment to instant communications, and the impact and opportunities this instant access brings to our industry. Charlie, charged with helping to oversee the break-up of the Bell-System, brings a special perspective to the need for immediate information during tumultuous times.

Chapter 11

Utility "Reregulation": The ESCO Fit

No one can think energy, and more particularly energy efficiency, these days without wondering what the impact of utility deregulation and competition will be on his or her operation. Suddenly, owners must get smart about buying power and making choices. The complexities inherent in this new era make what was learned through the deregulation of the telephone and natural gas industries look like rehearsals for the command performance.

Before we look at the ESCO fit in all this, one undergirding principle needs to be kept in mind. The popular nomenclature, has been "utility deregulation." The more appropriate term is reregulation. Anyone, who has seen the Federal Energy Regulatory Commission's Order 888, will have difficulty believing we are on the eve of deregulation. The term deregulation will continue to be used, but keep in mind that a bevy of orders, regulations and new federal intrusions are apt to come with the utility restructuring.

We have also been warned by Mr. Ashley Brown, former Ohio utility commissioner, that competition and deregulation are not synonymous. As Mr. Brown has observed, the airlines have been deregulated for many years, but in Atlanta today the choice of airlines is Delta ... Delta ... or Delta. Competition at Hartsfield Airport comes close to a choice among 747s, 727s or maybe an L1011.

For years the facility owner has flipped the switch and the electric power was there. Little thought was given to the whole process. Purchase options were severely limited, as owners were captive customers of the monopoly utility that served the territory. Customer protection was offered to some extent by state utility commissions and the Federal Energy Regulatory Commission.

Owners now have no choice but to become educated consumers. The first option will be whether to designate, and develop, in-house expertise to follow the day-to-day changes in the utility market place and their implications. Or, to gather a general knowledge of what is needed and outsource this "watch dog" function.

"Reliability" and "power quality" will become new words in most electric consumers' lexicon. *Reliability* has been pretty much taken for granted; and, for most, *power quality* has been an unrecognized factor. It may be a rude awakening but we are apt to soon learn what Mr. N.K.P. Salve, India's Minister of Power, meant when he said, "No power is costlier than *no power.*"

Consulting engineers, especially energy engineers, will need to develop their own supply expertise and/or develop strategic alliances with a firm that can provide this resource. Utility deregulation offers engineering firms a new burden or a great opportunity. Or both.

For ESCOs, the whole scenario becomes a crucial part of doing business. There is no question that changes in the new utility market place will have a significant impact on the way ESCOs do business.

The market segments an ESCO strives to serve will change. In the near term, large industrial customers will have little interest in the relatively small action on the demand side of the meter when rate/price negotiations on the supply side can make a big difference in the utility bill.

And what will happen should the price of electricity drop well below a previously contracted floor price and stay there? Could owners find themselves paying more to save energy than to burn it? Customer apprehension, real or perceived, could put a pall on the ESCO market place. At least until the utility restructuring sorts itself out.

The part, however, that will make presidents and CEOs of ESCOs lose sleep will be the dancing payback numbers that could vary by the hour. How will guarantees work? How will ESCOs cushion the risk? Will energy diminish in the performance contracting field while water performance contracting and other services grow? Those responsible for developing the operating blueprints of tomorrow will need superb sources of information, great computer programs ... and big erasers. Conversely, the new utility industry could offer ESCOs some exciting new opportunities and tremendous growth potential.

DUSTING OFF THE CRYSTAL BALL

The best fortune teller would have trouble wading through the mire of political, legal, regulatory and industry prognostications to accurately foretell how the utility scenario will ultimately play out. The most appropriate approach seems to be to take wording from the adage: She who lives by the crystal ball must learn to eat broken glass.

With a big supply of digestive relief on hand and mindful of the hazards, an assessment of a few short term and long term implications still seem to be warranted.

STRANDED BENEFITS

Much has been said, and will be said, about stranded costs or stranded investments. The other side of that coin (particularly for those who wonder how energy efficiency will fare under utility restructuring) stranded benefits are of equal concern.

In the monopolistic environment, utilities were directed (and sometimes offered) to provide special customer benefits. The utility services have been so pervasive that many government agencies have forgotten that they are often dealing with private companies. As utilities shed their quasi-government role and focus on competition, only those services that induce customer retention are apt to survive in utility hands *per se*. Unregulated subsidiaries of utilities, including utility affiliated ESCOs, will pick up some of the slack.

For analysis procedures, the stranded benefits are apt to sort themselves into three areas:

1. Economically viable services, such as cost-effective energy efficient measures. These services are apt to be found in utility-affiliated ESCOs, or ESCOs with established relationships with a utility.

2. Services that are not self-funding, such as more costly renewable measures. These measures may earn their way by being amortized over a longer time period. Some, which are deemed to carry social good, may receive subsidies.

3.   "Welfare" services, such as low income energy assistance pro-
     grams, will probably require more direct government intervention
     to persevere.

THE ESCO FIT

The ESCO of tomorrow, and most likely today, will need at least
some built-in expertise in power marketing and/or a strong alliance with
power marketers and independent power producers (IPPs). The ESCO,
which cannot reach across the meter and serve its customer's supply
concerns, will be at a disadvantage in the market place.

Many owners will be happy to dump the whole supply/demand
energy question on someone else; energy purchasing economies and use
efficiencies are not central to most managers' missions. The appeal of
ENRON's early foray into chauffage (selling conditioned space for 10
years at a set price per square foot) was an instant marketing success.
Unfortunately, the appeal was apparently greater than the company's
ability to deliver at this early stage in the chauffage evolution, but this
leader in the industry is still expected to stay on the cutting edge of
combined supply/demand offerings.

ENRON's vision marks the anticipated larger role ESCOs can, and
will, play in providing all its customers' energy needs. Ultimately, we
will have a seamless market of energy efficiency and supply. The supply
and demand distinctions in a competitive market will be less important
as time goes on.

The market demand for chauffage offerings, which will effectively
remove the supply meter from customer's conscientiousness, will move
the industry in this direction. As utilities negotiate supply prices, they
will realize that their own people, wearing the ESCO hats down the hall,
or in the next building, are negotiating guaranteed efficiency savings.
Soon a combined effort will emerge. Unfortunately, the first contracts are
apt to be cumbersome attempts to combine the separate legal conditions
of supply and demand contracts. Early on market increased share, however, is apt to go to the ESCO, which is customer sensitive enough to
provide simpler contracts. The basic contract, from the owner's perspective, need only establish operating parameters; i.e., temperature, humidity, air changes, light level, etc., and establish ways to deal with major
anticipated and unanticipated variables. A reopen clause to negotiate the

impact of unanticipated events will become even more common place. ESCOs will have a greater challenge to manage the risks and deliver the results, but how this will be done is not central to the owner's concerns. Nor, is it part of the contract language customers want to sign.

If emerging utility-affiliated ESCOs can move out from under their parent company's traditional monopolistic mind-set and develop a strong marketing and financing approach, they will be in a preferred position to develop chauffage. The "in-house" supply expertise already resides in the parent company.

For a short time, utilities—and to some degree their ESCOs—will continue to enjoy the quasi-government image they have held. As long as the federal government continues to regard utilities, even private ones, as quasi-government, the utility-affiliated ESCOs will continue to have some advantage. When the federal government no longer allows the utilities to pre-qualify ESCOs for its agencies, the playing field will even out. But the "level playing field" may not be so easy to achieve, particularly if utility-affiliated ESCOs wisely use this respite to cement their market position.

For the non-utility affiliated ESCOs and engineering firms, wanting to assure a strong position in this changing world, the learning curve will be steep and demanding. The trick will be for ESCO management to realize what they *don't know*, find reliable sources of information or strategic alliances, and integrate these new data and affiliations into their operations for effective application.

"Wanna-be-ESCOs" may find a more secure, and profitable, approach in serving the ESCO industry rather than becoming part of it. Two niches already exist that could prove very lucrative in serving performance contractors. They are:

a) *Investment grade audits (IGAs)*. Engineering firms can build on their existing auditing expertise by refining the traditional audit and incorporating the risk assessment component. (See the discussion on IGAs in Chapter 9, "ESCO Risks and Management Strategies.") Energy engineers, who can offer a quality IGA with predictive consistency, are in great demand now and the need is increasing.

b) *Measurement and Verification (M&V)*. Owners are increasingly aware that the savings they are paying for should be verified, preferably by an impartial third party. Thanks to the leadership of the U.S.

Department of Energy, a widely accepted protocol exists. (See Chapter 4 for more information on M&V and access to the DOE material.)

ANTICIPATING THE NEED; FINDING THE SOURCES

Both engineering firms and ESCOs, who wish to serve customers effectively, need to realize the struggle in the market place began long before the first legal and legislative actions took place. Whether we point to California as the first deregulated state because of its legislative effort or Massachusetts' attorney general's plan which claimed to have beaten California to the punch by a whole three hours (favored by the time difference) on the stroke of 12:00 on January 1, 1998, many *customer retention* maneuvers were already history.

On the other hand, wise customers were already active in establishing their bargaining positions. One of the end user visionaries was, and is, Lindsay Audin, who began gathering key facility data and researching options early. He urged his colleagues to collect and manage load information, to experiment with time sensitive tariffs, to analyze and redesign (at least on paper) present loads, to consider aggregate purchasing with other end users and to issue RFPs for market-based power.[1]

Those who listened to Audin did not sign long term contracts and are now in a position to work the new competitive market to their advantage. The Audin advice to his end-user colleagues can equally serve engineers and ESCOs, who wish to be in a position to serve their customers more effectively. Engineers and ESCOs routinely get some of the recommended information, such as demand profiles for load shedding analysis. The ability to assess rate options, changes in operating schedules, and the impact on energy-using equipment are part of any investment grade audit. This information can now be seen as preparation for comparative shopping and negotiating strategies.

Three of the tariff-sensitive options, listed below are generally available now. The fourth will soon be more common. They give owners, and those who wish to serve them, a glimpse of what the market offers:

* time-of-day (TOD) or time-of-use (TOU) rates—charges vary seasonally and with the time of use; typically peak use is penalized and off-peak provides incentives to shift loads;

- interruptible electric service, which gives the utility the flexibility to reduce power supply beyond a defined level and/or for a defined period in exchange for lower rates;

- curtailable rates, sometimes referred to as energy manager rates, allows the utility to reduce loads upon advance notice for which the utility offers incentives—and penalties for non-compliance; and

- real time pricing (RTP), which is relatively new, typically offers price by the hour with 24-hour advance notice.

THE NEW WORLD OF RTP

Owners, consultants and ESCOs will have to learn to manage RTP if they are to take full advantage of it. RTP can, and will, save money. Conversely, it will become equally apparent that a premium is assigned to set prices. The first question then is: How much price volatility can the business handle? Once the range of acceptable volatility is established, then maneuvering to gain RTP advantages will work.

The second aspect of working with RTP reflects the management of demand concerns we have all worked with for years, but now it is not just seasonal or TOD/TOU. The question turns on: How much price elasticity can a business have? Can loads be shed at the same time the utility has its late afternoon demand spikes? Department stores, for example, are apt to think of their constant lighting and air-conditioning needs and assert they have no elasticity. A careful study of customer traffic, however, is apt to show a major drop during the dinner hour. If air temperatures in the summer were allowed to rise a couple of degrees during the dinner hour, there would be negligible impact on the comfort level and the store would be in a very strong position to negotiate a better contract.

Presumed rigidity in energy demand may be replaced with considerable elasticity if all conditions are examined with an open mind.

Understanding how various utilities respond to load variations now will lay some groundwork for more sophisticated purchasing agreements when the time comes. In the same vein, load profiles (average demand divided by peak demand) and load management can enhance a customer's attractiveness to the utility.

ESCOs, or their power marketers, who understand this new market, will be able to take advantage of tariff structures, particularly poorly designed tariffs, by working the wholesale market through buy-backs and selling procedures. But these "new opportunities" are not for the faint of heart and require good and constant research.

Utility restructuring in the United States and around the world is on fast forward. Sources of information to keep abreast of the times are discussed in the "Parchment to Internet" chapter and a few select references which have been cited.

The hazards of writing about the volatile era of deregulation reregulation are profound. The utility perspective of all of this adds another layer of complexity and a unique perspective. The authors are indebted to representatives of Edison Electric Institute (EEI) for providing their insights of the changing energy market place. The remainder of this chapter reflects their viewpoint.

THE CHANGING
ENERGY SERVICES MARKET: EEI[1]

THE "OLD" ENERGY SERVICES GAME

Prior to the Energy Policy Act of 1992, there were five key players in the energy services market. The key players were as follows:

- Utilities;

- Energy Service Companies;

- Energy Management Control System Companies;

- Equipment Manufacturers; and,

- Consulting Engineers and other Consultants.

Utilities were involved in the energy services market through their offerings of energy audits, training seminars, technology promotions,

---

[1]Mr. Richard McMahon and Mr. Steve Rosenstock, P.E., of Edison Electric Institute authored the remainder of this chapter. This contribution does not necessarily signify any concurrence or agreement of EEI or these contributors with the earlier chapter comments offered by the book's authors.

load management programs, and energy efficiency programs for all classes (residential, commercial, industrial, and agricultural) of customers. Some of the programs provided technical support, while other programs offered financial support in the form of rebates or loans. In this arena, the utilities were vertically integrated and regulated on a state-by-state basis.

Energy service companies (ESCOs) provided project management and equipment installation for a variety of commercial and industrial customers. In a few cases, these companies were started as unregulated subsidiaries of electric (or combined gas and electric) utilities. In other cases, energy service companies were bought out by utilities that wanted to diversify. However, most of the energy service companies were operated independently of utilities.

Energy management control system (EMCS) companies, such as Johnson Controls and Honeywell, added energy services to their portfolio to gain a competitive advantage over other EMCS companies. The installation of an energy management system or building automation system was combined with energy-efficiency upgrades to enhance the value of their product and to quicken the payback period for the client.

Original Equipment Manufacturers (OEM's), such as Osram-Sylvania for lighting products and Trane for central air conditioning equipment, also joined the energy services market by providing analysis software, project financing, and equipment installation and maintenance service contracts. However, the equipment manufacturers were very specific in their applications, and usually did not perform services for equipment manufactured by other companies.

Consulting engineers and other consultants have served as project managers and sources of independent analysis for customers. In these roles, the consultants were able to recommend specific equipment, or obtain multiple bids, without any bias towards one type of technology or one particular manufacturer.

Under the old game, there were certain programs that were offered by utilities and other players to their customers:

- Energy Efficiency Programs;
- Load Management Programs;
- Load Shifting Programs;
- Interruptible/Standby Programs;

- Information Programs; and,
- Financial Programs.

The first four items fell under the demand-side management "umbrella" provided by many utilities. Energy efficiency programs included prescriptive rebates for specific equipment (lighting, motors, chillers, etc.) and comprehensive incentives for new construction design and total renovation of existing buildings.

Load management programs included equipment cycling or shutoff of residential equipment, such as water heaters and central air conditioners, along with commercial and industrial curtailment programs where the utility provided a signal to the customer to reduce loads.

Load shifting programs included thermal energy storage, electric thermal storage, time-of-day rates, and other programs to encourage customers to shift usage patterns to times of reduced system loads.

Interruptible/Standby programs provided significant incentives and discounts for those customers who could switch to other sources of energy during utility requests. The customers were usually large commercial or industrial facilities that had self-generation capabilities for redundancy or economic reasons.

Most of the players in the "old" game provided informational programs, such as energy audits, training seminars, or equipment information. They also provided financial programs such as loans, shared savings arrangements, or performance contracts for the installation of specific equipment.

However, with the passage of the Energy Policy Act in 1992, along with other changes in the gas and electric industries which started with competitive wholesale markets, the market for energy services began to change.

THE "NEW" ENERGY SERVICES GAME

Along with the "old" players listed above, there are many new players in the energy services market. Some of these players are new types of organizations, while others are the subsidiaries or descendants of the old players:

- Power Marketers;
- Exempt Wholesale Generation Companies;
- Investor-Owned and/or Private Generation Companies;
- Investor-Owned Transmission Companies;
- Independent Transmission System Operators (ISO's); and,
- Investor-Owned Distribution Companies (UDC's or LDC's).

According to the Utility Data Institute (UDI), the number of power marketers licensed by FERC to buy and resell electric power increased from 70 companies in 1994 to 229 by the end of the second quarter of 1996. By February, 1997, there were 303 FERC approved power marketers. UDI also reported that in 1995, the top 20 power marketing firms sold over 26.1 million MWh of electricity in the United States. For 1996, *MegaWatt Daily* reported that the top 20 power marketing companies sold over 200 million MWh.

The definition of an Exempt Wholesale Generation Company is a wholesale power generator that is exempt from the provisions of the Public Utility Holding Company Act (PUHCA). This legal class of companies was created by the Energy Policy Act of 1992 in order to allow individuals, corporations, and registered public utility holding companies to own wholesale generation assets, which are leased or sell power to non-affiliates without subjecting the owners to regulation under PUHCA. According to the EEI EPAct Briefing Service, the number of domestic exempt wholesale generation companies rose from 0 in 1992 to 59 in 1993. By November, 1996, there were 320 approved exempt wholesale generation companies.

Investor-owned generation companies, transmission companies, and distribution companies are the descendants of vertically-integrated utility companies. As utilities re-define their roles, many are unbundling themselves into separate entities. It is likely that the distribution companies will have the most impact in the energy services market, since they will be under state regulation, and many states may impose a "public goods charge" requiring the distribution companies to perform energy services.

In the "new" energy services game, the old programs will most likely co-exist or eventually be replaced by the following services and programs:

- Customer-Specific Incentive Programs;
- Green Pricing Programs;
- Value-Added Utility Services; and,
- Service Aggregation.

In a deregulated market, certain types of customers may contractually demand incentives for the installation of certain equipment. To gain the customer's revenue, energy providers may have to provide financial incentives based on the customer's preferences. This type of specified incentive may become a common part of the marketplace.

In addition, there may be a niche market of customers who will have preferences as to the generation source of their electric power. Some electric utilities are already offering "green pricing" programs, where customers have a choice of obtaining power or investing in a "green" power production facility, such as wind or solar power.

Other utilities and new entrants into the energy services market will offer non-traditional or non-energy services as part of their package. Such services may include equipment maintenance, special equipment or facility upgrade financing, power quality equipment, security systems, internet applications, telecommunication services, and cable television services. Different players will offer different combinations of goods and services in the new market.

Another aspect of the new market will be service aggregation. Facilities such as college and industrial campuses, along with retail chains and large corporations, typically have multiple facilities in one or several locations. Some providers will aggregate services, such as monthly utility bills, to these separate locations. This aggregation may provide significant savings to the customer and allow the service provider to serve multiple facilities with one signed contract.

ECONOMICS IN THE "NEW" GAME

With increasing competition, there will be changes to the electric rates as well as the electric bills that most customers see. In the majority of cases, there may be more components to the typical electric bill, as shown below:

- Generation charge;
- Transmission charges;
- Distribution company charges;
- Power marketing charge;
- Competitive transition charge; and,
- Public goods/benefits charge.

In markets with retail choice, the generation charge may be assessed by the generation company that is chosen by the customer or power marketer.

Transmission charges will be established by the transmission entity (such as an independent system operator, or ISO). Some customers may have multiple transmission charges, depending on the number of transmission entities between the customer and generation company. This may result in a layered or "pancake" effect of transmission charges.

Distribution companies may continue to have portions or all of their charges regulated by a state agency. Charges may be divided into basic service fees and value-added service fees.

Power marketing companies will either charge the customers for their services or the generation companies for finding customers that will buy their electricity. In some cases, the power marketing companies will charge both the customers and the generation companies for their services. At this point, it is not clear whether this charge will show up as a line item on customer billing statements.

The competitive transition charge is also known as the stranded costs charge. During the first few years of deregulation in a particular state, utility companies will be able to recover stranded costs of power plants that were approved by the state regulators. In Rhode Island, the charge to all customers will be 2.8 cents per kWh. Other states may impose specific mechanisms and charges on utility bills to cover stranded costs, and some states, like California, will issue bonds to cover these costs.

The public goods/benefit charge has also been labeled the "stranded benefits" charge. This charge may be collected by distribution companies to continue operating programs that are seen as beneficial by state regulators. Such programs may include demand-side management programs, low-income programs, low or no-cost energy audit services, and other social programs that are currently performed by vertically integrated utilities. It is likely that these charges will be in effect as long as competitive transition charges are being collected.

One possible result of public goods/benefit charges is competition between distribution companies and energy services companies for energy service activities or contracts. This may force the distribution companies to compete against their subsidiary energy services companies for a project within the distribution company's service territory.

In the new environment, distribution companies and energy services companies will find that different customers will be receiving different pricing signals. Some customers may receive real-time or on-line pricing signals with a variety of features or lead times. For example, some customers will have prices that change on an annual basis, while other customers will have rates that change on a monthly, daily, or hourly basis. Customers that receive hourly rates may receive advanced notice from the day before, or minutes before, the beginning of the new hour. With the mixed pricing signals, different portions of the electric bill may have different peak seasons or peak times during weekdays. For example:

- The generation company chosen reaches a peak demand during the winter;

- The transmission company (or companies) has its (their) peak demands during the spring and fall, due to increased bulk power transactions; and,

- The distribution company sees a peak load on its distribution system during the summer season due to air conditioning and other loads.

With multiple pricing signals, it is likely that the economic advantages for load shifting programs, such as thermal energy storage and electric thermal storage, will be greatly reduced or eliminated. This will also change the nature of project analysis.

To perform an accurate analysis in the "new" game, energy services companies will need building simulation software. The software will have to model the building energy usage on an hourly basis, along with simulating the rates on an hourly basis (e.g., 8760 data points for energy prices). The use of "average" rates will likely create large errors in the economic analysis.

It is also likely that prices paid by commercial and industrial customer will decline over the next several years. Real electric rates have fallen for the past eight years, especially for industrial customers. As the prices decline, the internal rate of return (IRR) for energy efficiency projects will also decrease. This factor alone will change the market for energy services, as the IRR threshold for projects is usually above 20%.

Other areas with active and/or aggressive DSM programs will likely have similar results. For those customers that have not participated in DSM programs, and are in the market for energy services, there are several options. A customer may currently choose between a utility, an energy services company, a power marketer, transmission system operators, in-house staff, and generation companies for the following items:

- Basic electric service (generation, transmission, and distribution);
- Energy audits;
- Efficiency equipment rebate;
- Billing and/or rate information;
- Financing;
- Power marketing;
- Equipment installation; and,
- Equipment operation and maintenance.

Different players will have different advantages (and disadvantages) in offering the above products and services. Alliances will likely be formed to "bundle" products and services that are offered to customers. For example, in late 1996, it was announced that Honeywell (energy services company) and Louisville Gas & Electric Power Marketing, Inc. (a power marketing company) had formed a strategic alliance. Other such strategic alliances may be performed to increase the product and services diversity offered to customers.

As the electric utility industry becomes restructured over the next several years, there will be rapid changes to the energy services market. As with other industries that have a large number of suppliers, there will likely be more strategic alliances and mergers among energy services companies with each other and with other participants (such as power marketers and generation companies) in the competitive environment.

EEI References

Birnbaum, I., et al. "Reinventing DSM: Program Design for Competitive Markets," in Proceedings: Delivering Customer Value, 7th National Demand-Side Management Conference, EPRI, June, 1995, pp. 171-176.

Brown, M., *Summary of California DSM Impact Evaluation Studies*, Oak Ridge National Laboratory, October, 1994

Caffrey, R. and McMahon, T., BCS/96 - *The Building Control Systems Market (1995-2000)*, BCS Partners, Leonia, New Jersey, August, 1996.

Electric Power Research Institute, *1994 Survey of Utility Demand-Side Programs and Services*, EPRI, Donegal, PA, November, 1995.

McCoy, G. and Douglass, J., *Energy Efficient Electric Motor Selection Handbook*, U.S. Department of Energy, Olympia, WA, August, 1996.

Nelson, K., "Utility Funding to be Used by 29% of Buyers in '95," *Energy User News*, Fall 1995 Special Edition, p. 2.

Potomac Electric Power Company, *Quick Facts and Figures 1995*, PEPCO, Washington, D.C., 1996.

Randazzo, M., "Despite Ban, Study Shows CFC Phaseout is Slow Going," *Energy User News*, July, 1996, p. 6.

U.S. Department of Commerce, *Statistical Abstract of the United States: 1995*, U.S. Department of Commerce, Washington, D.C., 1996, pp. 743-744.

U.S. Department of Energy, *Electric Power Annual 1995 Volume II*, U.S. Department of Energy, Washington, D.C., December, 1996.

U.S. Department of Energy, *U.S. Electric Utility Demand-Side Management, 1995*, U.S. Department of Energy, Washington, D.C., January, 1997.

References

1 Audin, Lindsay "Positioning Your Facility for Utility Competition" Energy Engineering Vol. 94, No. 2, 1997 pp. 17-35.

Chapter 12

When "Energy" Isn't the Answer

Traditional performance contracting initially addressed the needs of educational, municipal, and institutional energy users. Perennial budget shortfalls, consistent daily and annual energy usage, and a classic aversion to risk are as predictable as the lighting, energy management systems, and HVAC modifications that are appropriately offered in response. In countless instances, universal needs have been met with proven solutions that have saved millions of energy dollars.

The concept of performance contracting became so compelling that it was soon being offered to virtually every market segment from supermarkets to refineries. The prevailing theory was, and it's still valid for many energy users, that a project capable of being funded from energy and/or operational savings within a reasonable time period was a sound proposition that should be embraced. However, the same logic that might have appealed to the local school board was often rebuffed in the industrial sector.[1]

There are so many variations of products, processes, energy costs, balance sheets, and market stability that we can only reference a "typical" industrial opportunity. Although the need set for any particular school district usually matches that of other districts, industrials' needs vary widely and require a much more demanding prequalification process. Traditional performance contracting, so efficiently applied to the predictable requirements of the institutional customer, has often missed the mark in industry because the customer's desired result is signifi-

---

[1]For the purpose of this chapter the term "industrial" refers to a major energy consuming facility such as an aluminum smelter, chemical processor, or automobile manufacturer.

cantly different from that of the institutional market that spawned and refined the concept. Where a typical school district might have a need to upgrade the learning environment through better lighting and temperature control, the industrial strives to increase shareholder wealth. Most "for profit" corporations will evaluate a performance contract as critically and methodically as any other major equipment or service agreement purchase.

REALITIES OF PRODUCTION VS. ENERGY

To the manufacturer, production is king. Energy costs in such process industries as chemical, aluminum and cement can be as much as 30 percent and in some industries as low as 2-5 percent of the typical manufacturing budget. When energy constitutes a small part of the budget, its relative significance to a company is diminished. Labor and materials may account for the largest cost elements and are often the focus of industrial engineers and process designers when cost cutting efforts are under way.

Although any reasonable cost reduction measure is welcome, the value of its implementation is always weighed against the risk of lost production or the potential for increased production. If the projected cost of lost production or reduced yield even speculatively outweighs the value of energy cost savings, the project will be rejected. Any negative impact on output quality will almost certainly cause the performance contracting proposal to be shelved.

Processes that operate 24 hours per day can benefit the most from energy savings but are also most at risk from process interruptions due to the installation of cost reduction measures. For example, installing energy efficient high pressure sodium lamps with their characteristic orange light might reduce energy consumption, but the quality of color sensitive processes such as printing or dyeing would almost certainly deteriorate. After a manufacturer's fixed costs are absorbed, ongoing production becomes considerably more profitable and any energy solution that might retard production after break-even is totally unacceptable. So, the term "risk" in an industrial performance contract becomes the risk of lost profits rather than the political risk of a poorly negotiated performance contracting in the municipal market.

A PERFORMANCE CONTRACT
THAT INCREASES ENERGY CONSUMPTION

If increasing energy consumption improves production and subsequent profits, an industrial performance contracting project is desirable when it remains self-funded at an acceptable rate of return. A manufacturer of automobile carpets produced from synthetic materials cured one side of the goods in a single pass through a natural gas-fired oven, rewound the carpet, and repeated the pass for the opposite side. A conversion to an electric infrared oven that heated both sides simultaneously increased the cost of energy marginally but doubled the production of the curing process resulting in a project simple payback period of 6 months. Traditional performance contracting in the public sector does not gain the benefit of this upside potential since improved learning does not generate additional tax income to pay for the increased costs of enhancing the learning environment. The industrial market allows an ESCO to propose solutions that make prudent business sense, not just reduce energy consumption.

A guarantee of performance is an integral part of the traditional performance contracting process but, contrary to the highly sensitive political environments of public institutions, the industrial customer usually does not find overwhelming value in an intensive long term measurement & verification (M&V) process. Risk taking is a normal aspect of the business climate and this customer is not likely to seek insurance on every business decision. However, this is also a prudent and savvy customer, who prefers to protect his investments by dealing only with companies that have demonstrated capabilities, long-term stability and substantial financial resources.

THE PERFORMANCE CONTRACTING TIME HORIZON

Yet another issue that impacts the desirability of performance contracting outside of the traditional markets is the contract period. In areas of the country where electricity or natural gas costs are relatively low, projects can be self-funding but may also require lengthy payback periods to support positive project cash flow. Although a municipality may expect to own and occupy its buildings for an indefinite period of time, the "time horizon" that an industrial will consider is much shorter due to economic uncertainties. Product obsolescence, market shifts, imports, mergers, and a host of other uncertainties can leave a business liable for payments for energy efficiency improvements that outlive the company's full utilization of the facility. Accordingly, this customer expects a quick simple payback and a contract period in the 3- to 5-year range as opposed to the 8- to 12-year range acceptable to most public institutions. In low to moderate energy cost areas, savings from energy costs alone will not be adequate to produce a performance contract period in the target range—a primary reason why energy use reduction alone is not always the answer!

THE ALL-PURPOSE ESCO

Traditional performance contracting usually has limited its scope to conventional energy conservation measures on the demand side of the energy equation. A new generation of "integrated energy service companies" will now offer energy efficiency, supply acquisition management, asset monetization (privatization), and energy accounting services with ESCO direct funding. Innovative financing allows an industrial customer to recognize positive cash flow throughout the contract. "One stop shopping" for all of these needs reduces purchasing costs and generates immediate earnings, avoiding months or years of delays in understanding energy markets and evaluating proposals that can cost millions of dollars in opportunity lost. Some ESCO's even offer an inducement of an initial cash payment at signing equal to the discounted value of the project's guaranteed savings cash flow stream. However, any bold action of this nature increases the ESCO's financial risk and translates into additional cost to the customer. Despite the penalty, an unexpected cash infusion from a trusted, reputable company is apt to be as gratefully accepted as the demand side management (DSM) funds, which were so generously distributed by utilities in a bygone era.

In order to reduce a demand, or energy efficiency, proposal to an acceptable contract period, savings may need to be accumulated from other sources. Supply acquisition management is an increasingly important tool as deregulation of electric utilities accelerates nationally. As with unregulated natural gas supplies, there is an optimum purchasing strategy that will result in the best value for the customer. Major national industrial and commercial companies with dozens to thousands of locations can "aggregate" their energy supply purchases to obtain the most favorable rates and reliable service. A new generation of ESCO's has emerged that are highly qualified to participate in national retail energy markets and now offer this service. Any assertion that ESCO's must choose to participate in either the supply or energy efficiency industries, since no company can excel in both, is a protectionist theme for myopic first generation ESCOs.

The second generation ESCO, once described as a "Super ESCO", will guarantee lower costs based on its ability to purchase supplies more effectively, particularly where the ESCO can exercise fuel switching on short notice. A manufacturing process that is designed to use either fuel oil or natural gas allows the ESCO with a staffed and active trading floor to take advantage of market volatility and execute spot purchases that are exceptionally economical for the end user. Few industrials have this staff and capability in their organizations.

Performance contracts, where the customer and ESCO both participate in actual savings, are increasingly being used as supply acquisition instruments. Just as the magnitude of an energy efficiency contract is determined by the extent of the customer's own previous efforts, the amount of guaranteed supply savings will be determined by the customer's existing skills at purchasing fuels and energy. As electricity markets unfold to deregulation, the skills required to purchase energy will escalate, leaving countless millions of dollars to be captured or lost to indecision.

STRUCTURING A BUNDLED SOLUTION

Now that the ESCO has identified opportunities to reduce energy consumption, increase production through process modifications, and to purchase energy more cost effectively, it is appropriate to broaden the scope even further. Consider the textile manufacturer that had been paying a flat fee of $100,000 per year to the local municipality to treat effluent from his fabric dyeing operation. At the time that the treatment plant was built by the town, this cash flow was substantial and contributed to reducing the town's debt; but, as the years passed, the costs of treating the plant's waste exceeded the payment. In a bold confrontation with its largest employer, the city increased the plant's sewage charge sixfold, to $600,000, to match prevailing rates in the area. In addition, the town required that the plant install $300,000 of flow metering equipment to accurately measure the actual flow. Unwilling to accept the new charges and determined not to divert capital from new production equipment, the company turned to an energy services company for a solution.

The ESCO explored many alternatives that included recycling the wastewater, building an on-site treatment facility, and pumping the waste to another plant three miles distant that had unused capacity available at a low cost. Recycling created an unacceptable risk of defective product caused by potential failure of the filtering equipment that removed colored dyes from the water and EPA permitting requirements for on-site treatment were prohibitive. However, property rights between the plants were owned by both companies and the cost of pumps and piping would allow recovery of the investment in five years. By installing heat recovery equipment on the 190 degree F wastewater stream and using the recovered energy to preheat the boiler make-up water, the ESCO showed additional savings that reduced the proposed contract period to four years. Converting the steam boiler to dual fuel and providing the lowest cost energy at any time of year at guaranteed maximum rates produced supply savings that further reduced the contract period to nearly three years. The ESCO provided a turnkey project including funding, design, project management, construction, and maintenance.

By applying the familiar concept of the self-funding proposition and structuring it within the fundamental industrial time horizon and production risk constraints, the ESCO addressed the company's business needs, rather than energy needs. Rather than deploying performance contracting as a financial vehicle for promoting the sale of the proposer's products or systems, it can be offered as a powerful tool to improve production and earnings.

OUTSOURCING AND PRIVATIZATION

Utility outsourcing, also known as "asset monetization" when the ESCO purchases existing assets, is yet another offspring of the performance contracting offering. A new focus on profitable core business, often coupled with corporate executive incentive plans that reward high return on assets (ROA's), encourages decision makers to dispose of assets that can be operated and maintained more efficiently and reliably by third parties. Steam, chilled water, and compressed air are typical processes that are essential to production but excellent candidates for an outsourcing agreement. The objective of the facility owner is to reduce and control his costs associated with using these media and processes.

The ESCO can calculate the facility's current cost of consumption of these commodities with a reasonable degree of accuracy. Savings, which will allow the ESCO to earn a profit and the owner to recognize a lower cost, come from several sources including:

- improved operational efficiency resulting from the ESCO's superior engineering resources;

- lower cost of fuel and/or electrical supplies; or

- lower cost of maintenance after equipment is upgraded.

The driving force behind the ability of the ESCO to engineer real savings is the fact that most facilities have grown in stages over the years so that plant systems are an assemblage of add-ons and quick fixes. The systems were rarely designed for their current capacity, resulting in major inefficiencies from undersized distribution conduits, piping conflicts, leaks, and other expensive deficiencies.

Another source of savings results from the ESCO acquiring capital at a rate lower than the customer's required rate of return, allowing the customer to reinvest the proceeds from the sales at a higher rate. A variation on this offering is to determine the current energy/capital consumption of the customer's product and offer a lower, guaranteed maximum cost per unit of production for the essential commodities on an outsourced basis.

As attractive as these propositions may sound, let's restate that production is king and also that any real or perceived threat to production from this transaction will shelve the opportunity. Accordingly, only ESCOs with a solid reputation for performance, specific outsourcing experience, and substantial access to capital will find this type of venture to be fertile ground.

In summary, traditional performance contracting is transferable to the "industrial" sector and other markets if the ESCO can gain a clear understanding of the customer's specific business needs, not only energy needs, and offer a broad range of solutions that meet those requirements. Energy alone is not the answer for a customer whose driving force is accelerated production, lower operating costs, and, most importantly, increased earnings.

Chapter 13

Parchment to Internet—
A Perspective

"Business is... a network that is accelerating the time of the decision-making process to something approaching the speed of light."

Elliot M. Gold

"Each day we face new technological realities that we could only imagine yesterday: A national information infrastructure, the information superhighway with on ramps and off ramps in every home, wireless communications, and more. Each day it seems we must change our behavior and adapt to such new information-dominated technologies as automatic teller machines, debit cards, the Internet, and interactive television. In moving to the information age, humankind is putting itself through a technological revolution reminiscent of shifts from hunting and gathering to agriculture and from an agrarian economy to a manufacturing one."

—Report by the Federal Electronic Commerce
Acquisition Team (ECAT)

How We Got Here

Distance—and time—have shrunk over the years by the introduction of technology, so as to practically eliminate them as a concern in the modern business world. Those of us engaged in the field of energy performance contracting have always appreciated the role of technology in what we sell and service. Now we are called upon to embrace new office technologies and the changes they bring to the way in which both we and our customers conduct our business practices. They may appear daunting, but embrace them we must if we are to remain viable players in the eyes of our customers and partners.

Commerce has always reacted to the advantages that technology has afforded it. We can trace the manifestation of technology on commerce through the ages, particularly in the area of communication, as communication is most affected by time and distance. Oral agreements, writing (whatever the medium), mail, clipper ships, pony express, telegraph, telephone, radio, fax machines—all have been employed to deal with distance and time. And the need for speed.

Contracts serve to record the understandings that have been reached by the involved parties. Contracts have been recorded on stone, the skin of animals (parchment), papyrus and paper. We are fast approaching the day when we envision that contracts will consist of digital information transmitted to and recorded on magnetic storage devices. Speed remains the imperative.

The term electronic commerce (EC) generally refers to the paperless exchange of business information in a standardized format: electronic mail, electronic bulletin boards and electronic funds transfer in support of business functions. EC is made possible by adherence to electronic data interchange (EDI) standards agreed to by the parties exchanging information or selected from a set developed by a recognized standards body; e.g., American National Standards Institute (ANSI) or the International Standards Organization (ISO). Purchase orders, RFQ/RFPs, quotations, invoices, and other paper forms have been successfully replaced with standard EDI transactions.

Our society has become based upon the ability to move vast amounts of information quickly over great distances. Text and data in all its forms have become our lifeblood. Commerce may have, at one time, driven this effort, but it has spread into society as a whole much more quickly than might have been predicted. All aspects of our lives have become ever more dependent upon quick access to information. The Internet and its World Wide Web component now serves as the primary instrument for this change.

The Internet has been defined as an open interconnection of communication networks that enables connected computers to interact directly. The Internet spans the globe and supports thousands of operational and experimental services. In the process, it makes virtually all of man's recorded information available to anyone with access to a computer. The World Wide Web component of the Internet allows users to browse through hypermedia presentations of text and graphics very easily using a "point and click" methodology.

An equally important aspect of the Internet is a service which it provides; "E-mail," which allows messages (be it an inquiry, an offer to sell or service, or a contract) to be sent to a person across the street or to Afghanistan in virtually the same amount of time. The ease of use, coupled with the ability to move information quickly has caused the Internet to be accepted into the world of commerce at a phenomenal pace.

Governments have played key roles in the formation, development and ubiquitousness of the Internet, which quickly allowed the user to harness the power of the computer. Born in the Defense Department Cold War projects of the 1950's, the recent explosion of its myriad uses makes it appear to have sprung up over night. A collaborative effort of government, universities and industry, the Internet has become what the late Ithiel de Sola Poole of MIT called "the largest machine man has ever constructed." Shortly after the "ARPAnet" (Advanced Research Projects Agency) had demonstrated its ability to move data, graduate students employed in its development devised an application to accommodate their need for personal messaging. From this work ("Usenet") evolved what was known as "bulletin boards" and finally E-mail. The rest is history and today we find that a vast network can, and does, connect most of the world's business firms, institutions and individuals.

An effective ESCO will discover ways to add the Internet to its "business tools" as a way to find customers, competitors and vendor partners. The Internet gives those who avail themselves of it a global presence, no matter how small their business may be. Those who are still in denial, saying it is all hype, should remember that is how the naysayers spoke of the facsimile machine, and before that, the telephone.

The uses to which the Internet can be applied to business are many and varied. In addition to the often over-overwhelming e-mail, many firms are deep into electronic publishing. Sales promotions, specifications, technical manuals, are all out there. Anything that is dependent upon frequent revision and updating can easily be handled in this computer accessible medium, rather than in the printed form, thus allowing the end-user to share the responsibility of keeping current and reducing costs by the "publisher." The Internet is a source of information of interest to business—details on government bids and contracts, economic reports and analysis, securities filings, patent records, IRS regulations and announcements, census information, latest government publications, the Federal Register—all can be found there. Of particular interest to those engaged in performance contracting are the web-sites maintained by the Department of Energy, World Energy Association, National Association of Energy Service Companies, Association of Energy Engineers and other sites, which contain current information pertinent to the industry.

The decision has been made for us. We must embrace the concept of electronic commerce if we are to meet the imperatives of an increasingly competitive environment. The need for speed must be accommodated by enabling the functional specialists within our business structures (marketers, buyers, design engineers, project managers, etc.) to perform their duties in a more efficient manner, accurately and reliably. The Internet provides even the smallest firms with the ability to participate and compete globally.

Manufacturers and service industries can use the Internet to find customers, work with suppliers, engineers, and end users; to design products and systems and bring them to markets. Updates to software are deliverable by the Internet. Notices of, and registration for meetings and conferences are routinely handled on the Internet. And finally, as a medium for classified advertising, the Internet can be searched easily by subject, location and price—which can bring customers to the firm.

Several groups are active in guiding the evolution of electronic commerce. The government still plays an important role; even as its funding of the backbone facilities is ending. The Computer Aided Acquisition and Logistics Support Organization (CALS) was formed by the Department of Defense with the aim of moving toward electronic commerce for training and technical manuals, contracting and logistic systems. James A. Abrahamson, former Chairman of the Board of Oracle Corporation and Chairman of the US CALS Industry Steering Group which was established to bring together commercial standards, protocols and methods of operation, likes to think of CALS as "Commerce at Light Speed." He goes on to say that the effects of the movement towards electronic commerce, CALS and standards for electronic data interchange are going to be profound. It will change the face of business, how it communicates, conducts business, and ultimately, how all people will communicate among themselves. He does not fear dehumanization, but sees the ability to communicate across nations and the world as enhancing human existence.

CURRENT TRENDS AND BENEFITS

On October 13, 1994, President Clinton signed into law the Federal Acquisition Streamlining Act of 1994 (P.L. 103-355)-(FASA). The legislation was designed to significantly change the way the government does business and will force changes in business practices of all who wish to sell to government agencies. Key to the improvements promised by FASA is the establishment of a government-wide Federal Acquisition Network (FACNET) to connect the many current acquisition processes overburdened by paper-work to a expedited EDI systems readily accessible to the public through value-added networks certified for that purpose.

While the government market is large, performance contractors cannot lose sight of the private sector. In a recent press release, the International Facility Management Association reported that U.S. commercial buildings spent more than $71.8 billion on energy consumption in 1992. Applying the concepts of electronic commerce in conjunction with the principles of performance contracting contained in this book will enable ESCOs to effectively and efficiently help business owners and facility professionals achieve goals in energy efficiency and save money. And the ESCO makes more money in the process!

What are some of the ways that participating in the movement toward electronic commerce can benefit an ESCO business? Here are a few:

1. Image: By your business' presence on the Internet, your customers know that you are aware of the benefits of the technology and are a part of the current movement.

2. Productivity: The ability to use e-mail for staff, and existing customers and to be reachable by e-mail by potential customers is a big saver in terms of time and expense.

3. Keeping current: Use the Web to stay on top of current trends in the business. The ability to search for data on almost any subject is one of the under-appreciated aspects of the Internet by business.

4. Reaching the Market: Your business story can be told in many formats on the Internet—and your potential customers are looking! You can highlight your products and services, provide responses to frequently asked questions and update material as often as you like. Perhaps more importantly, it offers the ability to find out in real time what your customers like and don't like about your offerings and develop an understanding of what they want.

5. Customer Service: Communicate directly with your customers, exchange utility billing data, access monitoring data—all are presently being done over the Internet!

This last point needs underscoring. Many ESCOs today, for example, are eyeing opportunities in the federal sector, particularly the Department of Defense (DOD). Reflecting on the history of computer access fostered by DOD, consider how an ESCO will be perceived by this customer if it cannot operate in the new electronic world.

So, to those of you who are just starting to consider how you can benefit quickly and become familiar with what electronic commerce, the Internet and the World Wide Web have to offer you, it is suggested that you invest a little time and effort in investigating what is available. If you have access to a computer with communications capabilities, you are already on your way. Below are examples of websites that contain information that may interest you and can get you started. As more of us take advantage of the growing effectiveness of the Internet in our day-to-day business, it will continue to grow and serve us in ways we could only imagine a short time ago.

A SAMPLER OF WEBSITES

Internet Address http://www.	Website Owner
aeecenter.org	Association of Energy Engineers
weea.org	World Energy Efficiency Association (WEEA)
aesp.org	Association of Energy Service Professionals (AESP)
afe.org	Association for Facility Engineers (AFE)
boma.org	Building Owners and Managers Association (BOMA)
bmvp.org	International Performance Measurement and Verification Protocol (IPMVP)
eia.doe.gov	Energy Information Administration
epa.gov	Environmental Protection Agency
eren.doe.gov	U.S. Department of Energy-Federal Energy Management Program
energywise.com	Energywise On-Line Services
eren.doe.gov/femp	Federal Energy Management Programs
ifma.org	International Facility Management Association (IFMA)
mfginfo.com	Manufacturers Information Net
crest.org	The Center for Renewable and Sustainable Technologies (CREST)
naesco.org	National Association of Energy Service Companies (NAESCO)
necanet.org	National Electrical Contractors Association (NECA)
intr.net/pma	Power Marketers Association (PMA)

References

Abrahamson, James A.; "The CEO's Corner"; website, EDI World Institute, May 9, 1995

Diamond, Edwin and Stephen Bates; "The Ancient History of the Internet." *American Heritage.* October 1995, page 34-35

Gold, Elliott M.; "Special Advertising Section" *Business to Business.* Spring, 1997

Goldman, Melanie D.; "Surfing the Web of Profit." *Business to Business.* Spring, 1997. pages 43-45

ATT Public Relations; "ATT Today—An Internal Newsletter for Employees." April 30, 1997

Special Report; "Internet Communities." *Business Week.* May 5, 1997. pages 64-85

Microsoft "Encarta" 96 Encyclopedia. Search on "Internet"

Special report; "Opportunities Ahead." "The Internet." *The Kiplinger Guide to Business and Investment Profits.* pages 25-26

Brock, Terry and Chaim Yudkowsky; "Practical tips make the Web part of the sales team." *Atlanta Business Chronicle.* May 9-15, 1997. page 7C

Wright, Robert; "The Man Who Invented the Web." *Time Magazine.* May 19, 1997. pages 64-68.

Wiederboeft, Heather Mclean and Shanda R. Boyett; "Study Reveals U.S. Commercial Energy Usage." The International Facility Management Association Press Release. April 11, 1997.

Special Section; "The Web Gets Down to Business." *Fortune.* May 26, 1997, pages S1-S17.

Section IV

ESCOs Go Global

Should ESCO's go global? The decision to participate in the global marketplace is one that takes considerable thought and planning. On the surface, it might sound simple. After all, a jet ride is a jet ride, whether from Atlanta to Seattle or New York to Prague. To get below the surface, we are particularly pleased to offer you some worldly thoughts from international leaders in ESCO development.

When Don Smith was asked if ESCOs should go global, his response was "That's a no brainer." Concise, but the complexities of the international market place demand a bit more explanation. Mr. Smith provides that explanation by posing and answering a number of questions critical to an ESCO making the decision to go international. Mr. Smith is a pioneer in performance contracting, having been President of Viron, one of the early ESCOs in the U.S. Now as President of Energy Masters Corporation, he brings that history and experience to the international scene, and here.

Jim Hansen, president of an international performance contracting consulting firm, Kiona International, with experience in more than 20 countries, brings practical insight to international issues. From cultural to political to financial considerations, Mr. Hansen provides words of caution, optimism and reality.

Anees Iqbal, Associate Director of Business Development for Symonds Power & Energy, a U.K. division Compagnie of Générale de Chauff of France, starts out this section by providing unique and important insights into the European roots of performance contracting. Even people who've been in the ESCO business for some time may be unfamiliar with the length of time performance contracting has been in existence in Europe.

Those of us in the U.S. involved in the struggles to have performance contracting accepted by the U.S. Department of Energy, particularly in the Southeast, will recognize the strange similarities in the struggles in the UK.

Peter Garforth, writing from Brussels, draws on his European experiences at Honeywell and Landis & Gyr, and more recently his experiences as an international energy efficiency financing consultant, to add his realities of doing business in a global economy. We believe the reader will gain a greater appreciation for the skills and abilities that must be developed in order to take advantage of opportunities world-wide.

Note to U.S. readers: Mssrs. Iqbal and Garforth, in chapters 14 and 17, refer to performance contracting in the residential sector. In many countries, particularly in Europe, district heating serves "residences" in large apartment buildings... an attractive energy savings performance contracting market.

Chapter 14

From International Roots into Tomorrow

The Evolving Shapes of *Energy Performance Contracting* (EPC)

EPC is the generic term for performance contracting on the international scene. It is referred to by various names in different countries. Some of the common ones are:

- Technology Performance Contracting (Belgium, Germany, and other EU states)

- Contract Energy Management (United Kingdom)

- Contract du Resultat; or Exploitation de Chauffage (France)

- Third Party Financing (United Kingdom and occasionally in the United States).

Whatever the name, the main components of the service provided are the same. In essence this comprises a totality of services, including not only the provision of energy, but those operational services which are necessary to implement improvements for the provision of efficient energy services and paid for on some measure of performance.

As in the United States, EPC services are normally offered by companies called energy service companies (ESCOs).

Common to all countries, an ESCO offers its client not only energy services but also all the technical, financial, commercial and operational services which are necessary (depending on the client's needs) to implement improvments in energy efficiency. The objectives of the ESCO are primarily to provide a package of services in the field of energy management and to invest in suitable projects which can yield an acceptable financial rate of return.

In the original European form of this concept, the EPC company made improvements to the energy services utilized by its client through efficient operation and maintenance, modifications to the plant controls or even completely replacing the old and obsolete plant with an energy efficient new plant. Typically, the EPC company secured all the capital for modifying and replacing the plant.

As described elsewhere in this book, the cost of EPC company's services and the cost of servicing the capital have historically been recovered from the savings achieved. Normally, the net savings achieved *after* the capital equipment has been paid for, and operational costs have been accounted for, are shared between the ESCO and its client in an agreed ratio. There is, therefore, a very strong performance element and the onus is very much on the ESCO to achieve savings.

There are many variations to the basic EPC concept. The range of services usually provided can be packaged separately or in combination. Typically, they are:

*   routine maintenance, operation and attendance;

*   provision of energy including payment of fuel bills;

*   provision of replacement spares under a guarantee contract;

*   provision of project finance, for plant refurbishment; and

*   specialist engineering services including feasibility studies, design engineering, implementation management, etc.

HOW IT GREW IN EUROPE

The performance contracting concept evolved simultaneously in several countries, which probably helps to explain the number of terms used to describe it. Most, however, agree that the first major impetus came from France.

France

EPC has been established in France for over fifty years, and the concept trades under the general title of Exploitation de Chauffage. The concept originated on a single hospital contract and has since developed rapidly, initially in the building sector (residential, health, etc.) followed by the industrial and other sectors. Now the total number of companies engaged in EPC in France are approximately 130, and the industry employs over 20,000 people.

At present the EPC industry in France manages some 80,000 MW of energy within the housing sector. The housing sector accounts for approximately 33 percent of the EPC business followed by industry at 12 percent and the other sectors combined account for over 50 percent. The hospital sector features prominently in the latter.

The EPC industry in France is one of the most mature and well organized in the world, and it is represented by the SNEC section of the Trade Organization FG3E.

The basic forms of standard contracts were originally developed in France and have now been adopted by EPC companies elsewhere. These contracts were originally of short (2 years) duration and were based on Maintenance and Energy Supply services. This type of contract still accounts for 60 percent of all EPC contracts in Europe. Gradually the need to provide total maintenance guarantees created a trend for longer term contracts (8-10 years). The latter type now accounts for the remaining 40 percent of all EPC contracts.

The extended lengths of these contracts enables not only replacement guarantees to be provided but has also made the injection of capital possible. Capital is almost always secured from external financing institutions.

As elsewhere in Europe, the industrial sector in France has also lagged behind in the uptake of EPC. This is largely due to the general view taken by the industry that it can best manage its own energy.

United Kingdom (UK)

During the late 1970's, the oil companies, most of whom were cash rich, felt that energy management was a growth sector. Their cash resources could yield a higher rate of return if invested in energy management. Royal Dutch Shell was amongst the first to bring the EPC concept across the channel to the UK. Shell created a Heating Management Services pilot venture, which was later launched as Emstar Limited.

Shell launched Emstar in 1984, which was to be their arm in energy management. Shortly afterwards, British Petroleum (BP) launched its energy management company, BP Energy Limited. Both Shell and BP saw this activity as their company's contribution towards the national need to improve energy efficiency. This activity encouraged organizations to consume less energy, which was contrary to the popular belief that oil companies were only interested in selling more oil. An added advantage of their entry into this market was the higher return on the large cash resources they received. So, in fact, it was a shrewd move on their part. These companies quickly added a range of complementary services (some in-house while others were brought in) to complement their investment activity.

Additionally, other organizations, previously providing only plant management or operation and maintenance as their core business, added financing services. Typically they did not have access to adequate capital of their own; so they secured capital from external sources, such as banks, finance houses, etc. In general, these early ESCO companies primarily made their profits on operation and maintenance of plant. By and large, the capital that they lent or secured for their customers, was done more as a "facilitator" rather than a means of making extra profit.

As demand developed, numerous other types of companies entered the market, under the general banner of "performance contracting," using other market entry points; e.g. Monitoring and Targeting services. These companies, however, did not necessarily offer the full range of Energy Performance Contracting (EPC) services.

Consultants also entered the market; offering services with fees relating to performance. The implementation and financing of the consultant's recommendations in such cases, however, remained entirely the client's responsibility. If the client could not implement the recommendations, perhaps due to shortage of finance, the consultants could not get paid. Hence, the consultants often introduced external financiers to their clients.

Many other organizations also identified energy management as a potentially large growth market. In actual practice, however, market growth fell way short of expectations; for just as the concept was taking hold, there was a 40 percent drop in oil prices in Western Europe.

THE FIGHT TO MAKE IT HAPPEN

In addition to the drop in oil prices, the concept also faced another uphill struggle to gain acceptance in the public sector in the UK.

It came at a time when a number of local government bodies were facing a squeeze on their capital budgets, and to circumvent this, many local authorities got around their difficulties by selling their assets, including such things as street lamp posts, etc. and leasing them back. The term "Creative Accounting" was coined and this naturally carried a negative connotation.

It was, therefore, unfortunate that EPC/Third Party Financing was painted with the same brush, and EPC was seen by Her Majesty's Treasury as another means of circumventing capital restriction; i.e., Ryrie Rules. The government believed that no private sector company could have the same borrowing power as the Treasury, and thus the cost of capital through the EPC would always be less attractive. As a result, public sector bodies were forbidden to take advantage of EPC. In some quarters of the National Health Sector, there was even a question of the legality of the concept.

The private sector meanwhile enjoyed EPC freely, and achieved substantial improvements in their energy efficiency. The vast potential for improving the energy efficiency in the public sector, however, lay untapped. The UK Department of Energy, was nevertheless quick recognize the opportunities being missed by the public sector.

EPC companies and their respective Trade Associations together with the help of the UK Department of Energy, fought tirelessly with the Treasury to get this barrier removed. It wasn't, however, until Mr. John Major, then Chief Secretary to the Treasury, gave his support by formally denouncing the Ryrie Rules, that the door became ajar. It was beginning to be recognized that EPC indeed brought a number of other benefits, such as transfer of risks and value for money, besides the injection of much needed capital.

Initially, EPC was opened to the public sector on a limited scale. The Treasury, which sought justification on a project by project basis, insisted on seeing the transfer of risks and value for money being demonstrated. At first, projects were approved for a total capital investment below a prescribed ceiling, but the ceiling was raised progressively.

Today, under the government's new Private Finance Initiative (PFI), the situation is reversed. Public sector bodies can now seek state finance for projects; however, they must demonstrate that all options of private finance have been explored.

Ironically, now the market has opened up due to the down turn in the European economy, the cash rich oil companies have been forced to divert their cash resources to their core business. As a result, some, such as Shell, have withdrawn from the EPC market all together.

Increasingly, the Third Party Financing (TPF) business is being driven by companies using finance merely as a facilitator. Financial markets have opened up in recent years, and clients can also raise capital from the money markets independently.

THE WESTERN EUROPE EPC PIONEER

From early struggles and permutations, EPC has become an established part of the energy efficiency industry. While you can find EPC activity throughout Western Europe, France remains its most active location.

Compagnie Générale de Chauffe (CGC) is one of the largest multinational EPC companies in France. It is part of the Generale Des Eau Group of Companies.

Embodying Esys Montenay, previously an independent ESCO in France, but now part of CGC, the Group is now a major force on the European ESCO scene. The deChauffe Group employs in excess of 29000 staff, and manages some 51000 MW of thermal energy, and 1000 MW of electrical energy.

CGC has presence around the world in some 29 countries. These include, USA, Canada, West Europe, Asia, Australia and Latin America. Countries in Europe include, UK, Germany, Austria, Belgium, Luxembourg, France, Monaco, Spain, Portugal, Italy, Netherlands, Switzerland, Hungary, Czech Republic, Slovakia, and Romania. In Asia, CGC is active in China, Taiwan, Singapore, Macao, Malaysia and South Korea, while in Latin America, it is active in Argentina. Elsewhere it also has presence in Israel, Ivory Coast, and Papua New Guinea. As the Group continues to expand, its presence in other countries will no doubt be further extended.

In the UK, CGC has a strong presence as an ESCO through its subsidiary, AHSEmstar. It employs around 900 staff, and is the largest broad spectrum ESCO in UK. AHSEmstar offers both demand and supply side energy management services and has a strong investment capability.

MOVING INTO CENTRAL AND EASTERN EUROPE

The energy service sector throughout Central Europe is under-developed compared to Western Europe. The circumstances giving rise to EPC are also different. Energy efficiency has not been a concern until very recently. Facilities desperately need upgrading and energy prices have had to be increased from the historical social costs. The most prevailing concern has been the struggle to move to a market economy with the inherent economic instabilities and limited domestic financing sources.

Czech Republic

The Czech Republic had the first performance contract in Central & Eastern Europe (CEE) and is considered the leader in EPC activity to date. EPC in the Czech Republic is showing potential in about 50 companies. They offer services ranging from simple boiler type maintenance operations by 5- to 10-men firms, to larger firms offering more specialized but limited range of skills, and up to what would be regarded in western countries as full EPC companies. Of the total potential EPC companies, 10-12 firms provide the sale of energy services under performance guarantees.

In 1994, there were only two companies providing the entire EPC range of service in the Czech Republic. These companies were EPS-CR and INTESCO. Both were formed by foreign parents, whose support and expertise helped them to start the business.

Hungary

In Hungary, energy performance contracting has developed slowly as investment organizations and entrepreneurs consider this type of business risky. The largest ESCO is a private company owned by five firms, including the Tungsram lighting company, which has concentrated its activities on street lighting facilities for municipal authorities. The most attractive market segment appear to be largely with local municipal bodies.

Most ESCO's are small and concentrate on a narrow segment of the EPC market. They have typically originated as subsidiaries or affiliated organizations of big western ESCO's (ENSI from Norway, SRC and HESCO from USA, Vattenfall from Sweden, Prometheus and Pervin from France). There are about 10 ESCOs that can undertake performance contracting for a fixed share of savings or a fixed fee.

Under a typical contract, the ESCO in Hungary conducts an energy audit at their own expense and if the customer agrees to the recommendations, project investments can begin. A contract is typically signed for 7-10 years. The profit from the project is shared between the ESCO and the customer for the first 4-5 years. Typically, the initial ESCO share is 90-95 percent with the ESCO share decreasing each year.

Market development of the EPC market is largely hindered by the continuing low energy prices, and the general uncertainty about the economy. New energy acts have, however, established a legal framework for energy efficiency services. Plans to increase gas and electricity prices over the next few years may stimulate future demand for EPC.

Poland

Poland has seen little development in EPC in the past. Stabilization of the economy, a continuing drop in inflation rates and a government policy to increase energy costs will create a more favorable environment.

Contract arrangements to date have been drawn up on the basis of 'first out' concept (discussed below). This is probably explained by the fact that high levels of savings are achievable and hence relatively low payback periods are possible. Capital investment has been in the region of $10-$30 thousand per project.

In 1994, Elektro Remont Serwis started EPC by installing heat meters on 14-months contracts. Customers had traditionally paid for heat by the occupied square meters. The first installation of heat meters showed a 15 percent cost savings. A more comprehensive district heating performance contract was undertaken by Landis & Staefa at Dzierzoniow. In addition to the work on the district heating system, energy efficiency work was performed on customer facilities.

EASTERN EUROPE

Movement is now underway for EPC to penetrate the countries of the former Soviet Union. EBRD is working with the Ukrainian government to set up a state ESCO. Under the aegis of US AID, studies of the feasibility of EPC are taking place in other countries. EBRD has announced its intention to develop a state ESCO in Russia (to be privatized later) if a private sector ESCO effort cannot be launched. EBRD is also helping to create an ESCO in Nizhny Novgorod with the support of the regional government and Gazprom, a large gas utility. At the same time, an American based ESCO, Energy Performance Services (EPS), has signed a performance contract with Karelsky Okatysh, a mining and iron pelletizing factory, in Kostomuksha in Northwestern Karelia, Russia.

TYPES OF EPC CONTRACTS

There are many different approaches to EPC in Europe and many different types of contracts. A range of contracts have evolved as the concept has matured in Europe over the years. In principle, there are two main types of contracts, but numerous variations have emerged to suit different conditions.

The two principal types can be very broadly classified as Demand Side and Supply Side Energy Management contracts.

DEMAND SIDE EPC

The ESCO gets closely involved primarily in the efficient utilization of energy. Activities in this type of EPC service includes such actions as:

- Introduction of more efficient processes;
- Conversion of old appliances to more modern high efficiency appliances;
- Heat recovery;
- Reduction of distribution losses, leaks, etc.;
- Introduction of high efficiency lighting; and
- Installation of modem control and monitoring systems, etc.

Shared Savings

Shared Savings was the original basis on which the EPC concept of Demand Side Management evolved.

The basic concept is simple and was previously explained in Section I. When the prices of energy were high and climbing (prior to 1986), it was a rather attractive project for ESCOs to implement.

In principle, the concept worked so that the host organization and an ESCO worked together to achieve savings. By working together, a partnership approach was promoted.

The EPC company on its part made the investment and maintained the plant. The end user was encouraged to be careful and not waste energy. To further ensure the end user's co-operation, an additional and larger share of savings were offered to the end user as an incentive beyond any agreed target to be achieved through joint effort. The "incentive savings" concept typically ensured at least the achievement of the target savings, which are sufficient for the EPC company to satisfy its investment criteria.

First Out

As a variation of the shared savings type of arrangement, First Out lets the ESCO take all of the savings until its investment is recovered. This procedure enables the ESCO to amortize its capital investment as soon as possible. Once the capital has been paid for, the host organization takes all the savings thereafter.

The main disadvantage of First Out is to the host organization, which has to forego all the savings in the earlier years of the contract. In both the arrangements, the Simple Shared savings and the First Out, it is assumed that sufficient savings will be available to amortize the capital invested.

In practice, as the price of energy fell, less and less savings were available to share, and contractual difficulties emerged. The simple concept also became difficult to apply to host organizations, such as hospitals and factories, where operational dynamics could change energy demand.

Fixed Fee or Targeted Savings Concept

Most of the difficulties set out above are successfully overcome by the Fixed Fee contract. Under this concept, a host organization and the ESCO agree on a target level of energy consumption, which could be even higher than the original consumption. The contract is designed on the basis that the ESCO would receive:

*   A fixed fee to recover costs of capital amortization, operation and maintenance costs, overheads, and profit;

*   An agreed annual charge to cover cost of target energy consumption; and

*   An annual reconciliation to adjust for fuel over or under consumption. See Figure 16-1 below.

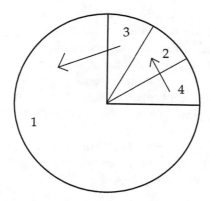

Figure 16-1. Targeted Savings Concept

Key:
1. Client's share
2. EPC company's share
3. Cost of additional savings reimbursed to client
4. Cost of additional energy consumed (e.g. by site expansion etc.) invoiced by EPC company.

This concept is particularly useful where capital investment cannot be paid out of the savings alone. One could argue, however, that under such an arrangement, there is little incentive for the ESCO to perform. Variations of this concept have, therefore, attempted to include the performance element. The most practical variation is the Heat Service Contract, which is predominantly applied in Supply Side Management EPC Contracts as discussed below.

SUPPLY SIDE EPC

Heat Service Contract
In the Supply Side of EPC, the ESCO is primarily responsible for more efficient energy production. The ESCO may supply energy across a metering point. The desired result is more efficiently produced energy at a lower unit cost delivered to the client for use as he wishes. The Supply Side ESCO does not normally get involved in the utilization end. The ESCO's activities are primarily confined within the boiler/power house walls.

The ESCO undertakes, for example:

- Purchase and administration of all primary fuels;
- Change of fuel, perhaps to a lower unit cost fuel;
- Installation of new high efficiency boilers;
- Installation of cogeneration systems;
- Upgrade of old boiler plant, fitting of economizers, etc.; and
- Provision of manpower for operation and maintenance.

In this arrangement, the ESCO supplies energy to the host organization usually in the form of steam (or hot water) under the two tier charging structure, which involves:

- A fixed charge to meet capital amortization, operation, manning and maintenance.

- A variable charge to meet the cost of actual fuel used and other consumables. The payment is in the form of an agreed price for steam or hot water (or electricity) actually used by the end user. Unlike the targeted type of contract, there is no need for annual reconciliation for over or under payment.

Minimum Off-take, or Take-or-Pay Contract

As explained above, a heat service contract has a two tier charging arrangement. In some contracts, this may be simplified into a single charge arrangement. However, to ensure that the ESCO continues to receive sufficient revenue to amortize its investment and cover its overhead should the host's demand for steam fall, the host organization agrees to take a minimum quantity of steam.

The performance element here comes in as the ESCO undertakes to provide a contracted amount of energy (steam, power or both) at a guaranteed lower unit cost (usually $/ton or $/1000 lbs) than the historical unit cost.

THE FRENCH MODEL CONTRACT

The French association of Energy Service Companies, FG3G, has developed an interesting contract format. To a certain extent, this form of contract can be applied both to demand side and supply side energy management services. However, and most importantly, it is a progressive type of contractual arrangement with which most clients feel comfortable.

It is a step-by-step approach, which leads an ESCO and a client to develop a contractual relationship from a simple O&M type of service to a full EPC contract. This model typically starts small with the O&M work and gradually adds larger measures, usually with progressively larger paybacks.

The contract is structured with three main sections:

- The main body
- Standard terms and conditions
- Obligations of the EPC company and the payments required.

The main body, which is client specific, and the standard terms and conditions remain unchanged. The last section is services and/or project specific, and it is only this section which needs changing as the range of contracted services develop.

THE MAIN OBSTACLES TO EPC IN EUROPE AND MITIGATING STRATEGIES

The EPC concept has faced many barriers during its evolution in Europe, and the concept of "Something for nothing" is frequently met with a degree of skepticism.

Some of the main obstacles encountered and the means by which some of them have been (or can be) overcome are listed below:

- *Customer's understanding* of the concept continues to be weak, and strong marketing and promotion is essential. Success stories from other countries (or other EPC locations in a given country) is an effective way to create better understanding and build up customer confidence.

- *'What is the catch' syndrome* is an obstacle. The offer on the face of it appears too good to be true, and puts some customers off. Showing customers how they will indeed pay for the services is actually a good marketing tool.

- *EPC as a totality of service* embodying everything from beginning to end can often be too much for many clients to commit to in one go. The French step by step approach can help.

- *Capital investment* offered has been a major attraction of EPC, but it can also create difficulties. As money markets mature, clients may delay signing up as they compare the EPC cost of money against theirs or an alternative source.

- *Long-term EPC contracts*, specially those involving finance, may require longer term commitments than customers want. This is a perceived barrier. The French concept of progressive contract development is an effective way of overcoming this.

- *Sector specific barriers* must be recognized. As mentioned earlier, process industry clients will be reluctant to get EPC companies involved in their processes, and may be reluctant to sign up Demand Side Management EPC contracts.

- *Lack of trust* frequently creates barriers. Industrial clients often express a fear that details of their confidential processes may pass to their competitors through the EPC company. For this reason, only Supply EPC contracts have found favor in such sectors over Demand Side EPC contracts.

- *"I can do it better" syndrome* is often a barrier. The biggest competition faced by an EPC company is from the client himself, particularly if he has the capital and also the perceived technical capabilities.

- *An Alternative Option Appraisals process* can be used to evaluate and demonstrate the benefits of EPC to the client. Option Appraisal is simply evaluating the net benefits to a project using the EPC option against other non EPC options, such as a "Do it Yourself" option. It is a powerful tool to convince clients (or government bodies) of the benefits of EPC. Total benefits are normally evaluated over the whole contract term and presented in present day monetary value (NPV).

- *Vested interests* can often be a barrier. Customer's staff may feel their jobs threatened by the involvement of an EPC company. This is seldom true, as EPC can often be demonstrated to be an extra resource for client's staff; thus, enabling them to do their jobs better. In certain cases, where jobs are threatened, as in the case of severe overmanning, it is often cost effective for some staff to be transferred to the EPC company's payroll. Their knowledge of the client's premises may be an asset to the EPC company.

- *Compensation for consequential loss* is often demanded by some clients. This presents a problem for EPC companies which cannot, and should not, take on this open ended liability. In fact, nobody should take this on.

- *Competitive tendering* (comparable to bid/spec in the U.S.) is a major barrier against Demand side EPC for clients in the public sector, where all contracts must be tendered on a competitive basis. Demand Side EPC is usually a partnership approach, and therefore does not lend itself to conventional competitive tendering; i.e., quantitative type tendering where contracts are bid against price. The cost of preparing bids as well as the cost of securing the contract can be unacceptable to EPC companies. Various ways are being tried to reduce the costs to both clients and EPC companies.

THE FUTURE OUTLOOK

The growth and continued development of EPC will not be a smooth process. It is an evolving industry, and clients will have to be educated along with the maturing industry.

The fact remains, however, that there is great interest in the European market place for EPC. Contracts are being sold successfully at all levels and in all sectors.

Contrary to common belief, the best customers for EPC will not necessarily be in those sectors which are the most energy intensive, even though they appear to offer the potential for huge energy savings. EPC is equally attractive for both large and small energy users, although the type of EPC service will have to be tailored to suit the client sector, the client type and the size of the client's energy bill. For example, the EPC contract may have to be structured for a demand side management contract, or supply side management contract, or a combination of the two.

Clear sectorial preferences for a certain type of service, and a certain type of contract will persist. In many client sectors, the reliability of plant operations will be more of a driving force for EPC than pure energy costs. In sectors such as industry, hotels, etc., plant unreliability can mean significant loss of revenue, and in the hospital sector, it can even result in loss of life of patients. When energy costs drop, plant reliability becomes an ESCO market. Indeed, this happened in Western Europe in the mid to late eighties; then, it became totally uneconomical to invest in energy efficiency. Throughout this low energy price era, the EPC industry was sustained largely by the need for enhanced plant reliability.

It is generally believed that in the medium to long term future, the energy efficiency industry in Europe will be more legislation driven, than price driven, although the former would also influence the latter. The issue of the environment and environmental legislation is to stay with us, and its influence is more likely to exert an upward pressure on energy prices.

Apart from the impact of legislation on energy prices, environmental considerations will inevitably also demand other capital intensive engineering measures to curb emissions from energy plants. EPC will, therefore, play a major role in helping to comply with stricter environmental legislation in the future.

Chapter 15

Weighing International ESCO Opportunities

To go international... or not to go? That is the question.

Paraphrasing the Bard doesn't make the decision to expand into the international market any easier, particularly for those in the complex energy-efficiency performance contracting business. Because energy services company (ESCO) projects carry certain risks, logic tells us an international setting would only magnify those risks.

True enough. But that is only *part* of the answer. The real question is: *Can you afford NOT to go international?*

Unlike Shakespeare's Hamlet, you HAVE to make a decision—especially in today's brutally competitive marketplace. To help with the decision-making process, I've broken it into the following general questions, which we'll explore in greater depth in this chapter.

1. *Is the international marketplace worth pursuing?*

2. *Is your company ready to go international? Can it handle an international venture without disrupting your domestic business?*

3. *Can you afford it financially?*

4. *Which countries will you target?*

5. *Should you have a local partner? What roles will you and your local partner play, both now and long term?*

6. *What value will your company bring to ensure a successful, long-term relationship and not just a short-term technology transfer?*

Q: *The international market: Is it worth pursuing?*
A: This is a no-brainer. For an energy services company to become a dominant player and maintain that position, the ESCO *must* participate in the international marketplace. Most recent studies show that the potential for ESCO services *outside* the United States *far exceeds* the U.S. potential, even though many countries need considerable development before an ESCO can become profitable there.

Q: *Are you ready to go international?*
A: To answer that question, you must first ask yourself this question: *Is your business in order in the United States?* Unless you answer "yes," you can't expect to add international business with any reasonable hope of success.

When my company decided to go international, we actually put international plans *on hold* for six months while we finished up some U.S. business first: achieving sales goals, making sure comprehensive business systems were in place, etc. Our reasoning? Developing an international presence takes so much time and energy that it's not feasible to catch up on the domestic front at the same time.

Q: *Has your company successfully developed its management, risk control, technical and other systems for its U.S. business and replicated them in remote U.S. offices?*
A: Key to success in the complicated business of energy services is developing and fine-tuning your technical, business and management systems to operate with consistency. You must be able to evaluate and manage risk and follow similar procedures each time, using the same forms and software for technical audits and analyses.

In addition, your technical, management and marketing systems should tie into your business accounting software to ensure that the entire company runs smoothly, seamlessly and profitably.

Project managers should use one project tracking and management structure consistently, enabling them to see in an instant precisely how their jobs are doing so they know when to adjust. Executives, likewise, must have up-to-date information to keep the overall business on track and make course corrections at the appropriate time.

More importantly, you must be able to replicate these systems in remote offices so that all of your people have access to the same information and do essentially the same tasks in the same way. Until your company does this successfully throughout the United States, you won't want to attempt it elsewhere.

The international equation is further complicated by different business cultures, customs, laws and languages, plus the great geographical distance separating employees from their home base.

Q: *Do you have in-house management expertise and time available to dedicate to international work?*

A: You must determine the management level and amount of management time needed for the task—and what you are willing to spare.

Further, ask yourself: *What tasks must be completed? What level of decision-making is required? How much management time will be spent abroad?*

Based on my experience, I can assure you that doubling or tripling your answers is prudent. Whatever your answers, can your company afford to lose key management time from your core business?

When we did this exercise for our first international venture, we determined we had to dedicate two man-months out of 12, or 1/6 of one key executive's time, the first year. Fortunately, we had international executive experience in house. In addition to this management commitment, we had to dedicate considerable technical and support staff to the effort.

Q: *Along with management and human resource expenditures, can you afford the financial expenditure? How much will it cost?*

A: Influencing cost are such factors as the actual international location, the partner, the market and others. Somewhere early in the planning stage, you've got to get a handle on cost.

The following are just some of the costs you'll want to consider. Some are better handled by local partners; others, directly by your company.

- Local office space and support staff
- Sales literature and other marketing support. (If you think the sales lead time for a performance contract is long in the United States,

think what it might be in another country, particularly one unexposed to the idea of performance contracting.)

- Sales expense
- Technical support for the sales staff
- Business plan development
- Travel and *per diem* costs
- Training personnel (your local partner's and your own)
- Adapting software programs to another country
- Project engineering and management
- General management and executive personnel

If you think your first international venture will make money or break even the first year, or even the second, *think again*. You should be prepared to fund the venture for a full year, and possibly two years or more, *with little or no revenue flowing back to your company*.

Q: *Have you evaluated your target countries?*
A: Once you've made the decision to go international, you must target a specific country or part of the world where you want to do business. This raises a whole new set of questions.

Q: *How big is the market for your services in the target country? Particularly, for the vertical markets that your company favors?*
A: The market must be large enough to make your venture worthwhile. One way to assess market size for energy-efficiency performance contracting is first to examine the total energy market, or the amount spent for electricity and fuel to operate, cool and heat buildings—and then make some assumptions.

For example, assume the country you're interested in has a total energy market of $1 billion. Your research further shows that half, or $500 million, is used for commercial buildings and the other half, for residential and industrial.

If you're interested solely in commercial, you can concentrate on the $500 million number. In the course of your research, you've also determined that few or no energy retrofits have been implemented in commercial facilities and it would be reasonable to achieve a 20 percent reduction in energy use by implementing cost-effective retrofits with three-year pay backs.

In this example, the potential total retrofit market for commercial facilities would be **$500 million** × .2 × 3 = **$300 million**.

The really big question is how much of this market could your company secure on an annual basis? A one percent (1%) penetration would yield $3 million; 5 percent would yield $15 million; 10 percent would yield $30 million, and so on.

The real answer, of course, lies with your sales and implementation ability, the extent of competition, local acceptance of performance contracting and a host of other variables.

Ultimately, you'll need good business planning and financial *pro formas* to determine if, and when, you can make a profit and how much.

Q: *Do you understand the laws and business customs of your target country?*
A: Certain issues are especially important, such as ease of repatriating money, taxes and other factors affecting an American company doing business in that locale.

Q: *What are the political and economic climates like now? What does the future hold?*
A: Ideally, you'll choose a country with a stable political environment, a good economy and positive, controlled growth. You don't want to be enmeshed in wars, political insurrections, runaway inflation and the like.

Q: *Is competitive project financing readily available?*
A: This is an extremely important issue and more than a little complex. You can't do projects unless readily accessible and competitive capital is available.

If you plan to deal primarily in the public sector, will special low-interest rates be available, such as tax-exempt rates in the U.S?

What are the prevailing rates in both the public and private sectors?

Will you use traditional third-party financing in which the customer signs a note directly with the financing institution, or are you looking at some form of shared savings?

Prevailing corporate returns also can determine whether a project is a "go." If companies can secure a 50 percent ROI by investing capital in their own core businesses, why would they want to invest in energy efficiency projects with a 30 percent ROI? In this scenario, the project sale may depend on off-balance sheet financing in which the customer truly is NOT investing any capital.

Q: *Do American banks have a significant local presence?*
A: If American banks are already committed to investing heavily in another country, chances are better for having your performance contracting proposal embraced.

Can 100 percent project financing be secured, or will you or your customers have to make an equity investment in the project? Do the financial institutions in the host country understand the concept of performance contracting, and are they willing to advance funds for both construction and permanent financing? What kind of terms are available? Will they go 10 years?

The above questions give you a flavor of the complexities involved with international project financing, which really is a subject unto itself.

Q: *Are the right factors in place to make performance contracting projects feasible?*
A: Here's a check list to review:
   • Energy rates: high, low or middle-of-the-road?
   • Are the buildings generally inefficient?
   • Does the government back energy efficiency?
   • Is financing available for energy-efficiency projects?
   • What is the status of the utility industry? Is it fully regulated or deregulated? What about load factors? Demand side management programs?
   • How good is the building stock infrastructure?
   • Are top-notch professional services available?
   • Are good subcontractors available? Are labor rates favorable?
   • What are the vertical markets like?

In some countries, like India, the market is more than 80 percent industrial. If your company's expertise and target markets lie elsewhere, then India may not be the best choice for your international venture.

Q: *How important is a local partner?*
A: A local partner is essential. Going international without a local partner would be worse than trying to do corporate taxes without an accountant or legal work without an attorney. There are too many things to learn, too many customer relationships to develop and too many unknowns for you to go it alone.

Before evaluating a potential local partner, you'll want to consider the roles you and your partner will play:

*   Since sales are built around developing personal relationships, you'll want your partner to have a significant role in sales even though you might be using your own proven sales process. If this is your approach, the ideal is to find a partner with a good customer base and sales personnel.

*   Since your own technical resources such as project engineers and managers, technicians and the like are limited—and the project's success depends on technical creativity and doing things right— you might want a partner with strong local technical resources.

*   Because these projects will be at a great distance geographically, with more variables and unknowns than you're accustomed to, you might want to share financial risks with your local partner. This means you'll want to choose a partner who is strong financially.

You'll also want the following from your local partner:
*   positive reputation;
*   good management team; and
*   commitment to success.

Q: *What are some of the important issues in structuring the business relationship?*
A: These issues are important to consider:
    *   You'll want good input from your outside accountants and financial advisors on whether to form a partnership, joint venture or contractor-subcontractor relationship.

- How will you share profits?

- How will you share risks? Sharing profits probably will be somewhat proportional to sharing risks.

- Who pays start-up costs? Are they later folded into job costs and reimbursed?

- What steps must you take to ensure that you'll add value to the relationship year after year rather than simply transferring technology to your partners, which they'll later utilize on their own?

Q: How does one begin all this research?
A: You have lots of good resources: Your local public or university library, the U.S. Chamber of Commerce, banks, the National Association of Energy Services Companies (NAESCO), the U.S. Agency for International Development (AID) and other federal agencies; or perhaps you'll be able to hook up with a good agent to guide you.

The time to start investigating and analyzing is *now*. Others are moving forward already.

Chapter 16

Assessing International Opportunities

With the maturing of the ESCO industry in the United States, the advance of retail access, subsequent price volatility, rapid changes in the utility industry and the general move toward a "global economy" is it time for global ESCOs?

Many countries could certainly benefit from the introduction of performance contracting and the establishment of full service energy service companies. ESCOs from a number of countries are already "testing the waters" around the world. British, German, Austrian, French, and Australian companies, and others, are looking for business. Still others are already quite firmly established far from their homes.

International markets can be very favorable targets for an ESCO that is ready to broaden its market base. There is a long list of developing countries: the Central European nations, the new nations that once formed the Soviet Union, the "awakening giants" like China, Indonesia and India... all *ought* to be good opportunities for a growing ESCO to plant the flag of performance contracting... but are they?

The answer is yes... but.

Markets in the developing countries are different... just how different becomes evident when the hunt to explore business opportunities abroad begins. If a firm is serious about venturing forth into the global ESCO marketplace, it will pay handsomely to first make an internal assessment of the firm's capabilities and

resources.

Those who have ventured into the global market and have found success will all agree with a few general statements: It will take longer than one thinks. It will require much more administrative time and effort than anyone thought reasonable. And the final result will be far different from what was visualized. (Please refer to the Chapter 16, "Weighing International ESCO Opportunities," for an excellent internal analysis of an ESCO firm contemplating international work by Don Smith.)

Not all international markets offer a real opportunity. Selecting and evaluating a "target" country is the first, and possibly the most important, task facing any firm that finds itself ready for international activity.

There is no "one size fits all" checklist to use in the evaluation of a potential target country. Over the years our firm has, through a lot of trial and some error, developed a broad protocol, which goes a very long way toward assembling the data needed to make a reasonably sound decision. After working in more than 20 countries, we are convinced that no list can remove all the risks. But our protocol removes many of the risks resulting from wrong assumptions. The format, which we have evolved, can be roughly divided into three broad areas: country analysis, in-country partner potential, and market assessment.

COUNTRY ANALYSIS

For a firm which is serious about entering the ESCO market in a certain country, there are several categories of information that deserve attention; some quite obvious and some rather subtle. While overlaps may occur, these general areas of inquiry provide a way to cross check data and help with interpretation.

Some of the needed information is readily, and publicly, available... and may even be accurate. Many other key pieces of information need to be developed in a visit to the country in question or through someone designated to conduct research on behalf of the firm. Reputable consultants are available who have the contacts and the knowledge of international business to get the answers and develop a plan from the basis of solid decisions. Needless to say, it is beneficial if the consultant has an understanding of the energy service business, so that the information generated is truly germane.

ECONOMIC ISSUES

First, of course, a careful examination of the economy is crucial to long term contracting; so it is essential to assess the overall economy and the political situation of the country in question. An initial reading on the stability and philosophy of the government and, in the case of a number of countries, the level of privatization, can be relatively easy to obtain. Much of this can be done "long distance" from sources that are quite readily available. In the United States, the U.S. Department of Commerce provides a constant flow of reports on the economy of most nations. This information is very good although, with some exceptions, it tends to be quite general. The U.S. Chamber of Commerce maintains a group of "Business Councils" consisting of business people with involvement in various countries. They publish valuable reports and provide the opportunity to meet with officials from their subject countries and other American businesses working in these countries. The World Bank and the other multilateral financing institutions also publish a great deal of material, which offers an economic analysis of most countries. These sources are all useful, but time and effort are required to sort out the useful from the interesting (or boring).

Beyond this broad economic assessment, there are a number of more subtle "blanks" that need to be filled in: What is the real posture of the country's leadership toward trade, the economy, foreign-based business activity, energy, etc.? How stable is the political situation and are there important changes in the offing? What are the prospects over the next several years? Specific economic issues such as inflation and interest rates, convertibility of currency, repatriation and economic trends are all indicators of possibilities/limitations for business success.

The answers to these questions can only tell the prospective international ESCO whether the target country *might* be a possible market and *might* be worth further effort and expense. To use ESCO parlance, this serves as a "scoping audit" to see if the expenditure of more time and money is warranted and how the country in question compares with other opportunities. Securing further data, beyond the broad facts suggested above, becomes more costly, and the data more subject to interpretation. Each of the initial "facts" opens the door to more issues, which will require careful examination and expansion, before an intelligent business decision can be made.

There are other things about the government, the energy situation and the economy, that data from the U.S. Commerce Department and other sources will not tell you. Does the government policy encourage energy efficiency or do various rules and regulations make it very difficult to get anything done... if you are looking at the market in public facilities, this is a vital question. Public espousal does not always match the facts.

This essentially seamless inquiry leads to more basic questions: If we go into this country, what kind of a market will we face? What problems will we have to deal with? What resources can we call on to get the job done? At this stage there is only one certainty; it won't be like home.

LEGAL ISSUES

The legal systems in possible target countries may not yet be ready to handle some of the "everyday" matters that the U.S. ESCO industry takes for granted. Laws may be solid, but the time frame in which the legal process works may make contract enforcement nearly meaningless. The legal framework in India is solidly grounded in English common law, but the courts are so slow that almost anything can happen. In some transitional economies; e.g., Central and Eastern Europe, China and some others, the court system, as we would recognize it, barely exists. Contracts can be more than somewhat questionable.

Efforts are being made to build a solid court system in most of the transitional countries and it will get better; however, it will take time and progress is uneven.

ESCOs from the early 1980s may remember the problems with U.S. attorneys rather fondly once they try to explain a performance contract to attorneys in some countries. An important first step is to present a contract to an in-country attorney; then, discuss all the contract language with the attorney. Allow the attorney to fit it to the local laws; then, critique it to be sure the ESCO is protected and the potential customer's position is reasonable, keeping in mind various aspects of contract enforcement. For example, specific information as to product value can greatly facilitate court action in some countries.

BANKING ISSUES

Banking in some of the countries that seem to be attractive targets can be a problem. Typically, commercial banks in transitional economies are still in an organizational phase and not really ready to consider financing of long term projects. In other areas, a "long term" loan is two years or less… and this may be justified in an economy where the inflation rate is high. In most countries where performance contracting is a new idea, education of the banking community becomes necessary before support from local institutions can be expected. A Russian banker was not at all interested in energy efficiency financing. He commented, "Energy efficiency financing is money made of air." It will take some time, and education, before that banker becomes a booster of energy efficiency investments.

In countries where the multilateral development banks (MDBs) are interested in energy efficiency, other routes to project financing may be available. MDBs can support/educate and/or mitigate some risks through their involvement. The European Bank for Reconstruction and Development (EBRD) has taken the MDB lead in energy efficiency financing and moved with considerable success in parts of Central and Eastern Europe. The World Bank with GEF support has made significant progress in China. The Inter-American Development Bank is active in Argentina, Peru and El Salvador, and the Asian Development Bank is moving to foster energy performance contracting in Asia.

HOW "FOREIGN" ARE YOU?

Underlying suspicion or bias against the entrance of foreign businesses, investment or technology can be very real regardless of official policy, and what is published. It pays to look beneath the surface. If suspicion of foreign investment exists, the bureaucratic road blocks, all quite unofficial, can be almost limitless. Consider that a Kentucky Fried Chicken outlet in Mumbai (formerly Bombay) was closed for a time because "flies" (a shocking thought in Mumbai) were discovered. It took court action to "un-discover" the flies. Sometimes this sort of thing happens when cultural, local, or regional issues have arisen that stir the political pot.

ENERGY MATTERS

Moving beyond "Internet available" information, there is very important energy information to be garnered "on the ground," such as power availability by region and power quality. In thinking about energy efficiency projects, power shortages in a particular region and frequent outages are critical concerns. A problem or an opportunity? In India, power outages and wide power quality swings are facts of life. Cogeneration may be an important ESCO offering. In the Philippines and some Eastern European countries power curtailment is a daily, scheduled, occurrence. How will these "routine" events affect savings calculations?

A growing number of countries have horizontal stratification of utility services like the U.K. model; i.e., generation, transmission and distribution, are separate functions with portions of the business controlled by the state. A key question arises: Who loses when energy efficiency increases? A utility that believes it's revenue will fall if a customer's energy efficiency increases can find a lot of ways to make things difficult.

Utility structures, policies, and attitudes vary by country, sometimes by region and always by utility company. The incentives and/or disincentives that originate with a utility can make a huge difference in the possibilities for successful energy efficiency projects.

How is energy purchased? In Poland where district heating is a big factor, tenants in apartment blocks have historically paid for heat by the square meter; thus, they had no incentive for energy efficiency. Without metering, there was no incentive to save. If a "no payment crisis" exists, such as the 1997 situation is Russia, there is no incentive to use energy more efficiently. As one Russian leader put it, "When you are not paying, it makes no difference how much you are not paying." These and other factors have complicated the approach to energy efficiency marketing and have required some very innovative strategies.

The size of the global market is huge and the efficiency possibilities are almost beyond imagination. The way to tap that market may be different than anything you have seen before. Thinking "outside the box" is a necessity.

In some countries there is very little accurate metering of any kind. There may be demand schedules, but no time-of-use metering. One very large Indian utility knows when its peak load occurs, but does not know exactly which customers are pushing the top of the scale. Their solution to potential system overload is to call some of their "high tension" customers and ask them to cut their loads.

Due to the chronic, and growing, power shortfall, in some countries manufacturing companies have contracted for far more electricity than they need as "insurance" against the time when they need to expand. This can well mean a minimum monthly bill that cannot be changed when energy is saved, without a difficult contract re-negotiation. This poses a potentially serious disincentive for an energy efficiency project.

Gathering as many indicators as possible as to what is likely to happen in a country is key. Some guesses may not be entirely correct, but they can be important and, in conjunction with other data, are revealing. Are new taxes in the works, or are there tax breaks that could make a difference? What sectors of the economy are growing or shrinking and what sectors are being propped up by government at an artificial level? Will those props last? And, not incidentally, how do people feel about the economy. If people are optimistic, they are far more apt to be ready to accept new ideas and approaches. The optimists are much more apt to take advantage of energy opportunities. Perception often becomes reality.

IN-COUNTRY SUPPORT

If an ESCO is going to do business in another country, it needs to know what resources are available in terms of technical capabilities, business alliances, financial resources and markets.

In most transitional and developing countries, good technical people are in abundant supply. Technically capable companies, which are willing to work, and are well qualified to be involved in energy efficiency projects are plentiful. However, the "software," the knowledge about the business side of energy efficiency and more particularly knowledge about energy performance contracting, is usually lacking. The concept of full service energy service companies is growing, but to many it will be new.

In some countries the level of technical capability is more limited. In many instances, the "new" equipment they are most familiar with is of the '50s era.

Misinformation among the "informed" can also be a problem. Disassociating a utility DSM program from performance contracting can at times be a struggle. While the concept of a full service ESCO is readily accepted, the business approaches we learned almost at birth are new and often thoroughly misunderstood in some cultures. The language barrier can be far greater than the difference between English and Hungarian. Terms such as "return on investment," or even "profit" are still new in some of the former communist countries. The words may be part of the lexicon, but it is a mistake to assume that such terms are well understood. Some times they talk the jargon, use the business terms we are familiar with, but their ability to actually implement the concepts is seriously narrow and lacks a full understanding of economic implications. In such cases, a "foreign" business man in an unfamiliar country can make some very dangerous assumptions. Furthermore, there are "foreign" businessmen and American businessmen. They are not necessarily viewed the same. An in-country partner can provide valuable counsel.

These matters make a difference when you are trying to set up a deal. In some Central and Eastern European countries there is enthusiasm, but, even in the late 1990s, there is limited understanding about how to move ahead. It is easy to forget that for fifty years, forward motion was strictly by permission; not initiative.

Training, therefore, is a must. Both business and technical training will probably be necessary before any solid business begins to flow. Expect a time lag before positive financial results. Be confident that it will always take longer than expected. Understanding the technical and business sophistication available within a target country is one more important step before major decisions are made.

Very good, very astute business people can be found in any country; and, in those countries where the economy has been unleashed and given a chance to respond to markets, their numbers are increasing. The rapidly growing numbers of young people who have been exposed to the market economy and have grown up in a less regulated society will soon make a significant difference.

A WORD ABOUT CULTURE

Much has been written on the importance of understanding the cultural climate in a country in which you wish to do business. It is very important. It is equally important to realize it cannot all be learned, *absorbed* and understood instantly. It takes time—time, which you will be reluctant to spend, even when demands, such as evaluating potential markets, call to you.

The initial solution is a willingness to learn and an acceptance that Beijing, Tula, Warsaw, and Ahmedabad are not like home. This understanding coupled with a degree of reserve and a willingness to be flexible can carry you a long way. An official in Moscow commented, "It is easier to deal with Germans than Americans... they are more flexible... Americans think theirs is the only way to do things." For those of us who have always viewed the German approach as rigid, this comes as something of a shock, but some thought suggests a reason. Germany is surrounded by differing cultures and to do any business outside of their own country they have had to recognize differences and be sufficiently flexible to get along with their potential customers. Most Americans are rather new at this game.

So approach a new culture with interest and curiosity. Don't rush things, watch your hosts and learn. They will understand and appreciate your efforts, and overlook your mistakes. Verbal recognition, on your part, that procedures, which worked well some other place, will need to be modified to fit local conditions will be well received.

In some countries there is a regular ritual for the presentation of business cards. In many, some gestures that would pass without notice or comment at home can create real problems. Business discussions have a defined time and place in some cultures. These are all things that cannot be learned instantly. Advice and guidance of someone totally familiar with local custom can, and will, be extremely valuable.

FIND THE TIGERS

In many countries it will be possible to find a few "tigers"... people who immediately grasp the concept of full service ESCOs and performance contracting; people who have enthusiasm and drive and who see a personal, and/or national, advantage in making the concept real. People who have the power and the will to make things happen. These "tigers" may be in government, or may be highly respected industry or financial leaders. The existence of a tiger can help to balance other concerns, especially when it comes to getting around bureaucratic roadblocks or opening doors.

Recently, in China, Mr. Li, Director of the Energy Division of the State Economic and Trade Commission, attended a seminar on performance contracting. He asked questions (all translated from Chinese) and made comments. During a tea break he was enthusiastically explaining financial concepts to other class members, drawing furiously on a blackboard. We had found a tiger. Together with a young woman from a commercial bank who speaks English well and is every inch a tiger in her own right, they became invaluable in forging the creation of Chinese ESCOs.

IN-COUNTRY PARTNERS

Few ESCOs will make it in a foreign market without in-country help. A joint venture with an in-country partner, or at least a strategic alliance with a well established firm, is a must. A careful census of who is in the energy business and what they are doing is an important part of the data collection process.

It is fairly simple to find out who is in the energy efficiency business within a given country. Engineering or mechanical contracting firms who do turnkey energy projects and in some cases, savings-based projects, exist almost everywhere. In addition, thanks to the efforts of the U.S. Agency for International Development, quite a number of consultants offering energy audits are available. These may be likely competitors, or present opportunities for joint ventures or alliances. At the very least, they are apt to be the people an ESCO will need to count on for installation and operational help.

Discussions with a few of the firms in energy related businesses will quickly reveal what is happening in the efficiency market. But, be aware: *their definition of what an ESCO is, and what it does, is apt to vary tremendously from U.S. views.*

The criteria our firm has established as a way to judge the qualifications of a potential in-country partner are not very different from what one would use to select a partner close to home... with some important variations. Along with the technical capabilities and the strength required for project implementation and follow through, there is a critical need for a partner that has the contacts and the knowledge to navigate the regulatory maze of that country. In-country partners also need to know how to deal with the codes and standards that are the pride and joy of any bureaucracy. Finding the way through the government channels is not usually considered an engineering talent; so administrative ability is also an important consideration. This talent will frequently go beyond *what* the in-country partners know to *who* they know.

It helps if the in-country partner has been privatized (or is being privatized). The in-country firm needs to understand some basics like real costs, return on investment and the need for profit. These qualities are sometimes harder to find than one might think, particularly in those countries still trying to find their way out of a command and control economy.

An effective in-country partner will also know where, and how, to acquire and/or import material and equipment needed to move projects forward. Tariffs may be high but there may be "forgiveness" of tariffs for some types of energy equipment... if the partner knows how to work the system and use the rules to their advantage. In one country, we were told several times that it was almost impossible to take advantage of the low rate for energy equipment, then a young engineer said, "It's easy if you know how to write the description of the equipment you want to bring in."

Local knowledge of the availability, and quality, of sub-contractors who will get the job done is also a vital resource, which cannot be brought from home. In the final analysis, the in-country partner needs the know-how and the contacts to get the job done efficiently and effectively.

MARKET ASSESSMENT

Selecting a target market within a new country, and identifying opportunities within that general market, is far more complex than in the U.S. The abundance of statistics we take for granted in the United States, and in most Western industrial countries, is often rudimentary or non-existent in many countries. This lack of data extends from a good estimate of the energy requirements relative to production levels to the credit information that financial people want to talk about. The information generally exists *somewhere*, in some form, but it will often require extensive research in-country to get it. It is seldom available in neatly written form and it is very frequently suspect. Historically, countries, which existed on imposed "five year plans," frequently reported statistics to satisfy plans and not to reflect actualities. A tendency still exists to make all forecasts look rosy and all results outstanding. Healthy skepticism makes good business sense.

An ESCO, contemplating markets on an international basis, should first consider where its own strength lies. If the firm's management knows a lot about a specific industry, such as the cement industry, hospitals or office buildings, that is the place to start. The firm is better equipped to assess the data, the problems, the opportunities and talk the language.

A few key indicators are basic in determining whether a particular industry or market is worth consideration. Preliminary screening includes concerns as to what industry segments are apt to be viable over time. Heavy equipment plants in certain Central and Eastern European countries, for example, are often so obsolete that there is little chance they can survive at all without a long term (and unlikely) flow of subsidies. The state of privatization in that industry and/or the level of government subsidies for the industry are key issues. Many of the industries in transitional economies, which have not yet been privatized, are "buggy whip" manufacturers that will never survive on their own. Not good targets for long term energy efficiency projects.

The "flip side" of the privatization issue involves those facilities, which are apt to remain under state control, that may be quite viable as targets for energy efficiency. These are public institutions, such as hospitals, schools and other public facilities as well as industries "vital" to the government. In fact, these markets initially present the most stable, least risky, opportunities. The political and economic decisions have been made; they will be there over time.

Is the industry growing or is it declining (or perhaps dying out)? Who is investing in the industry, or in specific companies within the industry? If outside money is flowing in, it suggests that someone else has confidence in the long term viability of the industry. Within an industry, companies that have attracted substantial outside equity participation may be particularly attractive targets for energy efficiency work. Their management is apt to have a better appreciation of costs as well as the importance and advantages of increased efficiency.

The "deal killer" in market selection, however, is whether or not a market can keep its savings. If savings flow to another entity, neither the incentive nor the means to pay the ESCO exist. Before a potentially viable market is written off, however, it pays to look at the entire revenue stream.

As our firm brought together the parties to establish the first performance contract in Eastern Europe, all conditions seemed very positive until we discovered that the Bulovka Hospital in the Czech Republic could not keep its savings. Another means of accessing the revenue had to be found. After considerable research ... and discussion... we were able to access the National Insurance Fund which finances hospital operations. A way was found for the hospital to benefit from energy savings. The project went forward, and all parties, Bulovka, Landis & Staefa, Energy Performance Services and Kiona International are all proud to take credit.

TEST THE "FACTS"

All "facts" accumulated to examine market opportunities should be tested... a source that is *absolutely sure* of his/her knowledge of a market, very probably is not. Asking more questions and/or seeking other sources is critical. Generalities, which are readily available, can hide real problems or opportunities. It is easy to say that country "X," with a very high energy intensity, is a good prospect for energy efficiency; however, that bit of information does not tell you that the government bureaucracy makes it almost impossible to get anything done, or that energy users don't pay their bills. Much as a child stacks building blocks, each accumulated fact should contribute to the picture of a potential market. The stronger the building block base, the easier the decision to take it one step further. But test at every level.

There is a wide world of opportunity for an ESCO that takes the time to do careful, thorough "homework." It is necessary to accept from the start that doing business in India, China, Slovakia, Brazil or Ukraine will not be the same as doing business in Kansas or California. Only one assumption works: assume that most assumptions about those countries are wrong. Good people can be found in every country, who are eager and well qualified to act as effective partners. Finding them is the challenge.

An in-depth investigation of selected countries with limited risks can allow an ESCO to bring together the ingredients that can lead to success. An ESCO, which does not have the internal resources to make a careful business evaluation in a selected country, should secure outside consultation or stay home.

Chapter 17

International Financing
Of Energy Efficiency

An endless stream of studies over the last ten to fifteen years has concluded that there is an enormous potential international market for saving energy in a multitude of markets around the world. In 1996, the US Agency for International Development (AID) estimated the non-OECD market alone at between $8 and $20 billion. Individual market opportunities are seldom less than several hundreds of millions of dollars, and energy performance contracting is frequently cited as the sales approach of choice to successfully attack the market!

Theoretical Potential or Profitable Reality

Closer examination of the actual number of successfully implemented projects or programs yields a disappointingly small inventory of examples. Too often, examples cited as "successes" are small demonstration projects, heavily supported by grants or subsidies, which, in strictly commercial terms are "failures" when measured in terms of profit or return on investment. Others are the result of disproportionate efforts by a dedicated band of managers within a large company, where the true costs of the effort have been hidden, and a true reckoning on good accounting principles, would render most of these "profitable" projects somewhat less attractive. Most of the market potential is still more theoretical rather than real.

Fortunately, a small group of pioneers in energy efficiency marketing and financing are beginning to show the way to business and financing approaches that are able to generate profitable energy efficiency projects that can be implemented in increasing numbers. In this chapter key financing barriers will be explored; then, an attempt will be made to dispel some of the myths surrounding financing energy solutions by using the various forms of performance contracts described elsewhere in this book.

Before going any further, it is important to clarify what is meant by "international." In energy terms the world can be loosely divided into three groups:

1)   The early industrialized economies of predominantly Western Europe and North America have by far the world's largest use of energy, but when measured in energy use per unit of gross domestic product (GDP), can be seen as relatively efficient in economic terms. Their sheer size makes continuing improvements in energy efficiency essential for competitive and environmental reasons;

2)   The developing economies of Latin America and Asia need more and more energy to fuel their growth and to improve the living standards of their people. Unfortunately, the demands of rapid growth and long term energy efficiency are too often seen as being in conflict, and efficiency suffers; and

3)   The former communist economies in transition of Central and Eastern Europe have inherited vast, inefficient energy systems supplying energy inefficient building and factories. The technical inefficiencies are two to three time those found in the OECD countries.

By the first years of the 21st century, the developing and transitional economies energy use will exceed those of the developed OECD countries. These latter two markets present the greatest energy efficiency potential, but arguably the most difficult to finance, and it is on these markets that this chapter will mainly focus.

IS LACK OF FINANCING A BARRIER?

Lack of financing is frequently cited as the key barrier to widespread implementation of energy efficiency projects or programs, and integrated energy solutions,[1] especially in the emerging markets. In parallel the key international financing institutions (IFI's), such as the World Bank, the International Finance Corporation, Asian Development Bank, etc. have come under widespread criticism over the years for favoring investment in major additions to generating capacity and for failing to invest in energy use reduction. Commercial banks have not escaped the criticism of the non-government organizations and the energy services industry for failing to respond to the investment needs of energy efficiency projects. How many of these perceptions are based in reality, and how many in myth?

There has been an increasing understanding of the importance of the efficient use of energy as a means of reducing operating costs, reducing pollution and building sustainability, thanks largely to the efforts of a dedicated, but relatively small community over the past twenty years. At long last their message has been heard, and energy efficiency is entering the mainstream of the vocabulary of the financial community. As of the time of this writing, some estimates place the availability of potential capital for investments in energy efficiency in excess of $4 billion worldwide, and growing. While commercial banking is limited in come countries, there are numerous examples of funds and financial facilities that are grossly under-utilized.

What *is* lacking is a ready supply of "bankable projects" being proposed by credible companies or public bodies. If the right kind of project can be mated with the right kind of financing, there is an almost unlimited availability of investment resources. As in any market, success will breed success, and this pool of finance will expand as more and more successful projects are implemented.

WHAT MAKES A "BANKABLE PROJECT"?

As in any market, the solution being offered by the ESCO must meet the customer's needs. The international demands parallel much of the discussion in Chapter 5, Financing Energy Efficiency. For analysis here, these needs can be broken down into three main categories:

- technical measures to reduce the overall use of fuel and energy to achieve certain economic or social goals;

---

[1]Integrated energy solution is the implementation of an efficient solution minimizing energy use with the combination of small scale captive generation, blended with grid supplies and combined with demand reduction measures. Generation would typically be from either renewable or co-generation sources.

- service measures to ensure the measures maintain or improve their efficacy over the period of the performance contract; and

- financing solutions to ensure the necessary investment capital is available, and the cost of the services are affordable.

While technical and service measures will not be covered here, it's important to emphasize that the customer is increasingly looking for total energy solutions, including both supply and demand side measures. Figure 17-1 summarizes the various value levels of energy efficiency solutions.

From a business standpoint, the returns for both the customer and the ESCO are better when a more complete energy management package is offered. In the developing economies, the customer will have major short term demands on limited capital, and will be reluctant to invest in the more long term aspects of energy efficient operation. A critical as-

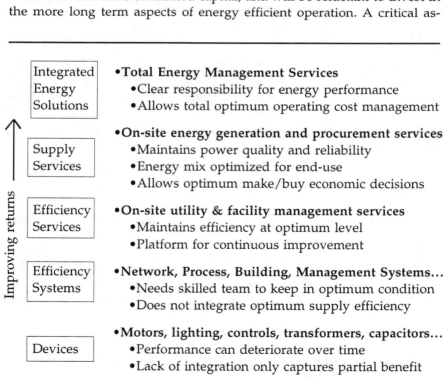

Figure 17-1. Trend To Integrated Energy Solutions

sessment of the energy efficiency of housing, hotel and commercial property in any Asian boom town will amply demonstrate this truth. However, as these markets overbuild, become more competitive, and energy prices increase, the need to lower operating costs will become a significant item on the local management radar screen.

These pressures are not limited to the private sector—municipal and public services are feeling the pressure of increasing expectations from their "customers." This pressure is exacerbated by limited operating budgets and little capital to invest.

In developing economies, the successful ESCO will offer a solution that frees up the customers own capital or credit rating to invest in his own business while simultaneously reducing energy related operating costs. In the transitional economies, the customers have an urgent need to immediately reduce devastating technical losses for economic, social and environmental reasons. Ironically, this is happening by default in the industrial sector as non-competitive Soviet era industries either go bankrupt, or are downsized and restructured to survive into the future.

The public and municipal institutions are facing a daunting set of energy related challenges requiring billions in investments over the next ten years to bring heat and electric services to acceptable standards, and to reduce the devastating cost of energy in-efficiency on national economies. In their own right, both industry and non-industrial customers have no significant capital to invest in energy efficiency measures, and generally have poor or no credit ratings. At the same time, in most countries energy costs are increasing; and, in early 1997, electricity costs in much of Central and Eastern Europe were approaching U.S. levels. In economies where salaries are still measured in hundreds of dollars a month and the prognosis for energy costs is upwards, governments face a political dilemma.

For economies in transition then, the successful ESCO may be called on to offer a solution that uses its own credit rating to provide investment capital for the customer.

The conclusion of this assessment is that the ESCO that wants to seriously succeed in these markets must be well capitalized, be prepared to take reasonable commercial and technical risks, and be committed to the market for the long haul.[2] To underscore the latter point, energy

---

[2]The examples of Compagnie Généralé de Chauffe establishing the Prometheus ESCO in Hungary, is a good example of a well capitalized company forming a successful ESCO.

services businesses must be developed over a long period of time. Only a fool would offer these services in a market where they believe the future to be unacceptably uncertain.

The other, equally obvious conclusion, is that the ESCO needs to understand the customer's business in depth, and recognize that the ESCO will become the customer's energy manager. As such, the ESCO will become more a part of the customer's management team than an outside vendor.

A further critical financial factor of success is that the ESCO fully understands the incoming and outgoing cash flows for a project, summarized in Figure 17-2. In developing and transitional markets, the accuracy and value of historical and current utility and cost records is of limited value. A very thorough technical/financial due diligence, combined with a healthy background knowledge of the overall political, economic and energy factors of the country or region is an essential element in preparing a successful bankable project. Since much of the value of the project will be based on assumptions about the future shape of these cash flows, a solid assessment of the future trends, and the customer's future viability must be carried out.

Figure 17-2. Understanding The Cash Flows

Last, but not least, the investments must be made in a country where the overall frameworks are friendly towards successful implementation of energy services programs. The previous chapter "Assessing International Opportunities," discusses a number of country parameters that an ESCO must evaluate before committing significant investments. They include the status of privatization, contract law, public policies on energy efficiency and environment, energy prices, economic indicators, management perceptions and the size of energy efficiency opportunities.

A systematic evaluation of these parameters, both in the present situation and expected conditions a year or two forward, should form a part of preparing bankable projects. The results are often a surprise to U.S. management, which may have a dated preconception of the market status of various countries.

Assuming a project is proposed by a credible company, with a credible customer, in a viable country, with a well constructed technical/ financial assessment of necessary investments and cash flows, the next step is to evaluate the financing options.

Financing Approaches For Different Energy Solutions

In general, the capital requirements for individual energy efficiency projects are relatively small by the standards of investment banks, while the projects themselves can be relatively complex, costly and time consuming to set up. The relative transaction costs to project size and complexity have dampened management enthusiasm and proved to be major barriers within financing institutions.

The project size barrier has all too often caused ESCOs to fall short of the mark set by financiers. The temptation to enter a new market by taking the approach of piloting a single, small project, has meant a large number of single, small ESCO projects have been tried. Given that the set up cost for a small or a medium project, or for a single or a multiple series, is much the same; a single small pilot, will almost certainly be unattractive from a financial standpoint. The successful ESCO needs to have the vision of a pipeline of similar transactions, based on a long-term commitment to the country concerned.

FINANCING MECHANISMS

Various financing approaches, which follow, have been developed to meet the key need of consolidating projects into a pipeline of similar transactions to reduce the management effort and costs on each project.

MULTI-PROJECT FACILITY[3]—THE ESCO AS FUND MANAGER

This model, outlined in Figure 17-3, was developed by the European Bank for Reconstruction and Development Energy Efficiency Bank-

---

[3]Facility in this context uses the banking terminology for a funding approach and does not refer to a building.

ing Team as a financing tool to implement multiple energy efficiency projects with capital requirements in the range of $1M to $15M. This investment range covers a wide spectrum of industrial, commercial, residential, utility and public projects.

Using the multi-project facility (MPF) approach, the ESCO will prepare, develop and close a number of similar projects, and will be given the authority by the investors to manage the financing facility on its own authority. In effect the ESCO is the fund manager. Clearly, the ESCO must be seen as credible by the investors, and may be an active investor itself.

The investors would generally be contributing both debt and equity capital, meaning that the development banks are sharing directly in the commercial risk of the projects.

This model can be used to combine development and commercial financing investments with the ESCO's corporate investments. It is equally suitable to 100 percent commercial financing.

The MPF is an excellent way of developing multiple, relatively large, energy service projects, where the ESCO will provide energy management for a number of years. While its application in the market is in a relatively early stage, the sharing of technical and commercial risk by the ESCO, and the political risk by the development bank, is giving cause for optimism that this will be one of the key financing tools to turn the theoretical market potential to reality. By early 1997, EBRD had con-

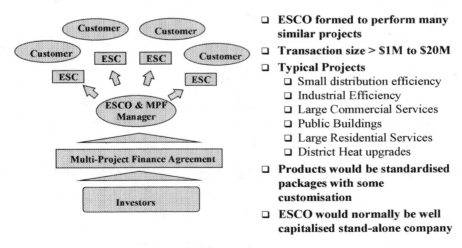

- ❑ **ESCO formed to perform many similar projects**
- ❑ **Transaction size > $1M to $20M**
- ❑ **Typical Projects**
  - ❑ Small distribution efficiency
  - ❑ Industrial Efficiency
  - ❑ Large Commercial Services
  - ❑ Public Buildings
  - ❑ Large Residential Services
  - ❑ District Heat upgrades
- ❑ **Products would be standardised packages with some customisation**
- ❑ **ESCO would normally be well capitalised stand-alone company**

Figure 17-3. Multi-Project Facility

cluded multi-project facilities for energy efficiency investments with Généralé de Chauffe, the large French ESCO; Landis & Staefa, the Swiss building controls manufacturer; and Honeywell, a U.S. controls manufacturer. The use of this financing approach is expected to increase. Aside from sharing the risks, and channeling capital to the market, this facility has a major commercial advantage. The ESCO sales team supported by such a financing facility is able to conclude deals much faster than their competition, and provide the complete technical/service and financial solution the customer is looking for.

LARGE LEASING COMPANY AS FUND MANAGER

Another whole category of energy efficiency projects is available through the multiple installations of low-cost energy efficiency measures (lighting, motors, power factor correction capacitors, etc.). Again, the "ESCO," or in this case a Leasing Company (or LeaseCo), will generally be a large, well-capitalized company, which is capable of establishing a multiple transaction leasing plan, with leases based on calculated energy savings. The investors, one of whom will generally be the LeaseCo, will delegate the disbursement of the leasing financing facility to the LeaseCo. The financing can be in the form of debt or equity.

Like the MPF, the offering to the customer comes complete with the

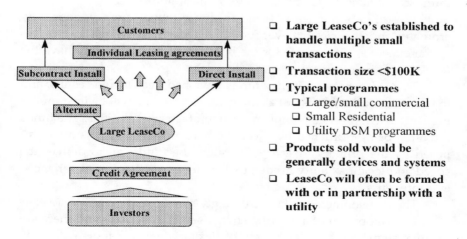

- ❑ **Large LeaseCo's established to handle multiple small transactions**
- ❑ **Transaction size <$100K**
- ❑ **Typical programmes**
  - ❑ Large/small commercial
  - ❑ Small Residential
  - ❑ Utility DSM programmes
- ❑ **Products sold would be generally devices and systems**
- ❑ **LeaseCo will often be formed with or in partnership with a utility**

Figure 17-4. Leasing Company As Fund Manager

financing, giving the ESCO a competitive advantage. This approach is well suited to widespread installation of small efficiency measures, with individual transactions from a few hundred dollars to some tens of thousands. This is the range that covers small industrial, residential and commercial programs. This type of facility is widely available from commercial and development banks to LeaseCos prepared to accept reasonable commercial and technical risks on their balance sheets.

FINANCING ESCOS VIA ENERGY EFFICIENCY FUNDS

Both the MPF and Leasing Company financing tools are ideal for larger companies, wanting to diversify into an energy services business; but, clearly, they rely on the ESCO taking risk on their balance sheet. The sheer scale of the challenge of encouraging energy efficiency investments has caused the major development banks to seek ways to support the development of strong, small locally capitalized ESCO's.

A whole raft of energy efficiency funds is being developed by the major development banks such as the Inter-American Development Bank, the Asian Development Bank, the International Finance Corporation and the European Bank for Reconstruction and Development. These funds are managed by local banks or financial institutions within the country of interest, and are charged with making available small to medium scale financing for smaller, less well capitalized ESCOs.

These funds frequently blend in donor money from various governments and agencies to cover fund management costs, reduce the fees or the effective interest rate for the borrower. They frequently have the flexibility to invest in equity as well as debt.

To date, energy efficiency funds have had very mixed results, and to some extent the jury is out as to how effective they will be in stimulating large scale, profitable implementation of energy solutions. The funds are often being burdened by excessive bureaucracy, which is often imposed by the primary investors. As such, the funds fail to deliver the speed and local flexibility needed to encourage smaller, less experienced entrepreneurs.

The development banks increasingly recognize the need to accelerate the development of a thriving energy services industry and there are positive signs that a wider variety of flexible financing tools will come into the developing countries' markets in the relatively near future.

WHAT ABOUT ENERGY EFFICIENCY SUBSIDIES?

Much debate on energy service financing in the developing world has focused on trying to persuade governments, trust funds and international institutions, such as the World Bank, to subsidize energy efficiency businesses. The subsidies have made it possible for a number of useful demonstration programs to be launched, providing clear local benefits and a wealth of technical information. The downside of this approach has been a sense that implementing energy efficiency is an added cost needing support, rather than an investment with a profit potential as a business in its own right.

Increasingly, subsidies are being recognized as having a greater value when applied to developing resources such as training people, developing public awareness, or being applied to assist ESCOs in the early stage development of their business structures and initial projects. Using subsidies to directly distort the cash flows of projects, and make them appear more attractive, is probably counterproductive to widespread market development. The future will probably see more use of subsidies in market and resource development rather than one-off demonstration projects, a healthy shift of focus.

MANAGING INVESTMENT RISK IN NEW MARKETS

The rules for managing risk in most markets are similar: take time to understand the country framework, select customers with a long-term future, employ quality local people, train them well, and apply good service quality control management practices and financial controls. Even with reasonable management preparation, any market has commercial and technical uncertainties, and an entrepreneurial ESCO must be prepared to accept these. Many of the developing markets, however, present political uncertainties, and these are largely beyond the control of the ESCO. Teaming with a development bank in one of the business models described above will give a certain amount of political risk insurance as well as access the wealth of local commercial and banking knowledge. Increasingly, political risk insurance for many developing countries is becoming available at very reasonable rates, and should be considered when putting together a project.

Energy efficiency has two interesting investment risk aspects that are often overlooked. In the developing and transition countries, the potential to achieve large technical efficiencies is much higher than in developed countries, with relatively less investment. This effect means the potential energy efficiency cash flows and operating cost reductions will generally be significantly higher in practice than are guaranteed in the performance contract. This acts as a buffer of risk for both the ESCO and the customer.

Second, the nature of an energy services contract is that the ESCO generally will have an extended presence on the site, and may be phasing in investments to achieve the contracted efficiency gains, usually over several years. This means there will be an increasing familiarity with the site, and investments can be adjusted or modified based on the gained operating experience. At the same time, the ESCO will develop closer relationships with the customer, will be better equipped to understand the customers continuing needs, and can adjust the energy management strategy to meet those needs. A solid working relationship with the customer, based on delivering mutual benefits will always, in the end, be the best risk management for the investments. Investments may need to be phased to have the early measures give the greatest early efficiency gains (and hence ESCO cash flows).

EXPECTATIONS OF THE OTHER "BANKS"

Banks are viewed as the main investors, but all too frequently a key investment barrier is closer to home. Often, an ESCO is a unit of a larger

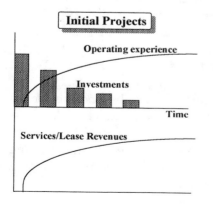

❑ **Initial investments should be set to capture quick-win efficiency and cash flow gains**

❑ **Adjust subsequent investments based on operating experience**

❑ **Adjust subsequent investments based on reliability of cash flows from service and/or lease revenues**

❑ **Over time, pipeline transactions portfolio will reduce risks**

❑ **Secure lien on energy system operation**

Figure 17-5. Phased Investments Minimize Risk

company trying to diversify. In the past, this has been the controls, lighting, motor, etc., manufacturers. As the energy market deregulates, traditional utilities have entered the game. As will be clear by now, these parent companies are key in being part of the investment plan, providing corporate equity, debt and guarantees. ESCO teams sometimes fail to sell this "Bank" as thoroughly as they sell to the real Banks.

EXPECTATIONS OF THE ESCO FROM THE BANKS

Whichever investor is being courted, the potential investor will expect the ESCO to:

- present opportunities that give acceptable returns;
- structure contracts clearly;
- define cash flows;
- have realistic resources to stay the course in the country selected;
- identify pipelines, not pilot projects; and
- have necessary commercial commitments.

Well prepared and properly supported investments plans in the developing and transition economies will generally receive favorable audience and a high probability of successful financing.

The ESCO, on its side, should expect to be able to work with qualified investment officers, who understand the special needs of energy efficiency financing. The Energy Efficiency Financing Team at the European Bank for Reconstruction and Development, with its depth of specialized expertise, provides a model answer to part of this need. The Environmental Projects Unit at the International Finance Corporation serves to strengthen the IFC's efficiency financing skills.

However, the depth of skills and energy efficiency understanding in the banking community is still developing; so the ESCO must be prepared to take some disappointments and to take on the role of evangelist from time to time.

Clearly, the financing of energy efficiency will require substantial amounts of capital, much of which must come from the commercial banking community. Over time, this financing must be substantially sourced from local commercial banks. Today, due to lack of experience in efficiency financing and to competing demands for capital, their participation is small. In many cases these local banks are allied to global players, some of whom are actively entering the efficiency market. It is to be hoped this expertise will be transferred to their local partners or affiliates in the developing and transforming economies. In the final analysis, cost-effective, local, commercial financing will be a key factor in creating widespread implementation.

CONCLUSIONS

The developing world represents a huge potential market for energy efficiency services, for the ESCO prepared to arrange fully capitalized integrated solutions. The international financing institutions and the commercial banks have a wealth of knowledge and available investment potential for well prepared projects. With the right project and business preparation, the risks are acceptable and can be managed.

The potential benefits of energy services to both the customers and the ESCOs are highly attractive and attainable.

CLOSING COMMENT

When Shirley Hansen's first book on performance contracting was published, EPC was seen as an exotic, somewhat dubious, market mechanism. Some years later, this image is not entirely dispelled, but the understanding of the potential benefits of widespread private sector investment in improving energy efficiency has spread around the world. In those same short years, the banking industry has gradually developed a set of financing tools suited to the energy services market. The world's utilities are going through the largest restructuring in their history, creating completely new market conditions and relationships. We are finally on the exciting road to the mobilization of billions of dollars of investments in the rational use of energy—profitably!

Glossary of Terms and Acronyms

Terms

BASELINE - Annually adjusted base year

BASEYEAR (historical consumption) - A recent year's, or average of years' energy consumption and operating conditions affecting consumption, used as a reference base to compute savings attributable to the energy conservation measures being financed.

CHAUFFAGE - Combined supply and demand efficiency services on a guaranteed basis; e.g., conditioned at a cost per square foot, or energy use per unit(s) of production.

COMMISSIONING - The performance verification, fine tuning, maintenance protocols, etc., associated with the new construction and/or major renovation of a building.

COST OF DELAY - The net loss from energy efficiency work not performed.

COST-BASE (applied to savings-based agreements) - The total cost of the equipment and related services provided to the customer plus a percentage fee to cover the energy service company's operating margin and indirect costs.

COST-BASED CONTRACT (or paid from savings contract) - A variable term based financing agreement in which a cap is placed on the total amount of payments to the financing firm. The cap is reached when the present value of all cumulative payments to the firm equals the cost-base plus a **pre-determined profit percentage**.

DEMAND SIDE MANAGEMENT - The efficient management of energy use on the demand (customer) side of the meter.

ENERGY PERFORMANCE CONTRACTING -Synonymous with the term performance contracting, more widely used in Europe.

ENERGY SAVINGS PERFORMANCE CONTRACT - A type of performance contract used within US federal agencies.

ENERGY SERVICE COMPANY (ESCO) - A firm which provides energy management services including an engineering evaluation of the building; installation of energy-saving equipment and maintenance procedures; arranges financing; and provides an agreed upon comfort level for a fee usually guaranteed not to be exceed the building's avoided energy costs.

ENERGY SERVICE PROVIDER - An energy service company or registered professionals, such as architectural and engineering firms, that provide the expertise, services, equipment, and financing without performance contracting guarantees.

GUARANTEED SAVINGS - Agreement, or contract clause, whereby a savings-based financing firm will guarantee that a piece of equipment, or package of energy efficiency measures, will achieve a minimum amount of savings over a contract period, or the firm will refund the difference between the actual and guaranteed savings (or otherwise compensate the customer).

HURDLE RATE - The point at which it becomes financially beneficial to the customer to use outside funds; usually based on present rate of interest earned on internal funds and related conditions.

INSTALLMENT/PURCHASE - An arrangement whereby the purchaser makes payments at regular intervals until the cost of the equipment has been satisfied. Unlike lease/purchase, ownership is predetermined and the contract may exceed a fiscal year without automatic renewal provisions. (Sometimes used interchangeably with the term "municipal leasing."; however, *municipal leasing* that the lessee be a tax-exempt entity.)

INTERNAL FINANCING - Financing with money available or retained by the organization without securing outside revenues.

INTERNAL RATE OF RETURN - The discount rate that discounts an investment's expected net cash flow to a net present value of zero.

LEASE - An agreement to make regular payments to a lessor (owner) over a set period of time in exchange for the use of a building or equipment.

LEASE PURCHASE (closed-end lease) - An arrangement whereby a lessee commits to making payments for the use of buildings or equipment for a set period of time. The lessee has the right to buy the property for a price agreed upon in advance, frequently a nominal figure.

LESSEE - The user of a leased asset who pays the lessor for the usage right.

LESSOR - The owner of a leased asset.

LOAD MANAGEMENT - Actions taken to reduce peak demand through load shedding and load shifting.

LOAD PROFILE - The average electric demand divided by the peak demand.

MINIMUM ACCEPTABLE RATE OF RETURN - The lowest rate of return that an investment can be expected to earn and still be acceptable; same as the investment's cost of capital.

NET PRESENT VALUE (NPV) (of energy savings) - The value in today's dollars (year zero) of future energy savings less all project contracting, financing, and operating costs. This measure takes into account the "time value of money."

OPEN-ENDED LEASE - A lease where there is no fixed price purchase option at the conclusion of the lease period. (Lease may indicate "purchase at fair market value", but no dollar amount is specified.)

OPERATING LEASE - A lease that does not meet capital lease criteria and is cancelable by the lessee at any time upon due notice to the lessor. Also refers to a short-term lease that is cancelable by the lessor or lessee upon due notice to the other party.

PAYBACK PERIOD - The amount of time required for an asset to generate enough net positive cash flow to cover the initial outlay for that asset.

PERFORMANCE CONTRACT - A contract with payment based on performance; usually a guarantee that costs will not exceed projected savings. (Also see savings-based agreement.)

POSITIVE CASH FLOW LEASE - A closed-end lease (lease/purchase) in which payments made to the lessor are kept below the level of savings derived from the leased equipment (for each leased payment, a specified time period, or the total lease period.)

POWER MARKETING - Managing products and services associated with electrical power; their delivery for fixed or variable prices without a given franchise area.

PRESENT VALUE - The value of money at a given date (current or today's dollars) that will be paid or received in future periods.

PRIME RATE - Interest rate charged by banks on short-term loans to large low-risk businesses.

PROJECTED SAVINGS (in a savings based financing agreement) - Refers to the expected annual dollar value of the reduced energy consumption due to implementing conservation measures.

RATE OF RETURN - The interest rate earned on an investment; may be the actual rate or expected rate.

RE-REGULATION - A realistic way to look at the "deregulation" of the utility industry.

RISK SHEDDING - Procedures used to assign risks to another party.

SALE AND LEASEBACK - An arrangement under which the user of the asset sells the asset and then leases it back from the purchaser.

SALVAGE VALUE (residual value) - The money that remains in an asset after it has been held/used for a period of time.

SAVINGS-BASED AGREEMENT (OR CONTRACT) - Arrangements by which energy service companies agree to provide services and energy efficiency improvements in a client's building or industrial process with the repayment to come from savings generated by the improvements.

SAVINGS-BASED FORMULA - The formula (calculation of savings procedure) specified in the contract which is used to determine savings. Usually involves four steps: (1) determine actual historical usage and contributing operating conditions to form a base year; (2) adjust base year (usually annually) actual usage for variations (temperature, occupancy, etc.); to form a baseline; (3) subtract actual usage from adjusted baseline consumption; and (4) calculate savings by multiplying the units of energy saved by the current cost per unit. Calculations for electrical demand savings are considered part of the formula but computed separately.

SELF-FUNDING - A project or program financed through savings achieved by project actions or measures taken.

SENSITIVITY ANALYSIS - Analysis of the effect on a project's cash flow (or profitability) of possible changes in factors which affect the project (e.g., level of predicted savings, energy price escalation, etc.).

STRANDED BENEFITS - societal, environmental and economic benefits provided by utilities voluntarily or by order, which are or will be lost when utilities are restructured and will operate in a competitive environment.

STRANDED COSTS - debts incurred to construct generating capacity which have not been fully retired.

SUPPLY SIDE MANAGEMENT - the efficient management of electrical generation, transmission and distribution to the customer's meter.

Acronyms and Abbreviations

ADB   Asian Development Bank

AID   U.S. Agency for International Development

A&E   architectural and engineering services, or firm

ACEEE   American Council for an Energy-Efficient Economy

AEE   Association of Energy Engineers

APP   adjusted payback period

ASHRAE   American Society of Heating, Refrigerating and Air-Conditioning Engineers

BAFO   best and final offer; (also B&F)

BAS   Building automation systems

Btu   British thermal unit

CFC   chlorofluorocarbon

cfm   cubic feet per minute

CMMS   computer based maintenance management system

COD   cost of delay

DD   degree days (HDD for heating degree days; CDD for cooling degree days)

DOD   U.S. Department of Defense

DOE   U.S. Department of Energy

DSM   demand-side management

EBRD   European Bank for Reconstruction and Development

ECI   energy cost index

ECM   energy conservation measure

EPC   energy performance contracting

EEI   Edison Electric Institute

EMS   energy management system; or energy management control system (EMCS)

EPA   U.S. Environmental Protection Agency

EPACT   Energy Policy Act, U.S. 1992

EPRI   Electric Power Research Institute

ERAM   electric rate adjustment mechanism

ESCO   energy service company

EUI   energy utilization index

FAR   Federal Acquisition Regulations

FEMP   Federal Energy Management Program, (U.S. Department of Energy)

FMS   facilities management system

HBI   Healthy Buildings International, Inc.

HUD   U.S. Department of Housing and Urban Development

HVAC   heating ventilating and air-conditioning system

IAQ   indoor air quality

ICP   Institutional Conservation Program, U.S. Department of Energy

IDB   Inter-American Development Bank

IGA   investment grade audit

IPMVP   International Performance Measurement and Verification Protocol (replaces NEMVP and BMVP)

IRP   integrated resource planning

kW   kilowatt

kWh   kilowatt hours

LCC   life-cycle costing

M&V   measurement and verification

MBtu   thousand Btu

MCF   thousand cubic feet

MDB   multilateral development bank

MMBtu   million Btu

NAESCO National Association of Energy Service Companies

NGO   Non-governmental organizations; typically non-profit, may have some government sanction

NIOSH   National Institute of Occupational Safety & Health, U.S. Department of Health & Human Services

NOAA   National Oceanic and Atmospheric Administration

OECD   Organization for Economic Co-operation and Development

OEM   original equipment manufacturer

O&M   operations and maintenance

OTA   Office of Technology Assessment, Congress of the United States

PC   performance contracting

PDL   portable data loggers

PM   preventive maintenance

PSC   public service commission

PUC   public utility commission

PUHCA   Public Utility Holding Company Act

PURPA   Public Utility Regulatory Policies Act

RFP   request for proposals

RFQ   request for qualifications

ROI   return on investment

RTP   real time pricing

SBS   sick building syndrome

SCF   simplified cash flow

SPP   simple payback period

SSM   supply-side management

TOD   time of day

TOU   time of use

TFC   termination for convenience

TPF   third-party financing

TRC   total resource cost

UDI   Utility Data Institute

UDR   universal data recorders

VOC   volatile organic compound

Appendix A

MODEL LANGUAGE FOR
REQUEST FOR QUALIFICATIONS AND
PLANNING AGREEMENT

The Planning Agreement and RFQ language presented in this appendix does not purport to cover all conditions or eventualities that may arise. It is intended only as a model document that must be modified to meet specific concerns, circumstances and conditions unique to a given facility or complex.

The request for qualifications (RFQ) appearing on the following pages offers suggested language for securing energy services and financing. The RFQ can also be modified to become a request for proposals (RFP) by including the technical provisions shown at the end of the appendix.

BOARD OF EDUCATION OF ALPHA BETA CITY

REQUEST FOR QUALIFICATIONS: ENERGY SERVICES

SCHEDULE OF EVENTS

REQUEST FOR PROPOSALS	XXXXXXX, 1992
PRE-PROPOSAL CONFERENCE: Date:	XXXXXXX, 1998 Time: 2:00 p.m.
LOCATION:	Board of Education Alpha Beta City, Anywhere 21000
PROPOSAL DEADLINE:	XXXXXXX, 1999 2:00 p.m. local time

SUBMIT TO: Mr. Administrator,
                                                  Director of Purchasing
                                                       123 Main Street
                                          Alpha Beta City, Maryland 21000

PROPOSAL OPENING: XXXXXXX, 1999

SELECTION OF FIRM: XXXXXXX, 1999

BOARD OF EDUCATION OF ALPHA BETA CITY

REQUEST FOR QUALIFICATIONS: ENERGY SERVICES

I.   PURPOSE AND SCOPE

The Board of Education of Alpha Beta City (hereinafter referred to as the "Board" or "Owner") and by reference the Alpha Beta City school system (hereinafter referred to as "ABC") is a public school system interested in receiving proposals from qualified energy services companies (hereinafter referred to as ESCO, firm, proposer, contractor) for comprehensive energy management services the purpose of providing.

Proposals are requested from firms capable of providing equipment and/or services and supporting equipment necessary to achieve cost-effective energy efficiency, reduce the district's operating costs and to serve other district facility needs.

Evaluation procedures will consider not only the performance contracting experience of the firm and its assigned personnel, but will weigh the technical feasibility, economic viability, soundness of project financing arrangements, and the estimated net financial benefit to ABC.

The district intends to award a negotiated contract to one firm to provide the services and equipment under terms and conditions ABC considers to be most favorable among those offered.

A.   SCOPE OF WORK

The company selected as a result of the combined qualification and technical evaluation will be expected to:

1.   Provide comprehensive energy management services for all ABC facilities, including but not limited to:

   •   an investment grade energy audit, comprehensive in scope
   •   the design, selection and installation of equipment systems, and modifications to improve energy efficiency without sacrificing comfort or existing equipment performance or reliability;
   •   the training of district's operations and maintenance personnel in energy efficient practices;
   •   the maintenance and service of the installed measures;
   •   24-hour monitoring and associated field support; and
   •   financing for the transaction.

2.   Assure that any payments for energy efficient improvements or services related thereto are contingent on energy savings; so the Board will not have any financial obligation that exceeds the district's share of the avoided utility costs.

   Any costs or obligations incumbent on the board that will not be covered by guaranteed savings must be explicitly stated in the proposal.

3.   ABC is also interested in capital improvement work, which may not meet the standards for cost-effective energy conservation measures. The district does not wish to incur any negative cash flow in order to accomplish this work. The proposer is asked to suggest any additional measures that could be performed that fits these conditions.

4.   (Optional) The district has the following equipment/modification needs [chiller, roofing, etc.], which it recognizes may not be covered by savings, but requests the proposer to offer procedures for incorporating these measures into the scope of work and to suggest

financing arrangements that might be made to cover costs in excess of savings.

II.   FACILITIES

The ABC buildings for which energy efficiency services are requested are listed in Attachment A. These facilities occupy approximately XXXXXX square feet and have an annual utility bill of $XXXXXX. Attachment A offers pertinent utility data and information on the facilities in order to provide the ESCO information upon which to judge the economic viability of the project.

ESCOs will be asked to consider all potentially cost-effective energy efficiency improvements in these facilities.

III.   RFQ PROCEDURES

A.   ISSUANCE, CONTRACTS, QUERIES

This RFQ is issued by the Board of Education of Alpha Beta City. The following persons should be contacted for additional information regarding this RFQ.

Alpha Beta City school system administration, governance, or financing:

_____
_____
_____
() ____ - _____

ABC physical plant and/or energy data:

_____
_____
_____
() ____ - _____

Proposal procedures:

<u>   </u>

<u>   </u>

<u>   </u>

() ___ - _____

[District personnel or consultant if one is involved.]

Verbal communication will be offered as a matter of clarification; however, such communication by employees or representatives of ABC school district concerning the RFQ shall not be binding on the district and shall in no way excuse the competitor of obligations as set forth in this RFQ.

Any inquiries received in writing on or before eight (8) working days prior to the deadline noted in Section III. D., wherein a response is deemed valuable to the process, the question(s) and response(s) will be sent to all ESCOs of record.

B.   SUBMISSION REQUIREMENTS

Proposers should submit an original and eight (8) copies of their proposal. Each proposal should have a Qualifications Section and a Technical Section. The Qualifications Section should be limited in length to thirty (30) pages, exclusive of the Appendices and Attachments as described in Section V, B.

The "Project Summary Sheet" in the original proposal must be signed by an official with authority to bind the proposer contractually. The name and title of the individual signing the proposal should be typed immediately below the signature.

C.   PREPARATION OF PROPOSALS

Proposals must be in correct format and complete. Elaborate proposals and brochures are not desired. Clarity and concise, orderly treatment are important. ESCOs must address each item in the order in which it appears in Section V, "Proposal Format, Content and Specific Criteria," of this RFQ and note the appropriate section heading being addressed at the top of the respective page.

The ESCO is expected to respond to all items in as much detail as necessary for ABC administration, its representatives and consultants to make a fair evaluation of the ESCO and the proposal for ranking. ESCOs should respond directly to the points raised as concisely as possible.

Proposals, which are incomplete, not properly endorsed, do not follow the requested format, or otherwise are contrary to the guidelines of this RFQ, may be rejected as non-responsive.

D.   DEADLINE FOR PROPOSALS

Proposals must be received on or before 2:00 p.m., XXXXXXX, 1998 at the following address:

ATTN: _____

_____

_____

The Board reserves the right to disqualify proposals received after the time and date specified. Proposals by facsimile or e-mail are not acceptable.

Proposals and all conditions therein shall remain in effect for at least ninety (90) days from proposal submission date.

E.   DISPOSITION OF PROPOSALS

All proposals shall become the property of the Board and will be returned only at the Board's option and the proposer's expense. In any event, one copy of each proposal will be retained for the institution's official files.

F. PROPRIETARY DATA

If a proposal includes any proprietary data or information that the respondent does not want disclosed to the public, such data or information must be specifically identified on each page and will be used by ABC administration, and their consultants solely for the purposes of evaluating proposals and conducting contract negotiations.

All proposals, exclusive of supplemental sheets designated "Proprietary Data," will become a matter of public record once a contract is signed with the selected ESCO.

Each ESCO agrees by submitting a proposal that ABC administration has the right to use any or all ideas or concepts presented in any proposal without restriction and without compensation to proposer thereof.

G. MODIFICATION OR WITHDRAWAL OF PROPOSALS

Any proposal may be withdrawn or modified by written request of the proposer provided such request is received by the Board by the deadline and at the address as stipulated in Section III, D. Modifications received after the due time and date will not be allowed.

The district or its representatives reserves the right at any time to request clarification from any or all contractors submitting a proposal.

H. PRE-PROPOSAL CONFERENCE

On XXXXXXX, 1998 at 2:00 p.m., the Board of Education of Alpha Beta City will hold a Pre-Proposal Conference in the following location:

_____

_____

_____

The ABC school administration, representatives and its consultant will be present to answer questions regarding the RFQ procedures and the overall project. Floor plans, available as-builts and other pertinent information will be made available at the conference. Those attending the conference will be given an opportunity to walk through three representative facilities.

Attendance is not required and will not be a factor in evaluating proposals. Printed information provided at the conference will be mailed to prospective proposers upon request.

ESCOs interested in attending the pre-proposal conference should contact _____ at (___) ___-____ [phone number] no later than XXXXXX, 1998.

I.   RIGHT TO REJECT

This RFQ does not commit the Board to award a contract or to pay costs incurred in preparation of a bid in response to this request. The school district reserves the right to accept or reject in part or in its entirety, any bid as a result of this RFQ.

J.   COST OF PROPOSAL PREPARATION

The cost of preparing a response to this RFQ is not reimbursable to proposers or the selected contractor.

K.   CONTRACT REQUIREMENTS

Standard construction contract provisions, such as OSHA laws, conditions of site, acceptance, permits, inspection provisions, cooperation with site personnel, indemnity, liability insurance, workmen's compensation, blanket fidelity and the like will be part of the contract terms.

The following conditions will also be incorporated in the contract.

1.   Taxes

The district will forthwith pay all taxes lawfully imposed upon it with respect to the equipment. The ESCO will forthwith pay all taxes imposed upon it with respect to the equipment.

By this section, the district makes no representation whatsoever as to the liability or exemption from liability of the ESCO to any tax imposed by any government entity.

2.   Choice of Law

The agreement shall be governed in all respects by the laws of the State of XXXXXX.

3.   Performance Bond

The Board may require the submission of a performance bond by the successful proposer upon agreement of the measures to be implemented, equal to eighty percent (80%) of the listed purchase price of the equipment. The bond will then remain in effect and be subject to forfeiture for non-performance until the equipment is accepted by the district.

4.   Systems Integration

A proposal will not be acceptable unless the proposer expressly indicates an intention to be responsible for systems integration, testing and maintenance of all installed hardware and systems level software. Integration of newly installed equipment and controls with existing equipment is considered a critical aspect of implementation.

5.   Negotiations

The district reserves the right to negotiate with the successful proposer any additional terms and conditions, which may be necessary or appropriate to the accomplishment of the purpose and scope of this RFQ.

6.   Sample Contract

ESCOs are required to attach to their proposals a recently executed contract with a non-profit institution, preferably a public school, for work similar to that requested herein.

7.   Upgrade Assumptions

It should not be assumed when developing the proposal that the district will be able to upgrade or make modifications to existing building equipment. The contractor should include in his proposal all costs to modify, upgrade or fine-tune any building equipment which the contractor feels is necessary to achieve the projected savings.

8.   Representative Investment Grade Audit

Under separate cover, the proposer will submit an investment grade audit (IGA) which the ESCO has performed on a facility(ies) similar to ABC facilities. By its submission, the proposer attests that the sample IGA is representative of the comprehensiveness, technological sophistication, formulas, calculations and detail it proposes to use under this scope of work.

The district reserves the right to make this sample IGA a part of the contract by reference as a standard of practice.

Each ESCO must state that its contract with the Board will contain the information specified in this section.

L.   PROPOSAL EVALUATION AND SELECTION PROCEDURES

All proposals will be evaluated by an ABC district committee and its representatives and consultants. The proposals will be evaluated according to the criteria listed in Section IV and delineated further in Section V.

The evaluation committee will make a recommendation to the Board for their approval. Upon approval, a letter of intent will be sent to the selected ESCO. The selected firm and those representing the Board will then seek to negotiate a satisfactory contract within sixty (60) days. If the parties fail to agree on terms of a contract within the (60) day period, the Board reserves the right to terminate all negotiations and either select one of the other finalists or issue a new RFQ.

IV. SELECTION CRITERIA

Evaluation will be made according to the following weighted criteria:

CRITERIA WEIGHTING

A. Proposal presentation (5)
   - adherence to format requirements
   - completeness and clarity

B. Proposer's Qualifications (40)
   - management plan
   - experience in similar facilities and demonstrated ability
   - personnel qualifications for designated responsibilities and availability for project implementation

C. Technical Quality and Range of Services (20)
   - technical approach
   - comprehensiveness of approach
   - baseline methodology and calculations
   - measurement & verification approach

D. Ability to Implement Project Properly (10)
   - management
   - quality assurance
   - schedule of implementation

E. Financial Considerations (25)
   - net financial benefit to district
   - savings calculations; previous experience in meeting predicted savings
   - penalties for failure to meet agree upon schedule; bonus for early completion.

V.   FORMAT, CONTENT AND SPECIFIC CRITERIA

Proposers will follow the format and content outline presented below and each section must be clearly labeled as to the section being addressed. Numbers on specific criterion are used for organizational purposes only and should not be taken as indicating any relative importance of that criterion.

PROJECT TRANSMITTAL LETTER—a standard cover letter

A.   PROPOSAL PRESENTATION:

Criteria:

1.   clarity, conciseness and completeness of proposal presentation; and
2.   responsiveness to RFP requirements.

B.   PROPOSER'S QUALIFICATIONS:

Management Plan. Describe the proposed organization briefly, noting management responsibility for the following areas:

1.   Financing
2.   Engineering design
3.   Construction and/or installation
4.   Operation and maintenance; training
5.   Measurement & savings verification procedures
6.   Other major activities

Qualifications. Describe your ESCO's: (1) corporate capabilities; (2) number of years firm has been involved in providing energy services and number of energy services contracts entered into; (3) years the firm has been involved in providing energy services to schools; and (4) the financial condition of the firm, including a 10 K for publicly held firms, or an annual report for private or closely held companies.

Also provide information on methods, techniques and equipment used by the ESCO in such matters as design preparation, systems installation, on-site coordination, system operation and monitoring staff training, maintenance and the like.

Demonstrated ability. Provide a brief description of the five most significant recent or current projects of a similar nature conducted by your firm. Include documentation of project approach, management, technical configurations, arrangements, energy savings projections and results achieved, and other pertinent information. Present the information on each project as follows:

1. Client (name, address)
2. Client contact (name, title, phone number)
3. Project title
4. Project description
5. Projected project costs and actual costs.
6. Energy and cost savings projected/achieved
7. Proposed schedule (from _____ to _____) and implementation achieved (_____ to _____)
8. Total project cost $_____

Personnel assigned. Indicate the personnel that will be assigned to this project and their specific project responsibilities. Indicate their qualifications to assume the assigned responsibilities, including degrees, special training, licenses, years of experience, projects where they carried similar responsibilities and any special areas of expertise that will enable them to meet these responsibilities effectively. Indicate the percentage of time each individual will devote to the ABC project during its initial phase. A full resume for each assigned person should be included in Appendix B of the proposal.

Criteria:

1. Firm's background and experience; including direct experience in performance contracting with school districts; quality of references;
2. Documentation of ESCO's financial condition and stability;

3. Proposer's experience and reputation in similar projects to that described in this RFP;
4. Assigned personnel's qualifications; project availability
5. Overall ability to maximize benefits and minimize risks to the institution.

C.   TECHNICAL APPROACH AND RANGE OF SERVICES OFFERED

Base Year Methodology. Describe the methodology typically used by the firm to compute the energy base year. Attach a sample computation from a previous job done by your firm which documents methods, assumptions, and input data used to adjust the base year for annual baseline calculations.

Range of Services. Describe the complete range of energy services being offered by your firm; e.g., auditing, equipment selections and installation, operations and maintenance, measurement and savings verification (M&V) etc.

Discuss the mechanism proposed, which will guarantee the local support services necessary for fulfilling the contract terms. Include any contemplated changes to the physical parameters in the facilities; e.g., temperature, lighting levels, humidity and ventilation.

Specify any exceptions or waivers to the contemplated scope of work as set forth herein.

Criteria:
1. Quality of technical analysis and recommendations;
2. Adequacy of services or equipment to accomplish scope of work;
3. Method of selection of energy efficiency equipment;
4. Monitoring of energy usage;
5. Technical field support; emergency response provisions;
6. Reporting procedures;
7. Maintenance on installed equipment; on any additional equipment;
8. Measurement and verification procedures
9. Training; and
10. Other services.

D.   ABILITY TO IMPLEMENT PROJECT PROPERLY

Management. Describe the specific responsibilities, lines of communication, and authority of the management structure. Note interfaces with the ABC district personnel.

Indicate typical procedures for identifying problems and preventing schedule slippages and cost overruns.

Quality assurance. Provide a plan for assuring quality of workmanship and provision of services. The plan should indicate who will review work in progress and work products, the schedule for reviews, how top management will be kept informed, and how corrective action will be identified, implemented and reviewed.

Implementation schedule. The proposer's projected implementation schedule of the tasks and responsibilities outlined in the proposal should be included in the proposal as part of this subsection. Any time required to secure financing, start up date, and rate of installation should be included.

Criteria:

1.   Plan to provide effective management procedures and quality assurance;

2.   Required time frame for ESCO to obtain financing and initiate the project; and

3.   Implementation schedule.

E.   FINANCIAL CONSIDERATIONS

Financial arrangements. Describe the financial arrangements you propose to fund the cost-effective energy conservation measures you recommend. If an outside funding source is used, discuss the general nature of investors with which you have had experience and the procedures you would expect to pursue.

Note any previous experience with financial arrangements of this type if not covered in Section V. B. Also note any tax or legal issues or uncertainties known to you which might affect ABC's cost savings.

Baseline adjustments. Include an explanation of how the base year will be adjusted to reflect changes in weather, occupancy and use; e.g., addition or removal of energy-consuming equipment, changes in the hours or level of occupancy, etc.

Savings calculations. Clearly show calculation procedures relative to quantity consumed, include procedures to share savings related to demand and time of day cost adjustments.

Measurement and savings verification. Describe the procedure that will be used to measure actual energy cost savings and the value of such savings attributable to the contracted services.

Share of savings. Propose a method of allocating the value of any energy savings above the guarantee between ESCO and the institution. Clearly state the number of years that savings will be shared and the proportional allocations of savings each year. Explain any assumptions used.

Sample calculations. Present sample calculations for a seven-year project with $2,500,000 equipment acquisition and installation costs (not total project cost) with a projected payback of three years. Include maintenance on the installed equipment and other proposed services. (Label Option A.)

Using the same parameters set forth in the above paragraph, describe the financial arrangements that might be used to provide the capital improvement items mentioned in Section I, B, 3. (Label sample calculations Option B.)

Penalties and Bonuses. The district will look with favor on ESCOs who state their intentions to comply with a penalties and bonuses provision.

The Cost of Delay (Cod) per day based on projected savings will be calculated. A bonus will be paid of 90 percent of the daily Cod pro rata for each day the project is completed ahead of the contracted schedule. A penalty at 100 percent pro rata will be charged for every day the project exceeds the contracted schedule unless the delay can clearly be attributed to the actions or inaction of the ABC school system or to force majeure.

Buyout, termination, and contract continuation. Explain the conditions under which this contract might be continued, extended, or amended beyond the contract years. Describe how the equipment and servicing responsibilities will be affected at the conclusion of the contract. Should it be a factor in the suggested financing approach, describe how the value of the equipment will be calculated upon contract expiration. Provide a buy-out schedule for Option A and Option B as described under Sample Calculations above.

In the event of contract termination, describe provisions for assuring that all affected district facilities will be restored to conditions at contract origination, or better, related to any work rendered under contract.

Contract conditions. State the firm's willingness to comply with the contract requirements discussed in Section III. Note any exceptions to this compliance and the rationale for exclusion.

Submit a sample contract which was recently executed with a similar institution.

Criteria:

1. Potential net economic benefit as evidenced in sample material and calculations;
2. Innovative energy financing procedures;
3. Liability and casualty tax insurance on the equipment and personnel involved in providing the service;
4. Source(s) of financing;
5. Protection against poor performance;
6. Calculation of savings — procedures for addressing such variables as changes in building use, utility rates, weather fluctuations;
7. How the baseline is adjusted; how energy and consumption data is derived;
8. Compliance with penalties and bonuses provision;
9. Value of extended services;

10. Methods used to determine amount of ESCO's compensation;
11. Termination and buyout provisions;
12. How equipment is valued at end of contract; and
13. Contract renewal options.

APPENDIX A.   **RESUMES OF ASSIGNED PERSONNEL** (RE-QUIRED)

APPENDIX B.   **SAMPLE CONTRACT** (REQUIRED)

APPENDIX C.   **ANY EXTENDED DESCRIPTION OF FIRM'S QUALIFICATION AND EXPERIENCE GERMANE TO THE PROPOSED WORK** (OPTIONAL)

ATTACHMENTS

SUPPLEMENT: **SAMPLE INVESTMENT GRADE ENERGY AUDIT** (REQUIRED)

PROPRIETARY INFORMATION (OPTIONAL)

REQUEST FOR PROPOSALS

The difference between a RFQ and a request for proposals (RFP) procedure usually rests on greater emphasis on precise technical detail, usually a test investment grade audit (IGA). The RFP may be used as the second phase in a two phase selection process. The two phase procedure is generally designed to pre-qualify bidders so that more exacting requirements are only imposed on a short list of bidders.

A RFP procedure is not recommended unless the project is very large, very complex, or unique.

The RFQ presented above can be converted to a request for proposals (RFP) by adding reference to the test IGA and/or a two phase procedure. Instructions to potential proposer's as to the purpose of the two phase process; i.e., a test audit, and exactly what will be expected in the second phase. This information will help the ESCO decide whether or not to bid.

Language eliciting technical competence should set the auditing and financial parameters.

Should the administration decide they wish to have a RFP procedure in order to assess the final bidders' abilities to approach unique problems through a test audit on given portion of the facilities, language similar to the following could be inserted in the above document. The language shown in capital letters is model language; lower case is explanatory language.

In the RFQ, insert:

TWO PHASE PROCEDURE:

THIS REQUEST FOR QUALIFICATIONS (RFQ) CONSTITUTES THE FIRST PHASE OF A TWO PHASE SELECTION PROCEDURE. THE INTENT OF PHASE 1 IS TO PRE-QUALIFY BIDDERS FOR THE MORE TECHNICAL REQUEST FOR PROPOSAL BY SELECTING _____ [A number may be specified if the intent is to narrow the number of firms for phase 2.] ENERGY SERVICE COMPANIES, WHICH APPEAR TO BE MOST QUALIFIED TO DO THE WORK AS REQUESTED IN THIS RFQ.

SUCCESSFUL PROPOSERS FOR THE FIRST PHASE WILL BE ASKED TO SUBMIT A PROPOSAL IN RESPONSE TO A PHASE 2 TECHNICAL REQUEST FOR PROPOSAL (RFP). PHASE 2 WILL REQUIRE A FULL ON-SITE AUDIT OF TWO FACILITIES WITH APPROPRIATE DOCUMENTATION AND FINANCIAL CALCULATIONS. PHASE 2 EVALUATION PROCEDURES WILL NOT ONLY CONSIDER THE EXPERIENCE OF THE FIRM AND ITS ASSIGNED PERSONNEL, BUT WILL WEIGH THE TECHNICAL FEASIBILITY, ECONOMIC VIABILITY, SOUNDNESS OF PROJECT FINANCING ARRANGEMENTS, AND THE ESTIMATED NET FINANCIAL BENEFIT TO OUR ORGANIZATION. THE _____ [organization] INTENDS TO AWARD A NEGOTIATED CONTRACT TO ONE FIRM TO PROVIDE THE EQUIPMENT AND SERVICES UNDER TERMS AND CONDITIONS _____ [organization] CONSIDERS TO BE MOST FAVORABLE AMONG THOSE OFFERED.

In the RFP, insert:

INVESTMENT GRADE AUDITS (IGAs)

THE SUCCESSFUL CONTRACTOR WILL BE REQUIRED TO DO IGAs FOR EACH OF THE BUILDINGS IDENTIFIED IN THE RFP. THE PURPOSE OF THE RFP IS TO ASCERTAIN THE ESCO'S TECHNICAL EXPERTISE, AUDIT METHODOLOGY, ECONOMIC VIABILITY AND THE POTENTIAL NET FINANCIAL BENEFIT TO _____ [organization].

THE RFP WILL PROVIDE A BRIEF DESCRIPTION OF ANTICIPATED EXTENT OF SUCH AN AUDIT; INCLUDING THE LENGTH OF THE PAYBACK PERIOD, WHICH WILL BE AT LEAST THREE YEARS, THAT PROPOSER WILL USE AS A CEILING TO GOVERN MEASURES TO BE RECOMMENDED. ANY EXPECTED LIMITATIONS ON MEASURES TO BE CONSIDERED, NOT EXCLUDED BY LENGTH OF THE PAYBACK, MUST BE NOTED. THE IGA DESCRIPTION SHOULD BE REFLECTED IN TEST AUDIT PROCEDURES AND THE AUDIT REPORT SHOULD BE REFERENCED AS APPROPRIATE.

TEST AUDIT

BIDDERS WILL BE REQUIRED TO SUBMIT A SAMPLE AUDIT PROCEDURE AND FINANCIAL CALCULATIONS. AN IGA WILL BE CONDUCTED AT _____ [name of facility] AT _____ [address] AND SUBMITTED, AS A SEPARATE DOCUMENT. THE FINDINGS, RECOMMENDATIONS AND CALCULATIONS FOR THIS SITE WILL REPRESENT A SAMPLE OF THE FIRM'S PROPOSED AUDIT WORK. APPLICATION OF ALL PROPOSED SERVICES APPROPRIATE TO AN INDIVIDUAL FACILITY SHOULD BE DESCRIBED.

FINANCIAL CALCULATIONS MAY ASSUME WORK AT THE TEST SITE IS PART OF _____ [X number of buildings, or all the facilities]; ALL OTHER PROCEDURES SHOULD BE SITE-SPECIFIC.

BIDDERS MUST USE THE FOLLOWING FINANCIAL ASSUMPTIONS FOR ALL CALCULATIONS: ... [see RFQ, III, i]

TECHNICAL SELECTION CRITERIA

COMPREHENSIVENESS OF PROPOSED AUDITS
- ANY LIMITATIONS ON MEASURE TO BE CONSIDERED
- LONGEST INDIVIDUAL PAYBACK
- LONGEST COMBINED PAYBACK

CLARITY OF METHODOLOGY AND SAMPLE CALCULATIONS

METHOD OF SELECTION OF ENERGY EFFICIENT EQUIPMENT

RANGE OF ENERGY CONSERVATION OPPORTUNITIES IDENTI-
FIED; NEW TECHNOLOGIES

INTERFACE OF RECOMMENDED EQUIPMENT TO EXISTING
EQUIPMENT

ADEQUACY OF EQUIPMENT OR SERVICES TO ACCOMPLISH
SCOPE OF WORK

APPROPRIATENESS OF SERVICES OFFERED AS EVIDENCED BY
NEEDS CITED IN IGA.

QUALITY OF TEST SITE(S) REPORT

FINANCIAL CONSIDERATIONS

CALCULATIONS OF SAVINGS—PROCEDURES FOR ADDRESSING
SUCH VARIABLES AS CHANGES IN BUILDING USE, UTILITY
RATES, WEATHER FLUCTUATIONS

PROJECTED LEVEL OF TOTAL ENERGY SAVINGS

OTHER MODIFICATIONS

In converting the RFQ to an RFP, the document should be carefully
reviewed for any cosmetic changes needed to make the solicitation con-

sistent throughout. Other procedural changes, such as the time specified in the deadlines, should consider the longer time period required for an ESCO to do a test audit.

Whatever process is used, the key to effective solicitation procedures is to ask for only the information that will enable the administration to effectively judge the proposers' qualifications and competence to meet the organization's identified needs as reflected in the criteria.

PERFORMANCE CONTRACTING
GENERIC PLANNING AGREEMENT

_____

Customer Name

_____

Address or Location of Premises

_____

City   State   Zip

_____[ESCO] and the customer named above agree as follows:

1. Energy and Operational Assessment

ESCO agrees to undertake a detailed evaluation study of the CUSTOMER'S Premises identified above to assess energy consumption and operational characteristics of the Premises and to identify the energy efficiency measures, procedures and other energy-related services that could be provided by ESCO in order to reduce the CUSTOMER'S energy consumption and operating costs on the Premises.

2. Objectives

CUSTOMER agrees to provide its complete cooperation in the conduct and completion of the study. ESCO will provide to the CUSTOMER a written report within 60 days of the effective date of this Agreement. The report will meet the following objectives:

(a)   a list of specific energy efficiency measures that ESCO proposes to install with estimated acquisition and installation costs;

(b)   a description of the operating and maintenance procedures that ESCO believes can reduce energy consumption and operating costs at the Premises; and

(c) an estimate of the energy and operations costs that will be saved by the services equipment and procedures recommended in the report.

3. Records and Data

CUSTOMER will furnish to ESCO upon its request, accurate and complete data concerning energy usage and operational expenditures for the Premises needed for the energy and operational assessment, including the following data for the most recent two years from the effective date of this Agreement:

- actual utility bills supplied by the utility;

- other relevant utility records;

- descriptions of all energy-consuming or energy-saving equipment used on the Premises;

- descriptions of any recent changes in the building structure or its energy consuming systems, including heating, cooling, lighting;

- occupancy and usage information;

- descriptions of energy management and other relevant operational or maintenance procedures utilized on the Premises;

- summary of expenditures for outsourced maintenance, repairs or replacement on the Premises;

- copies of representative current tenant leases, if any; and

- prior energy audits or studies of the Premises, if any.

4. Preparation of Energy Services Agreement (ESA)

Within 30 days after the submission to ESCO of the report described under paragraph 1 of this Agreement, ESCO will prepare and submit to the CUSTOMER an ESA to implement the energy efficiency measures, procedures, and services identified in the report that could reduce the CUSTOMER'S energy consumption in the Premises.

5. Payment Terms

CUSTOMER agrees to pay to ESCO the sum, not to exceed $ _____, within 60 days after the delivery to the CUSTOMER of the report described under paragraph 1 of this Agreement. However, CUSTOMER will have no obligation to pay this amount if:

(a) ESCO and the CUSTOMER enter into an ESA within 60 days after the delivery to the CUSTOMER of the report described under paragraph 1 of this Performance Contracting Project Development Agreement;

(b) An independent engineer deems that the audit has not adequately assessed the CUSTOMER'S energy efficiency opportunities; or

(c) A majority of the recommended energy efficiency measures cannot be implemented without a negative impact on the CUSTOMER'S processes or comfort conditions.

6. Standards of Practice

The detail and quality of the ESCO's investment grade audit submitted as a representative sample of its work shall serve as a standard of practice for all work under this project.

7. Indemnity

ESCO and the CUSTOMER agree that ESCO shall be responsible only for such injury, loss, or damage caused by the intentional misconduct or the negligent act or omission of ESCO or its agents. ESCO and the CUSTOMER agree to indemnify and to hold each other, including their officers, agents, directors, and employees, harmless from all claims, demands, or suits of any kind, including all legal costs and attorney's fees, resulting from the intentional misconduct of their employees or any negligent act or omission by their employees or agents.

8. Arbitration

If a dispute arises under this Agreement, the parties shall promptly attempt in good faith to resolve the dispute by negotiation. All disputes not resolved by negotiation shall be resolved in accordance with the Commercial Rules of the American Arbitration Association in effect at the time, except as modified herein. All disputes shall be decided by a single arbitrator. The arbitrator shall issue a scheduling order that shall not be modified except by the mutual agreement of the parties. Judgment may be entered upon the award in the highest state or federal court having jurisdiction over the matter. The prevailing party shall recover all costs, including attorney's fees, incurred as a result of the dispute.

9. Assignment

This Agreement cannot be assigned by either party without prior written consent of the other party. This Agreement is the entire Agreement between ESCO and the CUSTOMER and supersedes any prior oral understandings, written agreements, proposals, or other communications between ESCO and the CUSTOMER.

10. Miscellaneous Provisions

Any change or modification to this Agreement will not be effective unless made in writing. This written instrument must specifically indicate that it is an amendment, change, or modification to the Agreement.

ESCO   CUSTOMER
By   By

_____   _____
Signature   Signature

_____   _____
Title   Title

_____   _____
Date   Date

Appendix B

Case Study:
Commissioning the
Flight Test Engineering Building

COMMISSIONING PLANNING

Project Background

The Flight Test Engineering Laboratory Facility is a 100,000 square foot, five story building designed and constructed for engineering laboratories. The types of laboratories include Pressure/Transducer Calibrations, Physical/Environmental & Force Calibration, Photography, Radio Frequency Standards and Hardware and Software Development labs. The new facility was built for the Flight Test organization to support the 777 airplane program. It also supports all new airplane flight testing.

Situation

In 1991, the team of Scott Jackson and Mike Prittie was formed to head up the project team to construct a new engineering laboratory facility to be used by the Flight Test Engineering Group at North Boeing Field. A large office building had just been completed for the same organization and was not functioning as designed resulting in numerous occupant complaints. The root of these complaints were inoperative or malfunctioning systems and/or equipment problems which had not been detected during initial building testing.

Target

The plan would consider all aspects of the building operation including the requirements of each individual lab group. The goal would be a document that verified each operational element of the building systems, the whole building would be tested against the design intent, and that each laboratory would have the needed environment necessary to perform its duties and tasks.

PHASES OF COMMISSIONING

Planning Phase

This is the most important phase of the commissioning process. The commissioning plan was developed by the design team using the requirements developed by each of the user groups. The user group requirements documented the specific performance criteria of each particular space of the building including the temperature, humidity, lighting, air changes, process cooling/heating, power, etc. The design team took this information and developed the building design. The commissioning plan was then developed to verify that the design would meet the user groups requirements and that building systems met design intent. It is during this time that decisions are made as to the level of effort needed to verify design intent and to identify which systems would be formally commissioned. The plan could include HVAC systems, pumps and related equipment, electrical systems, special systems and any other special testing requirements needed to have a complete functional building.

Construction Phase

During this phase normal monitoring of contractor work for design compliance and quality assurance was conducted. It should be emphasized that the level of quality obtained will determine the difficulty of commissioning the facility. Many construction problems can show up in the functional tests as poor performance of overall systems. This may appear to be a design flaw when it is really a construction quality issue and significant time can be spent determining where the problem lies.

Other important aspects of this phase include walk throughs with the maintenance group to identify maintenance accessibility and non conforming construction, review and implementation of QA plans from the contractor and major subcontractors, preparation meetings if needed to clarify design intent, design change documentation control and implementation and other related tasks.

Testing and Move In

During this phase of the commissioning plan, the functional test procedures are implemented. Each individual component and/or system is tested and compared to design intent, branch systems are tested and the overall system performance is evaluated. In the case of the Flight Test Engineering Laboratory we discovered around 250 items that were not functioning per the design documents. Almost all of these items were small by most standards, but taken as a group they would have had a significant impact on overall building function.

Benefits Derived From Commissioning

The realized benefits, of the process have been extraordinary. Upon original start up, no indoor air quality complaints were received. All the major building systems and equipment had a baseline performance documented that establishes future maintenance requirements and operation characteristics. This documentation also provided a background framework for future changes as user needs emerged.

The Boeing Company has a building that receives very high marks from its occupants in its ability to support the customers business plan and has very few complaints from the maintenance crews supporting the building. After over two years of operation, the building still continues to provide a highly reliable environment for occupants with minimal complaints and unscheduled system interruptions.

Other benefits include:

Verification of mechanical and electrical design.

Documented evidence of energy efficient design and operation.

Control systems that operate the building per the design.

A complete manual identifying the baseline operation of the building for reference and use throughout the life of the building.

Low maintenance costs and minimal call backs for warranty work.

Very few comfort complaints from building occupants.

Special process systems continue to support critical test needs.

The development of this process has provided expertise and lessons learned that are being used on other Boeing projects.

KEY POINTS IN THE COMMISSIONING PROCESS

Start the process in the Planning and Requirements Development Phase.

Include the designer, the user requirements (or the user), the commissioning engineer, and the controls contractor in the development of the commissioning plan.

Design the plan specifically for the building.

Develop the commissioning plan to verify energy efficient operation.

Impress upon the construction contractor the need for high construction quality and how this relates to the commissioning process. Note that commissioning is a big win for the various contractors as minimal warranty work is required.

Monitor construction closely to ensure design compliance and to eliminate as many problems as possible with installation quality.

Allow the dedicated time necessary to completely commission the building.

Use the commissioning plan to develop maintenance plan.

Use the commissioning process so that it is a win for all parties involved, including the various contractors.

Case Study: University Physics/Astronomy Building Controls[a]

THE PROCESS

The Physics/Astronomy building, completed in 1994, was the first project to fall under the University of Washington's commissioning program. The 256,000 sq. ft., $45 million project includes laboratories, class-

---

[a]This text is an abridged version of a 1996 Bonneville Power Administration publication titled *Commissioning The Physics/Astronomy Building Control System*, by Phoebe Caner, P.E.

rooms, auditoriums and a department library. Because the university's project manager and the mechanical design consultant were unsure of the value of commissioning, the scope of work was limited to the building automation control system.

Commissioning fell into two phases: point-to-point (PTP) and functional performance testing (FPT). PTP testing included checkout of each control point to make sure that it was properly identified by the system, and that the wiring wasn't reversed. This scope of work, included in the control specifications, was to be executed by the control contractor and observed by the university control shop staff, but the control shop ultimately performed most of the PTP, at a cost to the university of $39,000.

FPT procedures were written, observed and reported by an independent consultant hired directly by the university for $65,000. Because FPTs were added after the construction contract had been signed, the control contractor was paid $45,000 by the commissioning agent to execute the tests.

FPTs went smoothly, largely due to the even-handed style of the commissioning agent, who worked closely with the university staff, contractor and design consultant. The commissioning agent frequently referenced the design documents, so the relationship between the tests and the construction contract were well defined. Before each test, the commissioning agent reviewed the sequence of operations with the control contractor. In this manner, time was saved when the contractor knew in advance that the system would fail a test. Weekly written test reports listing the details of any problems found proved highly useful in moving toward solutions. To allow an objective assessment of the savings from commissioning, the university encouraged the commissioning agent to keep a record of problems corrected in the course of testing.

A few lessons were learned at Physics/Astronomy which may be helpful in developing future commissioning efforts.

- Engineering staff should work closely with operations staff in setting up their role as owner-witnesses.

- The owner witness, whether it is a commissioning agent or in-house staff, should keep a concise detailed list of problems found. The list should be given directly to the owner's project manager or staff engineer each week so they can support contract enforcement.

- The contractor shouldn't be allowed to correct problems during witnessed tests unless it can be done within a few minutes. Otherwise the labor costs for supporting such witnesses will be unreasonably high, and the witnesses may become frustrated by delays.

- Because they involve high labor costs, test procedures which are repeated a large number of times, as for zone level tests, should be carefully defined so that the level of rigor, the need for the test, and the intended follow-through for any problems found are clearly identified in advance. Data for such tests should be collected on separate compact spreadsheets, not procedure documents.

- Whether commissioning is performed by the owner's staff or a commissioning agent hired by the owner, the owner should make clear that the contractor is still to perform all tests required of him in the construction contract. A matrix summarizing the contracted testing requirements facilitates contract enforcement.

RESULTS

Table B-1 describes some of the problems identified during commissioning.

The success of commissioning for specific test findings can be rated qualitatively by examining:

a)   the potential adverse effects of leaving the problems found during commissioning unsolved, and

b)   the degree to which they were solved as a result of commissioning.

According to these criteria, commissioning at the Physics/Astronomy project was more successful in addressing some types of problems than others.

Table B-1. Summary of Findings

Description of Problem	Effects	Solution via Cx.
1. Steam valves: Error in AHU sequence of ops; first stage of heating temp rise > 20F.	Labor, energy, comfort.	Complete.
2. Steam valves: Leakage due to failure of sleeve connecting valve shaft to actuator linkage.	Labor, energy, comfort.	Valves still leak.
3. Valve: Heat Recovery control valve action backwards Due to programming error.	Labor, energy.	Complete.
4. Unstable campus cooling water valve control; staging of 1/3,2/3 valves reversed.	Premature wear on valve seat, labor.	Complete.
5a. Valve control error: a reheat coil valve begins to open before the VAV box damper has fully closed.	Labor, energy, comfort.	Complete for boxes tested.
5b. Valve: A reheat coil didn't close.	Labor, energy, comfort.	Complete for boxes tested
5c. Reheat coil valve action reversed on 5 coils.	Labor, energy, comfort.	Complete for boxes tested
5d. Two steam valves not hooked to controls.	Labor, comfort	Complete
6. Actuated dampers: None of the shafts square or hex per specs. Two linkages anchored to round shafts. Four clamps slipping.	Energy wasted due to loose out-side air dampers. dampers. Fan cap.	Brought to engineer's attention.

(Continued)

Table B-1. (*Concluded*)

Description of Problem	Effects	Solution via Cx.
7. Supply air leaks at air handlers.	Labor, energy.	Complete.
8. Failure of proof of flow switches.	Labor, comfort.	Partial.
9. Fan control under fire alarm: Software in non-	Safety.	Complete.
10. HVAC return to normal power takes hours.	Labor, comfort.	Complete.
11. Building pressurization problems: Floor-by-floor dampers fighting return fan.	Leaves blowing into building	Adequate.
12. Air handler discharge air temperature control sequence not per specifications.	Uncertain.	Partial.
13. Unfriendly software elements.	Labor, comfort.	Partial.
14. Inaccurate sensors.	Labor.	Partial.
15. Thermostat in space served by another zone box.	Labor, comfort.	Complete.
16. Air in water systems, cavitation at two pumps.	Labor, energy.	Improvement.
17. Freeze protection strategy not per specs.	Risk frozen coils.	Complete.
18. False trips at eight MCCs.	Labor comfort.	Partial.
19a. Chattering relays on three fan MCCs.	Labor comfort.	Complete.
19b. MCC: Two exhaust fan HOAs where A=hand and H=off	Labor.	
20. Loose wires, loss of communications	Labor, comfort.	Partial.
21. Faulty control boards.	Labor comfort.	Complete.

Solutions were most readily introduced for design and installation errors that could be corrected easily and inexpensively by applying a strong knowledge of HVAC design and the contract language of the specific project:

- Incorrect preheat coil sequence of operations (1)
- Loose damper linkages (6)
- Inability to return to normal power in a timely manner (10)
- Improper operation under fire alarm (9)
- Incorrect operation of the heat recovery run around loop valve (3)

If left undiagnosed until after occupancy, these errors would have caused confusion, compromised comfort and safety, and wasted energy.

The influence of commissioning on on-site calibration was less dramatic. Although commissioning expedited proper re-calibration, success was achieved only after the control shop was operating the building, by the control shop technicians. Calibration of flow switches (8) and motor control centers (MCCS) (18) falls under this category.

The solutions that were least successful involved the following:

- Faulty manufacturing, as with the steam valve extension sleeves (6)
- Design problems for which solutions are not easily developed, such as building pressurization (11)

Manufacturing problems may be difficult to solve because the commissioning agent (and often even the university mechanical engineer) does not work directly with the manufacturers' factory engineers. The factory engineers are often more capable than any other party of understanding the cause of failure and defining the least-cost avenues for a solution satisfactory to the owner. Solutions to manufacturing problems also tend to be more expensive, and may therefore meet with resistance from the party who would be responsible for paying for a successful change-out. The impact of commissioning on faulty equipment selection and faulty manufacturing depends to some extent on the owner's style of contract enforcement.

BENEFITS OF COMMISSIONING

Meeting Design Goals

At the Physics/Astronomy building, the design goals for the mechanical systems were (in approximate order of decreasing importance):

occupant safety, support for research, flexibility of space use, comfort (thermal and auditory), operability and reparability, and energy efficiency. With the exception of auditory comfort, commissioning of the Physics/Astronomy building improved the project's ability to meet all of these goals.[b]

Energy Savings

Although energy efficiency was a low priority in both the design and commissioning of Physics/Astronomy, a significant potential energy impact can be assessed for five of the test findings. Table 2 shows the estimated annual savings multiplied by the assumed duration of savings, which ranged from 0.5 to 3 years.[c]

The energy costs at the university are roughly $0.24 per therm for natural gas and $0.035 per kWh for electricity. The estimated total energy saving thus calculated is approximately $11,000. Had fatigue testing of steam valves been successfully introduced for both the installed and the replacement parts, the estimated energy savings from commissioning would have been $19,000.

Commissioning Appears To Be Less Expensive Than The Alternative

The following observations made in commissioning Physics/Astronomy suggest that the cost of solving problems through commissioning may be less than the cost of solving problems progressively over the years in response to occupant complaints.

- The contractor was present during testing, providing an opportunity to develop a consensus between the contractor and the commissioning agent about the nature of the problems observed.

- Commissioning formalized on-site observations, reducing the likelihood of disagreement about the nature of the problem, and increasing the likelihood of timely, effective corrective action.

---

[b]Nationwide development and application of standardized tests and third party testing to support certified submittal and nameplate ratings may offer a more viable long-run source of quality control for faults in manufacturing than on-site testing. In the foreseeable future, however, on-site testing is essential as a check to manufacturer ratings and to fill the gap where manufacturer ratings are not available.
[c]The duration of savings is defined as the length of time between when the problem was solved via commissioning and the time that it would have been solved otherwise.

Table B-2. Energy Savings

ID# from Table B-1	Description	Potential Elec. Savings	Potential Gas Svgs therms/yr	Potential Svgs, Gas +Elec.	Yrs. of Svgs	Total Potential Savings	Est'd Elec. Savings kWh/yr	Est'd Gas + Elec Savings
1.	Pre-heat coil valve control error.	0	30,188	$7,245		$3,623		$3,623
2.	Steam valve leakage.	81,824	20,958	$7,894	1.00	$7,894	0	Not solved.
3.	Heat recovery valve action backwards.	0	10,281	$2,467	2.00	$4,934	0	$4,934
6.	Damper actuator clamp slipping	63,120	0	$2,209	1.00	$2,209	63,120	$2,209
7.	Leaky duct penetrations.	921	580	$171	3.00	$513	921	$513
	Total	145,865	62,007	$19,986		$19,173	64,041	$11,279

- The commissioning agent contributed expertise which helped the contractor understand the design, and helped the designer identify weaknesses or errors in the design.

- As an independent party, the commissioning agent was effective in coordinating solutions between the controls contractor and mechanical design consultant.

- Solutions introduced after commissioning will be more difficult to document than solutions introduced when the designer is still available for input and the project documents are still being finalized.

- Both cost and inconvenience to occupants of corrective action would have increased after occupancy.

- Some problems found during commissioning, such as loose connections between the damper actuator linkage and the damper shaft, probably would have been corrected at the owner's expense by the owner's staff had they not been caught during commissioning.

CONCLUSIONS

Pre-occupancy on-site testing by an independent commissioning agent offers a highly effective vehicle for debugging software and installation problems and for correcting design errors for which a solution is easily found and inexpensively implemented. Commissioning brings a building closer to the original design goals, and introduces operations staff to the building before they become responsible for its operation. At Physics/Astronomy commissioning improved energy efficiency, comfort, and operability. The presence of the commissioning agent at emergency power and fire system tests also improved the safety of the building, as his HVAC expertise and inter-system interests contributed significantly to the test findings. Energy conservation was most readily accomplished by examination of the valve controls, which had a large number of problems that were relatively easy to solve.

There exist in the body of any construction contract a number of contractor start-up and testing requirements which should be carefully enforced so that such work isn't transferred inadvertently to other participants in the commissioning process. This lesson was learned as the university introduced use of the control shop staff in pre-functional testing at Physics/Astronomy. Subsequent work on other projects demonstrated that the mutual benefit to capital projects and operations from such participation is possible if it is carefully managed by engineering staff.

Index